INCORPORATING TEXTS INTO INSTITUTIONAL ETHNOGRAPHIES

Edited by Dorothy E. Smith and Susan Marie Turner

In *Incorporating Texts into Institutional Ethnographies,* Dorothy E. Smith and Susan Marie Turner present a selection of essays highlighting perhaps the single most distinctive feature of the sociological approach known as Institutional Ethnography (IE) – the ethnographic investigation of how texts coordinate and organize people's activities across space and time. The chapters, written by scholars who are relatively new to IE as well as IE veterans, illustrate the wide variety of ways in which IE investigations can be done, as well as the breadth of topics IE has been used to study.

Both a collection of examples that can be used in teaching and research project design and an excellent introduction to IE methods and techniques, *Incorporating Texts into Institutional Ethnographies* is an essential guide to the discipline.

DOROTHY E. SMITH is a professor emerita at the Ontario Institute for Studies in Education, University of Toronto, and an adjunct professor in the Department of Sociology at the University of Victoria.

SUSAN MARIE TURNER is an associate scholar with the Centre for Women's Studies, Ontario Institute for Studies in Education, University of Toronto.

Incorporating Texts into Institutional Ethnographies

EDITED BY DOROTHY E. SMITH AND
SUSAN MARIE TURNER

UNIVERSITY OF TORONTO PRESS
Toronto Buffalo London

© University of Toronto Press 2014
  Toronto Buffalo London
  www.utppublishing.com
  Printed in the U.S.A.

ISBN 978-1-4426-4703-9 (cloth)
ISBN 978-1-4426-1480-2 (paper)

Printed on acid-free, 100% post-consumer recycled paper with
vegetable-based inks.

Library and Archives Canada Cataloguing in Publication

Incorporating texts into institutional ethnographies / edited by
Dorothy E. Smith and Susan Marie Turner.

Includes bibliographical references.
ISBN 978-1-4426-4703-9 (bound).—ISBN 978-1-4426-1480-2 (pbk.)

1. Ethnosociology.   I. Smith, Dorothy E., 1926–, editor of
compilation   II. Turner, Susan Marie, 1948–, editor of compilation

GN478.I53 2014   301   C2014-900999-2

University of Toronto Press acknowledges the financial assistance to its
publishing program of the Canada Council for the Arts and the Ontario Arts
Council.

Canada Council   Conseil des Arts
for the Arts   du Canada

ONTARIO ARTS COUNCIL
CONSEIL DES ARTS DE L'ONTARIO
50 YEARS OF ONTARIO GOVERNMENT SUPPORT OF THE ARTS
50 ANS DE SOUTIEN DU GOUVERNEMENT DE L'ONTARIO AUX ARTS

University of Toronto Press acknowledges the financial support of the
Government of Canada through the Canada Book Fund for its publishing
activities.

In memory of
Ellen Pence (1948–2012)

Contents

Figures

Exhibits

Permissions

We acknowledge with thanks permission to reprint received from the following publishers of papers that appear, some in substantially revised versions, in this book.

De Montigny, Gerald, *Social Working: An Ethnography of Front-line Practice*, © University of Toronto Press 1995; extracts from chapters 8, 9, 10, and 11 have been revised and rewritten by de Montigny and appear here as "Doing Child Protection Work." Reprinted with permission of the publisher.

Eastwood, Lauren E., "The Activation of the Text: Conceptual Resources at Work." Republished with permission of Taylor and Francis Group LLC Books, from *The Social Organization of Policy: An Institutional Ethnography of UN Forest Deliberations* (2005). Permission conveyed through Copyright Clearance Center, Inc. The chapter is revised and rewritten and appears here as "Negotiating UN Policy: Activating Texts in Setting-specific Policy Deliberations."

Luken, Paul C., and Suzanne Vaughan, "Standardizing Childrearing through Housing." Republished with permission from University of California Press, from *Social Problems* 53, no. 3 (2006). Permission conveyed through Copyright Clearance Center, Inc.

McCoy, Liza, "Producing 'What the Deans Know': Cost Accounting and the Restructuring of Post-Secondary Education." Republished with permission of Springer, from *Human Studies* 21 (1998). Permission conveyed through Copyright Clearance Center, Inc.

Rankin, Janet M., and Marie L. Campbell, "Three in a Bed: Nurses and Technologies of Bed Utilization," from *Managing to Nurse: Inside Canada's Health Reform*, 45–64. © University of Toronto Press, 2006. Reprinted with permission of the publisher.

Smith, Dorothy E., "Exploring the Social Relations of Discourse: Sociological Theory and the Dialogic of Sociology," from *Writing the Social: Critique, Theory, and Investigations*, pp. 133–56. © University of Toronto Press 1999. This chapter has been revised and rewritten by Smith and appears in this book as "Discourse As Social Relations: Sociological Theory and the Dialogic of Sociology." Reprinted with permission of the publisher.

Smith, George W., "Policing the Gay Community: An Inquiry into Textually-mediated Social Relations." Republished with permission of Elsevier, from *International Journal of the Sociology of Law* 16 (1988): 163–83.

Turner, Susan Marie, "Rendering the Site Developable: Texts and Local Government Decision Making in Land Use Planning," from *Knowledge, Experience, and Ruling Relations: Studies in the Social Organization of Knowledge*, edited by Marie Campbell and Ann Manicom, 234–48. © University of Toronto Press, 1995. This chapter has been revised and rewritten by Turner and appears here as "Reading Practices in Decision Processes." Reprinted with permission of the publisher.

Warren, Leanne D., "Organizing Creation: The Role of Musical Text," from *Studies in Cultures, Organizations and Societies* 7, no. 2 (2001). Reprinted with permission of Taylor and Francis Group (www.tandf online.com). Permission conveyed through Copyright Clearance Center, Inc. Page 1 of the score from "Joseph Haydn: Concerto in C major for Violoncello and Orchestra – Hob. VIIb: 1, edited by Sonja Gerlach, Urtext of the Joseph Haydn Complete Edition, TP 291© by G. Henle Verlag, Müchen; Bärenreiter-Verlag, Kassel" is reprinted with permission of G. Henle Verlag, Müchen; Bärenreiter-Verlag. The chapter has been rewritten by the author and appears here as "Text in Performance: The Making of a Haydn Concerto."

Acknowledgments

The editors want to express our appreciation of Stephan Dobson, whose assistance in sustaining organization in the making of a work depending on multiple sources and interchanges was essential to the existence of the book you now see before you. We also want to acknowledge the work of Douglas Hildebrand of the University of Toronto Press in guiding us through the editorial and review processes towards significant improvements in the final version of the book, and we thank him for his ongoing support and commitment.

INCORPORATING TEXTS INTO INSTITUTIONAL ETHNOGRAPHIES

Introduction

DOROTHY E. SMITH AND
SUSAN MARIE TURNER

Incorporating Texts into Institutional Ethnographies collects examples of how institutional ethnographers have introduced observations of texts in action into their ethnographic practice. Working from the writings of Dorothy Smith and others who have used the approach known as institutional ethnography for over thirty years, the selected examples illustrate diverse fieldwork-based investigations into how texts coordinate and concert people's activities across time and place. The book presents research models, each with distinctive ethnographic strategies appropriate to the researcher's project and the institutional sphere being explored. The selection emphasizes the variety and difference among possible ethnographic practices that bring texts into view, including interviews about work and practices, observations of naturally occurring activity, a strategy for experiential ethnography, and strategies for investigating text–reader conversations. Each chapter illustrates an ethnographic strategy and its analytic payoff, discovering and extending ethnography into the organization of institutions beyond the immediately observable. Together, they provide a "toolkit" of strategies, inviting the reader to borrow and improvise in new projects.

Moving beyond the immediately observable is a major research innovation and significant change in ethnographic studies. For the most part, when reaching beyond what lies within people's direct experience, social science is stuck with a transition into theory or into an abstract language of categories and concepts that cannot be anchored back into the world of actual people. Terms such as "power," "large-scale organization," "transnational relations," "governance" and so on make regions beyond the local and that dominate it nameable and speakable, but not observable. Institutional ethnography repairs, or perhaps better, simply bypasses, this break in social scientific inquiry. It does so with an ethnographic method of inquiry that has discovered how to explore, learn about the workings of, and explicate the relations that organize our lives beyond the immediacies of local settings.

Institutional ethnography's discovery is of how replicable texts are integral to the relations constituting the objectified modes of consciousness and organization that are deeply and yet undramatically embedded in how our societies are put together. Marx (1973) argued that money had come to organize a distinctive order of social relations overriding and, indeed, overpowering direct relationships among individuals. Now we confront *objectifying* relations mediated by texts that stand over and against our local everyday worlds and lives and yet permeate, penetrate, and organize them. Indeed, money is no longer the material entity that it was when Marx theorized in the mid-nineteenth century. It, too, has largely been resolved into the textual modes that organize our contemporary world. A transnational financial order, for example, exists primarily in an electronic mode; there are complexes of international *agreements* (see Lauren Eastwood's chapter on the United Nations Forum on Forests negotiations) and *regulations* implementing them at various levels of government. In agriculture, for example, there is *certification* of types of product (see Katherine Wagner's chapter on the certification of organic production), also involving texts; producers must be able to produce the texts of their *accounts* as part of demonstrations of having conformed to regulations – and so on and so on. At every point in such an institutional complex there are people who devise and negotiate the wording of governing texts; who check out with forms whether regulations are being followed; who produce reports; whose record-keeping is accountable (i.e., read by someone who supervises and who is supervised). The introduction of new forms of public administration that conform to a managerial rather than a bureaucratic model involves changing textual organization and the introduction of new textual technologies of information and communication that enable, for example, people's front-line work to be translated into the technical language of accountancy (see Liza McCoy's chapter).

What Is a Text?

The notion of texts that institutional ethnography works with has two aspects that differentiate it from how texts are taken up elsewhere in discourse analysis (see, for example, Norman Fairclough 1995, 2003), or in social research more generally (see Lindsay Prior's 2011 four-volume *Using Documents and Records in Social Research*).

First, texts are material objects that carry messages – stone carvings, sand sculptures, writing or pictures on walls, paintings on canvas, writings on cloth, parchment, paper or on computer screens, music recorded on records, CDs, or on tape, images on film, television, and so on. The texts that are of particular relevance to institutional ethnography are those that are or can be reproduced many times, so that different people can read the same text in different places or at different times; it is their *replicability* that is central. Of course not every text is replicable. The message on a birthday card wishing the recipient "best wishes and happy returns with love from" is not what is meant by a replicable text. We are talking about texts that can appear again and again in different places and at different times and for different people to read, watch, or listen to. The replicability of the texts does not mean that every copy or occurrence of a text is read in exactly the same way; the making of or reading (watching, listening to) a text is something being done in an actual sequence of action at a particular time and in a particular place. But the recognizable identity of a text from one site of activation to another is integral to the text's distinctive form of coordinating ruling relations, and hence is also significant for the development of ethnographic practices exploring the social relations extending across, coordinating, and regulating multiple sites and settings of people's work.

Second, texts are never to be treated as objects of research in and of themselves nor as separate from how they coordinate people's doings. They must be conceived as occurring in definite actual settings of people's everyday/everynight living. They are incorporated into ethnography as they enter into and play their part in ongoing sequences of action coordinating them with action going on at other places or at other times. Institutional ethnographies exploring the complex and varied social relations are discovering and making observable just how texts enter into, organize, shape, and coordinate people's doings as they/we participate in the objectifying relations of ruling.

Some Historical Background

We could start with the invention of writing, but perhaps more dramatic in the extraordinary reconstruction of social relationships is the invention of print. Texts, defined as material forms mediating human communication, have been around perhaps ever since anything we could call human has existed. Think of handprints on the walls of caves and on rocks, of markings which have not survived on tree trunks, of arrangements of stones, and, as skills and tools developed, of paintings, carvings, notations, and eventually script. All have this extraordinary and powerful magic; they create expressive bridges across time and space.

But with the invention of printing, something else happened. It was not fully realized in the early forms of printing created in China, in part because the replication of a given text was etched on stone, laborious, slow, and hence, radically limited in its distribution. In Europe in the fourteenth and fifteenth centuries, however, with the advantage of alphabetic script, technologies of printing were developed which could reproduce a given form of words and even of images with an ever-increasing facility, so that many copies of a given text could be produced. Different readers in different places and at different times were finally able to see and read the same words. No need to imagine that they read them in the same way, but for each the form of words would be identical. If the translation of the Bible into the vernacular was a major historical event, no less significant was how print made possible its circulation beyond the traditional hierarchies of the priesthood. The very existence of the standardized texts created the ground for questioning and resisting the authority of the church and at the same time generated radical differences in, and arguments about, interpretation.

As texts, replicated and replicable, became ubiquitous, new forms of consciousness and organization emerged, progressively independent of particular speakers or hearers connecting face to face. The transition is from utterances, in M.M. Bakhtin's (1981) inclusive sense and use of this concept, relying on the authority of speakers, to utterances that appear in a material form, in-text, without a present and embodied speaker. Even though an author or source may be identified, she or he is not there, face to face with the hearer. The utterance in-text stands alone. It has no specific personal destiny, no specific other it is addressing – though it may be written or imaged as if indeed it were addressing itself just to you. Here is the practical reality of objectification as something people do; taking up, activating, and making such texts enters and is integral to the creation of a world of messages that are materially grounded and must be created and/or activated by actual people in actual settings. But at the same time, those texts are not, and cannot be, simply located there, tied there. Such objectified and objectifying utterances always hook and engage makers and readers in a complex of relations, coordinating a given moment of utterance or reading or watching or listening with what others are or will be doing elsewhere. Institutional ethnography's ontology is distinctive among approaches to texts and to the ethnography of texts in its reliance and focus upon the coordination of subjectivities, consciousnesses, activities, and relations among people rather than a reliance on an ontology of the social as organization produced by motivated individuated subjects.

The Collection

Institutional ethnography as a social scientific approach develops and evolves through its practitioners' ongoing research. This book collects and brings into focus how in their research institutional ethnographers have been discovering the way the texts on which they focus coordinate what people do – create, put together, and build – in different sites of our contemporary world. We have designed the collection to make available just how integral texts are to the organization of the trans- or extra-local relations that we participate in but cannot observe from our local sites of being. We also wanted to provide an opportunity for others to learn, as we have been learning, about what can become observable when texts are incorporated into ethnographies of regions of organization and ruling in contemporary society.

What we have brought together here are institutional ethnographies illustrating different ways texts are incorporated as integral to the ethnography. Putting together this collection has been a pleasure for us. We have enjoyed the task and the work of the contributors, learning how they have gone about putting together their ethnographies. Though we had read most of the studies included here before imagining this book, they were read separately and over a period of several years (the span is 1988 [George Smith's] to 2008 [Katherine Wagner's]) and many are not easily accessible. Reading them again, this time as models of different strategies for how to incorporate texts into ethnographies, and bringing them into dialogue with one another as chapters in a book, has meant learning more and differently about how institutional ethnography proceeds as a discourse, how it has developed based on empirical explorations of ruling relations, and is developing new ethnographic techniques as the different terrains and forms of organization demand new approaches.

The chapters of this book explicate in various ways how texts coordinate the settings and sequences of action that are the focus of the ethnographies. They are grouped into five "parts" to bring out some of the distinctive ways in which institutional ethnographers have worked with texts in varying institutional settings and using varying approaches. We have assembled them as we have to bring into view some of the distinctive discoveries that have been made about text-mediated organization as well as how to incorporate texts into ethnographies thereof: (1) the discovery of "institutional circuits," originating in George Smith's investigation of an ideological circle; (2) how to develop institutional ethnographies involving technologically specialized texts; (3) ethnographies drawing on the ethnographer's own experience of institutional workings; (4) how activating texts as readers can be examined close-up and in detail; and, finally, (5) a rather special ethnographic venture into regions ordinarily assigned to political economy, a historical exploration starting from people's experience that explicates the coming of the suburb and its relation to child-rearing practices in North America. Notice, throughout all and across the different parts, that each ethnography always recognizes that texts only become alive, active, or "occur" as people bring them into place in institutional sequences of action. Of course, some ethnographies would fit into more than one grouping under a particular heading. We have assembled them as we have so that those collected in each group are brought into something like a dialogue in which they reflect on one another. Bringing institutional ethnographies together in this way gives emphasis to some of the distinctive ways in which texts can be brought into ethnographies that reach into regions formerly beyond ethnographic grasp.

Exploring and Explicating Texts-in-Action

In institutional ethnographic practice, nominalizations such as "organization," "institution," or "discourse" are not left standing or endowed with agency in the ethnographic text. The focus is always on uncovering what people are actually doing, and the activity and coordination that are implicit in such terms. This exploration also involves working ethnographically to discover just how the characteristic objectifications of organizational and institutional discourses are locally accomplished. Terms such as "UN policy," "the city's decision," "organic certification," and so on, when substructed ethnographically, are shown to locate forms of the social that rely on texts. Making visible what people are actually doing in sequences of action substructs the objectifications of organizational and institutional discourses; it returns the abstract nominalizations that attempt to capture these dimensions of the social to the observable and experienceable of everyday life and of people's doings. The institutional ethnographies collected here show exactly how this is achieved in investigations of how texts organize the discursive transcendence of the local and ephemeral. The tricky matter for practice is to locate texts in time as participating in actual courses of action. The social act unfolds in time as well as in actual local settings. Note the plural form we are using here. The texts articulate what is getting done in local settings and at particular times within social relations that extend beyond any one setting and any particular time. The texts thus must be recognized as "occurrences" at the moment of reading that enter into the reader's next doings or "responses." And so long as the ethnographer avoids attributing agency to them (they can only come into play as they are activated by someone), they are seen *as they are*, involved in some course of action, in talk or in writing/reading/watching/listening as organizers of local settings, aimed at, and governing, the ongoing development and concerting of activities.

Themes and Threads

There is not just one line of discovery to be found in these chapters. As we, the editors, read and reread, we became aware that there were themes and threads of ethnographic practice working with texts that recur and are developed over the collection as a whole. This led to the parts into which we have assembled the various ethnographies. Collecting and differentiating the ethnographies emphasizes some of the distinctive aspects of how ruling relations are coordinated that become visible when the textual organization is brought into focus, as well as some of the distinctive ways in which institutional ethnographies are developed. However, though we have broken the collection up into parts, juxtaposing each study with others that tie into a common theme, we know that there are other connections to be made that bridge our thematic divisions. Assembling ethnographies that have distinctive features in common with one another is intended to bring those features into focus. It is not intended to blot out other aspects of how texts are brought into play in any particular ethnography.

Part 1: Institutional Circuits

Part 1 brings together three ethnographies that show texts in action in organizing institutional circuits. We have stressed earlier that discovering how to incorporate texts into institutional ethnography has been an essential innovation and that it has made possible the extension of ethnography beyond the local that ordinarily confines it and so to open up the investigation of how ruling is organized textually in contemporary society. One such discovery recognizes how the objectified modes of coordinating people's action are organized as institutional circuits. "Institutional circuits" is a term that locates sequences of text-coordinated action making people's actualities representable and hence actionable within the institutional frames that authorize institutional action. In institutional circuits, institutional work comprises mining actualities selectively to identify aspects, features, measures, and so on that fit the governing frame (sometimes called a "boss text"). The textual representation then produced can be interpreted in terms of that frame and become, in this way, articulated to an institutionally mandated course of action. The three ethnographies in this first section make visible different aspects of such circuits: George Smith developed his investigation of the circuit involved in "policing the gay community" from the notion of ideological circles originating in Dorothy Smith's 1973 paper "The Ideological Practice of Sociology." He takes a step, which he celebrates, of moving out of theory into a scientific investigation of, in this paper, just how gay men enjoying their sexuality in a steam bath could be charged under Ontario "bawdy house" laws. Texts are central to his ethnographic account, first of a report prepared by detectives on the basis of an investigation of the steam bath when gay men were present and active and of the textual fitting of their actions with sections of Ontario's "bawdy house" law – and then how that textual fit unleashed the "mandated course of action" leading to the arrest and charging of the steam bath owner, its manager, and those "found in" it at the time of the police raid.

The second paper in this group, Katherine Wagner's ethnography of how organic farm production is certified, brings into view the actual work involved for small organic farmers in governing both their production and their record keeping as well as how the inspector goes about the interchange with farmers to meet his accountability to government. Third is Lauren Eastwood's ethnography that shows the work processes involved in the writing of a governing text as she describes her experience of participating in the attempts of a non-governmental organization (NGO) to control the wording of the United Nations Forestry Forum's forestry policy. Noteworthy in this part is the way in which each inquiry shows an aspect of how texts in action are put together to construct an institutional circuit. George Smith's ethnography is built directly from the texts of an institutional circuit and shows both the relevant categories of the governing or boss text and how the textual reality is constructed to fit them. Katherine Wagner's study focuses on the work of creating texts integral to a circuit which includes organic farming as a performance designed to conform to the certification procedures. Then Lauren Eastwood breaks open the work concealed behind those governing or boss texts known as "policy," making visible the skills and contentions of negotiating the language that will come into play in the representations of actualities they will govern.

Part 2: Diverse Textual Technologies

The second section emphasizes the variety of textual technologies that ethnographers can encounter. We have emphasized here the importance of the invention of print in the historical development of the ruling relations, but this section recognizes specialized technologies that, in one case, at least – that of the musical score on which Leanne Warren's study focuses – has only an uncertain relation to the history of print as explicated here. Liza McCoy's ethnography can be read as an institutional circuit which she shows as having reorganized relations among managers, deans, and departments and instructors in Ontario community colleges. But we include it in this section because the reorganization that brings the educational objectives and practices of the colleges under the control of financial government involves fitting the work of instructors into the framework and discourse of accountancy. McCoy teaches the reader how to read a key type of specialized text that brings departmental instructional practices into a commensurable relation with others and with other costs and benefits in the college. Warren's ethnography shows how the musical score of a Hayden cello concerto comes into play in coordinating the rehearsal performances of orchestra members, soloist, and conductor and how the score catches up the performance into the historical trajectory of musical tradition. And again, the reader is taught how to read the text, in this case, a musical score. In both of these cases, then, we have to learn how to read the text in order to trace in the ethnography just how these texts come into play. Marie Campbell and Janet Rankin's chapter shifts the focus to a technology with a hidden textual (electronic) system generating readable text that likely ties back into much the same language as that introduced to us in McCoy's paper. But here that which might be accounting language translates into instructions for nurses whose responsibility it is to ensure hospital conformity to the managerial criteria of bed utilization.

Part 3: Experiential Ethnography

There is a distinctive use in some of the ethnographies of accounts based on the ethnographer's own experience. These are particularly valuable when texts are playing a focal role in an ethnography. One difficulty in discovering how texts coordinate social relations is that major aspects of textual work are not spoken and are not in any simple way visible to an observer. Hence the special value of what we have called "experiential ethnographies," that is, ethnographies written from within the ethnographer's experience. Gerald de Montigny provides a vivid account of how the categories and concepts of the social work discourse in which he had been trained organize his selective attention to a dirty and smelly domestic situation reported as being one of suspected child abuse. The observations he makes orient towards the production of a formal report eventually presented in court that justifies the removal of the child he had found there from that foul domestic setting.

Though Montigny's chapter is distinctive in his use of experiential ethnography, the uses of experience are also to be found in other chapters: Janet Rankin and Marie Campbell's ethnography of the workings of new computer software in managing hospitals draws on Janet's own work experience (see part 3); Susan Turner's drawing on her experience of participating in the municipal government decision setting; and Dorothy Smith's investigation of her own experience of a sociological text–reader conversation in sociological discourse (both in part 4). Each shows the researcher's own experience as an important resource for the institutional ethnographer.

Part 4: Text–Reader Conversations

To locate the moment of reading as an active interchange between text and reader, institutional ethnography has introduced the notion of a text–reader conversation. The idea here is to be able to see the moment of reading as one in which the reader activates the text as well as responds to it. In a sense, the reader becomes the text's proxy, taking on what is written or otherwise represented. Hence, the text organizes the reader's subjectivity in how she or he responds. Two ethnographies are included in this section: Susan Turner's explication of how a particular text can be read very differently, and what that looks like, takes up text–reader conversations as these became observable in a public meeting where elected municipal officials were considering plans for a development proposed for a ravine and were reading and speaking about a diagram representing the site. She shows how different ways of activating the text enter into the talk producing "the city's" decision making; Dorothy Smith's study of her intertextual engagement with sociological theory is explicit in how becoming the text's proxy enters into her experience; she shows how she herself in her reading of a passage from the work of sociologist Anthony Giddens becomes its agent in excluding other text-grounded voices with which she was engaged.

Here again, there are instances of text–reader conversations explored in other chapters: Lauren Eastwood explores text–reader conversations in policy negotiations (chapter 3); Leanne Warren's account of how a cellist works with the cello concerto score in a rehearsal clearly involves a text–reader conversation (chapter 5).

Text–reader conversations are troublesome to investigate because they are generally done in silence: Eastwood draws both on her own experience and on observations of talk; Warren did interviews in which both she and her respondent knew the text; Turner makes use of her observations and recordings of a public meeting; Smith draws directly on her experience. Another research strategy was developed in Liza McCoy's (1995) study of how wedding photographs can be read. She brought together a group of three people, including herself, to talk about one of the participants' wedding photographs; how the three talk about the texts produces an observable text–reader conversation that McCoy uses to unfold how such texts may be read.

Part 5: Extended Institutional Ethnography

Paul Luken's and Suzanne Vaughan's study opens up new institutional ethnographic possibilities. They begin with women's experience of resettling in Phoenix, Arizona before the Second World War and delve deep into how models and ideals of suburban housing were developed in complex initiatives of the federal government, health and psychology professionals, and the construction industry. Their historical ethnography incorporates both written and pictorial texts. It is an innovative study, one that extends the reach of institutional ethnography into relations being designed and put in place in the past that have laid the groundwork shaping the ongoing (and changing) of our present, an investigative strategy that we hope to see taken up by others.

The Possibilities for Institutional Ethnographic Practice

In identifying some of the themes that emerge from the studies collected here, our intention is to open up the range of possibilities for designing and doing ethnographies that explore what may otherwise be ethnographically impenetrable aspects of institutions and organization. Each chapter opens a door into relations present in but extending beyond our everyday by showing concretely how various texts are brought into action in coordinating with the extra-local what is being done in local settings. Each chapter shows the distinctive aspects of organization the ethnographer has discovered and the innovative ethnographic strategies she or he has used to move into the institutions and relations whose workings were to be understood. And each shows how to write creatively of what they have discovered. What they bring into view for readers is the operation of texts in distinct institutional forms such as child protection, hospitals, and nursing homes, in financial accounting in education restructuring, in land development processes and international governing negotiations, in sociological discourse and discourses reorganizing family practices in a critical historical period, and so on. The chapters also bring into view the potentialities for discovery beyond the particular instance on which each focuses. We invite you into the worlds and settings of work and method of inquiry that these chapters present, and we invite you also to explore texts-in-action wherever there are organizational and social issues that concern you.

PART 1

Institutional Circuits

1 Policing the Gay Community: An Inquiry into Textually-Mediated Social Relations[1]

GEORGE W. SMITH

First published in 1988, this is one of the earliest empirical studies of a text–work–text course of action. It illustrates the procedures described in Dorothy Smith's The Everyday World as Problematic *(1987), and marks the distinctive shift to the alternative sociology that is now known as institutional ethnography (it had not yet assumed that name when George Smith wrote). Setting aside the "speculative explanations" of his AIDS activist colleagues, he delved into the textual work that organized the legally mandated police bathhouse raids and then the criminal charges of the owner, the manager, and the "found-ins" that rocked the gay community in Toronto, Canada, in 1981. Instead of asking* why *the bath raids took place, the alternative Smith posits directs readers towards discovering just* how *they came about. George Smith's focus on inscription practices allows us to see them as the particular feature of police work that displays the internal relations between a police report and its organizational context. The analysis of inscription also reveals how a police investigation is organized and conceptually coordinated by the Criminal Code. He tracks the text-based procedures that enter people's experiences into the documentary forms of a governing institution, fitting them into the frames of institutional discourse and thus making them actionable in the terms of a particular institutionally mandated course of action.*

Outlining inquiry and discoveries, Smith provides a distinctive set of procedures:

1 *locate a text/document/account in a particular textually-mediated course of action; in this case, making an investigation of a bathhouse under the provisions of the Criminal Code;*
2 *analyse the social organization of the text/account (i.e., how it is put together) to bring into view its work process and extra-local organization (its part in a larger institutional operation/function);*

3 *examine textual practices such as inscription as central to the work prac-*
  tices by which events in the ordinary world are reframed and entered into a
  documentary reality (and thus can be read) as "facts"; and
4 *examine how the inscription encodes actualities to intend the governing*
  conceptual schema – in this instance, the Criminal Code's conception of a
  "bawdy-house."

He presents sections of the Criminal Code and the pre-trial disclosure docu-
ment and its account of the "first visit" undercover officers made to the bath-
house, as "exhibits"; then examines the sections of the code that define a bawdy
house, its offensive acts (179 (1)) and an owner/agent's responsibility (193 (1))
to show how these texts provide the "discourse frames" or "structure of rel-
evance" police and judges orient to and rely on in the course of producing their
actions and written reports. Investigating authorized texts that were integral
to police actions and the laying of charges, Smith enters the inner workings of
what he calls a ruling "regime" in order to, as he says, provide a "scientifically
adequate" account of how the policing of gay men works.

Gay steam baths can be found in most major cities of First World
countries, especially in North America. Steam baths in Canada were
originally a feature of turn-of-the-century European immigrant communities. As these communities assimilated and residential plumbing
improved, these baths catered more and more to gay men. During the
1970s, gay-owned baths supplanted these European saunas, offering not
simply a steam bath, but a variety of facilities including weight rooms,
swimming pools, lounges with cafeterias and televisions, professional
massage areas, tanning equipment, sun decks, and whirlpools. Most
importantly, these clubs provide gay and bisexual men with a venue
for sex with other men. Although steam bath sex is often referred to as
"anonymous sex," in Toronto at least, the baths have much more of a
communal character, somewhat like the relation European-style baths
in Canada originally had with their immigrant communities. Because
the baths in Toronto are located in the gay ghetto, they have come to be
places where people keep in touch with friends and acquaintances and
often have sex with regular partners. They have thus become a feature
of the social organization of the community.

   Near midnight on 5 February 1981, the intelligence bureau of the
Metropolitan Toronto Police raided four downtown gay steam baths
and arrested more than 300 men as being either keepers or found-ins
of a common bawdyhouse. The scope and violence of these raids made

them a cause célèbre. Three years earlier, after a similar but smaller raid, gay people in Toronto had established the Right to Privacy Committee (RTPC) to defend men arrested in Toronto steam baths under the bawdy-house law. These raids were an attempt by the police to regulate the sexual lives of gay men in Toronto.

From 1980 to 1984 I sat on the executive of the RTPC. The writing of this paper comes out of this period of my life. It is contextualized in the broadest way by the generalized experience gay men have of the police and their work of regulating sex. Following Dorothy Smith's Marxist-feminist method and its project of creating a sociology *for* women rather than one that is merely *about* them (Smith 1977), I have attempted here to create a sociology that does not take gay people as object, but rather starts from their location as subject – a sociology that is *for* them. This line of inquiry requires a different method of research from that ordinarily used in contemporary social science, one that begins from outside the institutional relations which order, regulate and otherwise govern society.

While the bath raids created a serious confrontation between gays and the police in Toronto, serious enough, in fact, for Toronto City Council to commission a special study of the problem (Bruner 1981), the raids themselves were merely a very dangerous crevasse in what, for gay men, was an already uneven and treacherous terrain. For decades the Toronto police had arrested men, often using entrapment techniques, who were engaging, or who the police thought might engage, in homosexual activity. Nonetheless, for the majority of Toronto's gay community, the raids were perplexing. Why they were carried out was a matter of constant speculation. One steam bath, at least, had been operating in the city for nearly twenty years. According to the managers and owners of these clubs, most were visited by officers from the morality bureau which oversaw and permitted their operation. Why the police had arrested so many people was another question raised continually. If "cleaning up" or closing down the baths was the purpose, this could have been accomplished without arresting hundreds of individuals. Indeed, the bath raids were the largest mass arrest of citizens in Canada since the federal government declared the War Measures Act to cope with terrorism in Quebec.[2] And finally, why had the police behaved so viciously? The owners of the clubs claimed that over $50,000 in damage was done to their establishments, and those arrested documented in graphic detail case after case of police abuse (White & Sheppard 1981: 12–14).

The answers to these questions were more than a matter of idle speculation. This was particularly true for the leadership of the RTPC, who had the responsibility of forging a politics that could respond publicly to the raids and to their aftermath while at the same time continuing to organize the resistance of the gay community. As relations between the police and the RTPC unfolded, this became not so much an inquiry into the raids themselves, as an ongoing piece of research into the police and the policing of gays in Toronto. At every point, including the production of this paper, it was a work in progress, constantly shaped by the everyday practical activities in Toronto both of the police and of gay people, including the RTPC.

Organizing Our Research: Starting from the Experience of Gay Men

The Experience of Being Policed

A major problem of organizing a piece of research of this kind is knowing how to begin. The knowledge which we, as gay people, have of the police arises out of our historic treatment by them as they carry out their work of regulating sex. Among us, accounts of the efforts of the police to administer our sexual lives circulate mostly by word of mouth, although they appear from time to time in the gay media, as well as in gay history and literature (e.g., *The Body Politic* magazine;[3] Hodges 1983; Preston 1983). A fundamental property of such accounts is that they arise locally out of our first-hand experience of being policed, of having our lives controlled and regulated by the authorities. In trying to make sense of what are for us often violent, brutal experiences, these accounts come to be told and recorded from the standpoint of gay people. They describe the reality of gay experience.

What is implicit in our experience of being policed is that the regulation of sex in our society is not only locally, but extra-locally organized. What I mean by its being extra-locally organized is that the organization of the work of the police is not something that is simply available at first hand such that it is completely observable and straightforwardly comprehensible within the ambit of a local setting – such as being arrested in a bath raid. Rather, what our experience on such occasions suggested is that our local, face-to-face treatment at the hands of the police is the result of a much more extensive organization located elsewhere that from time to time, and often at a completely unexpected moment, penetrates the local circumstances of our lives, casting them beyond our control. It is precisely this awareness of the opaque, extra-local character of policing that produces within the gay community, especially among activists, a continuously elaborated set of speculative accounts as to why the police behave as they do.

Speculative Explanations

In these accounts police oppression is sometimes seen as the result of the personal bigotry and brutality of front-line officers directly responsible for local law enforcement; a case of "homophobia simple." On other occasions accounts are constructed around the rationale of "clean-up" campaigns, etc., where gay people describe themselves as mere pawns in a larger political scenario such as a provincial election. Or they see the policing of gays, as one activist in Toronto put it, as a result of "the rule of the sergeants," where police oppression of gays is not viewed as a general policy of the force, but something instigated by local staff sergeants. Another activist, a lawyer by profession, elaborated what he called the "mini-economy theory" to explain police behaviour, whereby police harassment of gay people is described as arising out of a peculiar professional symbiosis involving the judiciary, the police, and the legal profession. The arrest and prosecution of gays, according to this explanation, is not fundamentally a matter of regulating sexual activity, but is a rather self-serving arrangement whereby judges have an easy day of it handling guilty pleas that are relatively simple to dispense with; the police get their clearance quotas – thereby assuring the "efficiency" of their division, bureau, etc.; and the lawyers, their sometimes extravagant fees, very often for simply pleading their double-charged clients guilty to the lesser charge.[4]

There are problems, of course, with these kinds of explanations. While the zeal and enthusiasm with which some officers enjoy arresting gays marks them as homophobic, the organization of the mass arrest of over 300 individuals in the Toronto bath raids clearly goes beyond personal bigotry. At this point homophobia or, perhaps better put heterosexism, takes on systemic proportions. Moreover, even though Ontario was heading into a provincial election and support for gay rights (which under the circumstances was tantamount to support for bathhouse sex) could have proved to be a difficult election issues for the opposition parties – especially for the social democratic New Democratic Party (NDP) who in theory supported gay rights as party policy, the attorney general/solicitor general at the time claimed on the floor of the provincial parliament not to have had any advanced knowledge of the raids, let alone to have ordered them to coincide with the provincial elections. According to the Tory government's account, the raids were not part of a master plan to win the election. Indeed, the staff inspector, head of the police intelligence bureau responsible for the raids, testified before the House of Commons Standing Committee on Justice and Legal Affairs that he, and he alone, was responsible for ordering them. It was precisely these kinds of problems with the speculative character of our explanations of the bath raids that demonstrated the inadequacy of our ability, within the scope of local events, to come to grips with the extra-local organization of the policing of Toronto's gay community.

An Ontological Shift

To return to the problem of how to begin our research, what the production of the speculative accounts in the gay community made clear from the start was that our interest in the police did not arise as a theoretical or legal issue, the way it might for the Canadian Civil Liberties Association, for example. Rather, it arose out of our generalized, everyday experience as gay people of having our sexuality denied and our lives overrun and sometimes destroyed by the police. Consequently, rather than speculate about *why* the police behave as they do, we realized that we wanted to know *how* it is that this sort of thing happens to us. Our interest, as it turned out, was practical and political, rather than theoretical and speculative. Realizing this was an important break not only with how gay activists ordinarily thought about this problem, but also with traditional sociological thinking.

Our experience of policing directed us to attempt to address as a problem the relation between gay men and the wider society in which we live. We wanted our study to assist us in understanding our world with a view to how it comes into being, and hence with transforming it. Toronto was not the first city where gays have had a problem with the police, and the RTPC was not the first organization to attempt to change the way in which the police treat gay people. By the late seventies, in fact, various jurisdictions across North American had proposed a number of solutions to this problem: the hiring of gay police, psychological testing to weed out homophobic recruits, gay–police liaison committees, better in-service training, etc. By the early eighties, however, it had become clear that none of these strategies held much promise for improving gay–police relations. Nonetheless, they provided the context for the political debate around what to do about the police.

The Everyday World as Problematic

Beginning with the experience of having our sexual lives regulated by the authorities, we decided to render this opaque feature of our everyday world problematic. We used the notion of "problematic" to set out a form of inquiry that, starting from the position of individuals in the everyday world, is directed at illuminating how their world is shaped and determined by social processes that go beyond it – specifically in our case, of course, the work of the police in regulating sex. This was to be a study not *of* gay people, but *for* them. An important assumption on our part was that the social processes which impinge on our lives do not appear miraculously, but are constituted in the activities of people, and that our experience of police oppression arises in how these activities are put together. Setting aside our speculative accounts of why things happen as they do, we insisted on an interpretation of events that took at face value, and thereby attempted to reveal, their structure of relevance. We depended, in order to do this, on our ability as members of our society to make sense of it. We wanted our research to begin not discursively with the theories of either gay activists or sociology, but with the realization that there is a real world out there, no matter how opaque it might be, that continually impinges on our lives, and over which we have very little control. We wanted our research to tell us more about how this world is organized. Our method was one of textual analysis that undertook to develop an archaeological reading of a police report with a view to recovering the lineaments of the social organization which brought it into existence.

Our Study of the Police: From Speculative Explanations to the Description of Social Relations

Organizing Our Research

For a number of months, the RTPC gathered data on the police as it was generated day-to-day out of the bath raids and their aftermath. This work was not initially seen in any technical sense as research. One thing we did, for example, was to keep an extensive collection of newspaper clippings related to the raids that reported on the activities and pronouncements of the police. A similar activity was to record raid-related TV coverage on a VCR. Our periodic meetings and discussions with the lawyers defending the found-ins and keepers also increased our knowledge of both police practice and the operation of the criminal justice system. Our understanding of the police was, in addition, supplemented by accounts provided by the defendants and the post-raid activities of the police in handling both anti-police demonstrations, and criticism of the raids in the media. As the cases of the found-ins ground slowly through provincial court, the work of the police and of the Crown attorneys was observed in court. As well, briefs were presented to various levels of government (e.g., the police budget sub-committee of Toronto metro council and the police commission). The RTPC executive, also, continued its study of policing by inviting experts to talk about their experience with and research on the police. These activities, too, increased our background understanding of policing. Sociologically speaking, these explorations constituted for us, as members of the setting, our background knowledge of policing, although they were never formally organized as an ethnography.

After the 1981 raids, the police continued, now and again, to raid the baths. Then, in the early summer of 1983, officers from the morality bureau arrested twenty-four individuals as keepers, found-ins, and inmates of a common bawdy house at the Back Door bath. The legal defence of those arrested in this raid resulted in the RTPC coming into possession of the preliminary disclosure documents that were provided by the Crown attorney's office to the defence attorneys as part of pre-trial preparations. This document, describing the pre-raid investigation of the bath, became an important set of data on the internal operations of the police.

How these documents were used to carry out this research on the police is what I want to describe now. I am going to use, simply because it is shorter, the disclosure document's account of the "First Visit" (see exhibit 1.1) of the undercover officers to the Back Door bath to illustrate these procedures.

Exhibit 1.1 The disclosure document's account of the "First Visit"

First Visit

Constables Coulis and Proctor attended at the premises, entering separately, where they approached the cash area. It was at this location that the officers first saw the accused; who was later identified as [John DOE]. [DOE] was the only employee that the officers saw that night. [DOE] was the one who permitted the officers access to the premises once they had paid the fee for either a room or a locker. When the officers first entered the premises they walked around and noted the lay-out of the premises as well as any indecent activity that was taking place at that time. It was at this time that both officers saw a number of men laying [*sic*] nude in their private booths with the door wide open. Some of these men were masturbating themselves while others just lay on the mattress watching as other men were walking about the hallways. The officers took periodic walks about the premises and they saw that the same type of indecent activity was taking place each and every time.

During the course of the first visit the officers made certain purchases from [DOE], who was working in the office area. The office area was equipped with numerous sundry items available to the patrons for a fee: pop, coffee, cigarettes, Vaseline and various inhalants. The officers watched [DOE] on two separate occasions when he left the office area to clean rooms that had just been vacated. On each of these occasions, [DOE] walked past a number of rooms that were occupied by men who were masturbating themselves. At no time did [DOE] make an effort to stop these men, or even suggest that they close the door to their booth so that these activities would no longer be visible to other club patrons.

Source: "Social Form" and "Social Relations": A Way of Investigating and Talking about Social Organization

The procedures used in treating this document as basic research data are those which Dorothy Smith has developed and advanced over the past decade as a method of textual analysis. This method takes as a basic premise that the social world in which we live depends for its continued existence on the practices and activities of people. In doing so, it reveals that the documents which people produce and use both *express and coordinate* the social forms of these activities.[5] "Social form" is used here to point out and investigate the ways in which people's activities are neither random nor chaotic, but rather constitute particular social relations. The notion of "social relations," in turn, is used to examine courses of action, developed intersubjectively and intertwined and extended over time, in which people participate, but which no one person both initiates and completes. For us the policing of gay people came to have just such a distinct social form: an institutional relation regulating our sexual lives that is constituted and reconstituted in the routine procedures and practices of the police. To think about policing this way is to see how it is that local events are situated within the structure of more extended social processes.

The notion of "social relation" is also used here to think and talk about the way in which the organization of a local setting is but a moment of an extended temporal sequence of human action. In this context, the notion of social relation does not operate referentially to stand for a thing that is to be investigated. Rather, it serves indexically as a methodological injunction, pointing to the social character of phenomena; to their temporal production in the practices and activities of people. Thus the notion of social relation is used here to talk about and investigate the actual practices of individuals, articulated to one another, as forming a social course of action where

> different moments are dependent upon one another and are articulated to one another not functionally, but as temporal sequences in which the foregoing intends the subsequent and in which the subsequent "realizes" or accomplishes the social character of the preceding. (Smith 1983)

Thus, the various moments of such a sequence are related internally rather than externally to one another; that is, social relations are *internally* organized.[6] Given this ontology, the touchstone of our method of research became one of employing our knowledge as members to investigate internal relations internally. Again, this procedure, like starting our research from the experiences of gay people, marked it off from traditional, positivist social science.

An important discovery of contemporary sociology, credited to ethnomethodology (Garfinkel 1967), is that documents are part of the makeup of social relations. Documents only make sense, in other words, within the social organization of their construction and use. Making sense of the disclosure document's account of the "First Visit," for example, depends on a taken-for-granted understanding of the organization of a police investigation. Thus, it became evident during the course of the research that to understand, for instance, why it is that the officers reported taking periodic walks around the bath and seeing the same type of indecent activity on each and every occasion required locating this account in a particular textually-mediated course of action: making an investigation of a bathhouse under the provisions of the Criminal Code. It is the Code's structure of relevance (to be examined shortly) that provides for the "common-sense" interpretive practices used by police officers (and for that matter, lawyers, judges, etc.) in constructing and reading the disclosure account. Its social organization is part of the work of the police because it is only the standard procedures involved in enforcing the law that make sense of the officers, as officers, walking around the bath and reporting seeing the same type of "indecent" activity on each occasion. Like the police and lawyers, etc., we too used our knowledge as members of the setting to understand these procedures.

One way of seeing this more clearly is to realize that these interpretive practices are not indigenous to what is going on in a gay steam bath. A gay bath is organized and experienced very differently by gay men. The social form of gay activity in a steam bath is not one of investigating and reporting "crime," but a social relation that aims at producing sexual encounters. It is this to which gay men are oriented. Coulis and Proctor's activities as police officers, however, are not concerned with having sex. The social organization of their work, oriented to the requirements of the Criminal Code, is located very differently. Its *mise en scène* is extra-local. While gay men in a bath would describe themselves as engaging in sex, even "hot" sex, and other erotic and eroticizing activities, they would not see themselves as engaging in "indecent" acts. To see what is going on as "indecent," in the sense in which the officers went around observing "indecent" acts, requires the contextual overlay of the Criminal Code. In analysing the social organization of the officers' account of the "First Visit," consequently, what comes into view is a textually-mediated work process, extra-locally organized, that transforms a scene of sexual pleasure into the site of a crime. It is in this relation that the sexual activities of the bath patrons are transformed into "indecent acts," and an ordinary individual, the bath attendant, eventually becomes "the accused." It is precisely how the "First Visit" account reconstructs a local event in terms of the structure of relevance of police work that displays it as an extra-local organizational accomplishment, and underscores its embeddedness in this organization which arises outside the local and particular.

The Social Organization of Gathering Evidence: Inscription

This analysis located Coulis and Proctor's report as integral to the social relation of "investigating crime" or "gathering evidence" as its context. It is important to keep in mind that in examining the account the police provide of their actions and of what they see, we are not investigating its "truth," but rather its social organization. We are not interested in reading through the text to a set of circumstances that lie behind it and which it is taken as representing. Within the context of "investigating crime," the report of the "First Visit" is a story about bath attendant John DOE, who lets the patrons of the bath he works in masturbate "in public." What creates this story are the legal "facts" of the report. These "facts," in turn, are created by the use of inscription techniques (Latour & Woolgar 1979; Lynch 1983; Smith 1984) that are an essential part of the work of gathering evidence, and therefore internal to the textually-mediated organizational properties of the report. "Inscription" is used here to point out the practices involved in producing an event or an object in documentary form as a "fact" about the world. Masturbation becomes the "fact" of "indecent acts" not because of what Coulis and Proctor see as such, but because of what they report. It is on the basis of what the officers report, rather than on what they simply see, that the bath is raided, for example. Were the officers to "turn a blind eye," there would be no raid. "Indecent acts" as a legal "fact" about activities at the Back Door bath only exist, consequently, as a product of their being inscribed in the report; and this is a textually-mediated process.

Inscription, in other words, is the means by which events in the ordinary world are reconceptualized, and entered into documentary reality (Smith 1974b). Because the "facts" of the report only exist by being inscribed they exist only as discursive objects,[7] textually-mediated to the world through the categories of the Criminal Code. These inscription techniques provide a new mapping of the activities and individuals at the Back Door, locating the "indecent acts" and the "accused" on paper, in documents. The fact that they exist only on paper should not be taken as indicating a kind of mystical quality. On the contrary, within a textually-mediated organization discursive objects, in this instance "indecent acts," provide a necessary coordinative capacity. It is as they are inscribed (i.e., mapped) in a police report as "facts" that these phenomena come to constitute a documentary reality that organizes the modus operandi of the police. It is because the officers *report* (i.e., inscribe) "the same type of indecent activity ... taking place each and every time" they walked about the premises, for example, that the police raid the bath, and that DOE is arrested, thereby becoming an "accused" slated for trial.

Before going on to analyse the ideological properties of police inscription, it is important to see how this technique, as a textually-mediated procedure and as an integral part of a policing relation, is able to penetrate our lives as gay men and in so doing articulate us to a ruling apparatus. This is the way in which individuals are transformed into legal "facts," and in the process entered into and held in the ongoing institutional relations regulating sex. Throughout the report of the "First Visit" the family name of the bath attendant is inscribed in uppercase letters, which not only emphasizes his centrality to the "facts" of the account, but, more importantly, this very activity of inscribing transforms him into a "fact," himself, about activities at the Back Door. It is by being inscribed and transformed in this way into a legal "fact" that he is "identified" to the authorities, and thereby caught up and held in the sequential moments of this documentary mode of action. By way of contrast, the individuals masturbating in their private booths are not named, consequently not identified, and therefore not swept up individually into this investigative relation. For the time being, all that is required is to observe and record their "indecent acts" as evidence (i.e., legal "facts") against the bath attendant. What these procedures for naming individuals in the disclosure document display, consequently, is that police inscription as a documentary procedure just does not simply describe, it picks out and secures an individual within an investigative course of action. In this way it not only coordinates and concerts an investigative relation, but in so doing it is an important means by

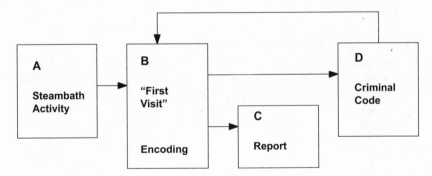

Figure 1.1 Smith's Ideological Circle applied.

which this extra-local, regulatory relation penetrates the local setting of gay men's lives.

The Social Organization of Gathering Evidence: Ideology

The next part of this study undertook to probe more deeply the social form of these techniques, specifically their ideological and conceptual properties. Following Dorothy Smith (Smith 1974a) and with an eye to the materialist foundations to this research (i.e., that the social world is constituted in the activities of people [Marx & Engels 1976: 31]), the notion of "ideology" was not used to reference personal mental states such as beliefs or, put more grandly, a political *Weltanschauung*. Nor, following the Mannheimian tradition of ideology, was it used to reference biased knowledge, tainted by class interests or whatever (Mannheim 1936), which is how it is ordinarily used in traditional sociology. Instead, the notion of "ideology" was used in a materialist sense to point out the social form of the textually-mediated reporting practices of the police. The procedures of interest at this point were the inscription techniques the police used to construct the "facts" of an investigation.

In the case of the Back Door, these techniques, as I have said, formally transformed a scene of sexual pleasure into the site of a "crime." In this process they appear as an "objective" form of knowing where the analysis and description arising out of them is not articulated directly to the actual social organization of the bath, but is constructed in terms of what is important about this setting for the purpose of ruling it (i.e., regulating sex). The organization of this form of knowing involves what Smith calls an ideological circle (Smith 1983: 321–31).[8] The ideological circle is a two-phase process: first, there is an interpretive phase where events are analysed as documenting an underlying pattern originating in a textual discourse (in this case, the Criminal Code's conception of "crime" – "bawdy-house," "indecent acts," "keeper," etc.); and second, a phase where the underlying pattern operates as part of the procedures for selecting, assembling, and ordering these "facts." In the Back Door bath case, an ideological circle is produced when the masturbatory activities of the bath patrons are treated as documenting "indecent acts," the Criminal Code conception of which is used in the first place to generate this "fact" about these activities. Each is used to elaborate the other. Figure 1.1 schematizes this form of organization. In it, the actual social organization of a gay steam bath, represented in box A, is transformed by an encoding process, represented in box B, into the legal "facts" of a police report, box C. The encoding process is governed by the interpretive schema of box D, which in this instance is the Criminal Code's conception of a "bawdy-house." What is important is that the account intend the conceptual schema by being read as referencing this underlying pattern of bathhouse activity.

Exhibit 1.2 Sections 179 and 193 of the Criminal Code (Greenspan 1984).

179. (1) In this Part ...
"common bawdy-house" means a place that is
    (a) kept or occupied, or
    (b) resorted to by one or more persons
for the purpose of prostitution or the practice of acts of indecency; ...

******

193. (1) Everyone who keeps a common bawdy-house is guilty of an
    indictable offence and is liable to imprisonment for two years.
    (2) Everyone who
        (a) is an inmate of a common bawdy-house,
        (b) is found, without lawful excuse, in a common bawdy-house, or
        (c) as owner, landlord, lessor, tenant, occupier, agent or otherwise
        having charge or control of any place, knowingly permits the
        place or any part thereof to be let or used for the purpose of a
        common bawdy-house, is guilty of an offence punishable on
        summary conviction.

In the disclosure document the "facts" about the Back Door bath (i.e., "indecent acts," "not stopping individuals from masturbating," etc.) are used to document an "underlying pattern" of a "common bawdy-house." It is, however, how a "bawdy-house" is defined (i.e., conceptualized) in the Criminal Code (see exhibit 1.2) that provides the procedures for selecting and ordering these observations (e.g., "indecent acts" + a person in charge who does not stop them = a "keeper of a common bawdy-house") as documenting this underlying pattern. The bath is not a "bawdy-house" as such. The Back Door is only describable as a "bawdy-house" in the report by virtue of how a "bawdy-house" is defined in the Code. The legal definition, as referencing an underlying schema of "bawdy-house," and the "facts" of the case are used, in this fashion, to elaborate one another. What is meant here by "ideology" is this circular organization of routine police practice that makes it possible to describe events and individuals located in the everyday world of a gay steam bath in the abstract, legal terminology of police work. In this process, the ordinarily pleasurable activity of jacking off comes to be described as an "indecent act." This transformation is not merely some sort of artful piece of trickery, but rather a procedure essential to administering sex under the Criminal Code. The textually-mediated social organization of this ideological circle provides the means of accounting for actual activities going on in the everyday world in terms of the formal categories which coordinate objectively, rationally, a ruling apparatus. It is in this sense that the legal conception of a "bawdy-house" is a ruling idea, and ideology, the practical means whereby this ruling idea is used to shape people's lives. What is central to this process is how it goes forward on paper, how it takes the form of a textually-mediated relation, which ontologically speaking is how it actually works.

The Social Organization of Gathering Evidence: A Mandated Course of Action

Our research, as a piece of textual analysis, aimed at substructing the social relations of the "First Visit" account. The investigation centred on how Coulis's and Proctor's report is structured by the work of gathering evidence. This led to focusing on inscription as that feature of police work which displays the internal relations between a police report and its organizational context.[9] In turn, the analysis of inscription revealed how it is organized ideologically; that is how a police investigation is conceptually coordinated and organized by the Criminal Code. The way in which the conceptual properties of the Code shape the organization of a police investigation is evident, for example, from how the "facts" inscribed in Coulis and Proctor's report are contextualized by very specific activities on the part of the two officers. It was when they "... *approached* the cash area," for example, that they first saw the bath attendant, John DOE. Likewise, it was in *walking around and noting* "the layout of the premises" that the officers saw "a number of men laying [*sic*] nude in their private booths" and that "some of these men were masturbating themselves" And of course, it was in "*taking periodic walks about the premises*" that they "saw the same type of indecent activity taking place each and every time." Similarly, the officers *watched* DOE, on two separate occasions, walk past a number of rooms that were occupied by men who were masturbating themselves and make no effort to stop them.

These actions are determined conceptually, legally, by the Code. Exhibit 1.2 reproduces two parts of the bawdy-house law, sections 179 and 193 of the Criminal Code. Notwithstanding that "indecency" is not particularly well defined in the Code, it was in meeting the investigative requirement of proving that the Back Door was a "bawdy-house" – that is, a place "kept, occupied, or resorted to ... by one or more persons ... for the purpose ... of indecent acts" – that Coulis and Proctor "walked around and noted" a number of men lying nude in their private booths with the doors wide open, some of whom were masturbating. Similarly, it was through the activity of entering, approaching the cash area, and paying their fee that Coulis and Proctor found the individual, later identified as John DOE, to be an employee of the bath. Later they watch him "on two separate occasions ... walk past a number of rooms that were occupied by men who were masturbating themselves," and at no time "make an effort to stop these men." This watching was necessary to the "facts" in the report alleging that DOE was an "agent ... having charge of [a] place," who knowingly permitted "the place ... to be ... used for the purpose of a common bawdy-house." Thus, it is the definition of a "bawdy-house" and the conception of a "keeper," etc., as they are elaborated in the Criminal Code, that determine this mandated course of action. It was in performing these activities that Coulis and Proctor carried out the work of the police.

This account of the actions of the two officers is obviously a very partial one because it does not describe their personal behaviour: perhaps hitching up their pants, having a smoke, going to the toilet, observing the bath's decor and so on and so forth. Indeed, the activities of Coulis and Proctor described in the account are very different from this sort of personal behaviour. The attachment of these activities to the bawdy-house "facts" of the account constitute them rather as "official investigative activities." They are, for example, the kinds of activities about which the officers could be cross-examined by a defence attorney in court, or which would ordinarily be treated as official "police facts" that could, for example, be reported in the press. What is interesting sociologically is that the "facts," in order to be official police "facts," are contextualized by the appropriate investigative (as opposed to personal) actions on the part of Coulis and Proctor. Thus, whether they are true or not, the "facts" must be reported in the context of a "mandated course of action" that is determined by the Criminal Code.

The notion of a "mandated course of action," in this context, indicates a textually-mediated social process whereby organizations appropriate as theirs the actions of individuals who "perform" the organization (Smith 1982). It is Coulis's and Proctor's investigative activities mandated by the Code that constitutes, as a feature of their report, their *performing* "the police" as an organization. These are not their personal but their official actions and, consequently, are reported formally, objectively by being described as independent of their subjectivity. This is done by inscribing these actions (again, yet another inscription practice), actually performed by two different people, in various areas of the bath premises and at different times, from the standpoint of a neutral third party observing "the officers" conducting their investigation. This practice is the social organization of the "objectivity" of the report. What is important is that its production depends on a "mandated course of action," the organization of which depends on the conceptual formulation of the Code. Thus, inscription techniques conjoined with a mandated course of action, as a tacit resource of police work, produce the objective character of the "First Visit" account. Together, they are integral to the officers' documentary method of interpreting the bathhouse setting.

Regulating Sex: A Textually-Mediated Relation

This research originally began with our generalized experience as gay men of having our sexual lives policed. The course the analysis took started with the work of Coulis and Proctor inscribing the "fact" of "indecent acts" at the Back Door bath. It went on, first, to the ideological features of this organization, and then to its properties as a mandated course of action. The next step the research took was to orient to the way in which the work of the police, as a mandated course of action, resides within the social relations of policing. In these circumstances, these relations consisted of a set of sequentialized moments: investigation–raid–arrest–trial, where former moments intend latter ones and in which the latter accomplish the former. That is, the investigation of the premises intends a police raid which accomplishes the purpose of the investigation; the raid, in turn, intends the arrest of individuals which accomplishes the raid; and so on and so forth. This work process, taking place across various sites of ruling – the legislature, the police investigation, the Crown attorney's office, the courts, etc. – is coordinated by texts such as the Criminal Code and the disclosure documents, among others. It is the way in which the various moments of these relations are knitted together and organized internally by documents that makes them textually-mediated relations.

Like the organization of inscription as a mandated course of action, documents not only link the various moments of these relations, they *concert them*. For example, in the account of the "First Visit" there are two sequences of inscription: the original report of Coulis and Proctor, and the reconstruction of this account in the disclosure document itself. The temporal sequence of this work can be seen in the initial identification of John DOE. ("It was at this location that the officers first saw the accused; who was later 'identified' as [John DOE].") Originally, he was just observed (i.e., reported on). Now, in the disclosure document he is "identified" as the accused, which means that in the interim the raid has taken place, DOE has been arrested and is presently awaiting trial. Thus, two moments of inscription central to this policing relation that are present in the disclosure document are, first, writing the police report at the time of the investigation, and then putting together the disclosure account as part of the preparation for trial. The way in which the category of "the accused" can be used retrospectively in the disclosure account displays how these sequences of inscription and the documents they construct concerts these relations by holding together the moments of "investigation" and "raid" while intending the moment of "trial." Thus, the social relations regulating sex are a form of organization in which a ruling apparatus is coordinated through time and space by documents.

The last step in this analysis was to embed the policing relations of investigation–raid–arrest–trial into the social organization "crystallized" in the Criminal Code. This required, at least in a cursory way, substructing the conceptual organization which this document expresses (i.e., its structure of relevance), and which the police are hired to enforce. The key concept here is "indecent," as in "indecent act." Under Canadian law all sexual acts, except those focused on procreation, are "indecent"; and even procreational sex is "indecent" if it goes on "in public" – that is, involving more than two people or in a public place. The organization, therefore, which this concept "bears" and helps enforce is the social relations of heterosexual sex taking place privately within familial circumstances. "Familial" should not be read here as strictly implying "marriage," but as intending various social forms that either tend towards (e.g., pre-marital sex), or approach in one way or another (e.g., common-law marriage), married life. It is thus organized within the ambit of home and family. Its antithesis is the social relation of anonymous sex in public.

What this analysis makes evident is that legal concepts such as "indecent act," far from being theoretical entities divorced from the practicalities of everyday life, constitute a fulcrum from which a ruling apparatus gets purchase on the lives of those it seeks to govern. Thus, incorporating the notion of "indecent act," the concept of a "bawdy-house," organized conceptually in the definitions of the Code, makes illegal any place that individuals might resort to for prostitution or acts of indecency.[10] As has already been shown, this concept organizes the investigative practice of Coulis and Proctor, which operates, using inscription techniques, to enter and secure individuals within the regulatory relations of a ruling apparatus. Thus concepts, in how they shape and determine policing practices, display the organizational properties whereby they control those aspects of life which they inform and order (Kress & Hodge 1979: 62–84). It is in this sense that the conceptual formulation of the Criminal Code intends a form of society that the work of the police accomplishes (i.e., a heterosexual society where legitimate sexuality is focused on procreative sex within private, familial settings). The bawdy-house law, in this sense, "crystallizes" a social form of life which is both the social organization of the Code's construction and the social organization which its application brings into being.

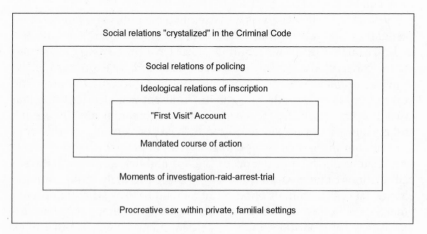

Figure 1.2   The social organization of the "First Visit" account.

As a piece of textual analysis, this research aimed to explicate the social relations of policing by substructing the organization of the "First Visit" account. It is, in this sense, a study in the social organization of knowledge. What it has revealed is that the social organization of the "First Visit" account resides in a set of textually-mediated social relations that are part of a ruling apparatus. The purpose of this apparatus is to enforce heterosexuality and to ensure that people's sexual activities take place in private familial settings. Figure 1.2 provides a diagram of the social organization of the "First Visit" account, displaying its embeddedness in a series of ever-widening, textually-mediated contexts. What this research demonstrates, comparable to early institutional analyses of ethnomethodologists (e.g., Zimmerman 1969), is that documents are an active constituent of ruling relations (Smith 1982).

Conclusions and Discussion

Implications for Sociology

At the beginning of this paper, I pointed out that this inquiry was not a study *about* gay men but *for* them. It does not, consequently, take gay people – or the police, for that matter – as object. Rather, starting from the standpoint of gay men, it undertakes to constitute and investigate their everyday world as problematic (Smith 1981). The method of work was to inquire into how our world is shaped and determined by social processes that go beyond its scope. The genealogy of this method lies in the work of Marx, Garfinkel, and, most importantly, Dorothy Smith. It is only in eschewing discourse and theory and starting from the location of actual individuals in the everyday world that it is possible to take up what in this particular instance is the standpoint of gay people. A major sociological finding of this study in the social organization of knowledge is the textually-mediated property of police work. Moreover, this analysis shows how a textually-mediated, investigative course of action operates, using inscription techniques, to enter and secure individuals in a regulatory relation. It is the categories of the Criminal Code, and hence the disclosure documents, that make the administration of sex possible. These documents, among others, concert the extra-local relations that penetrate our lives with the intent of regulating sex by knitting together the work of ruling taking place at various sites. It is in this sense that the conceptual formulations of the Code intend enforced heterosexuality in private. By insisting that documents are active constituents of policing relations, this analysis stands in contrast to traditional ethnographic accounts of police work, which usually adopt the methodological prejudice of emphasizing local, face-to-face relations. If policing relations are to be understood, however, documents and textual analysis must be integral to their explication.

Implications for Gay Politics

For as long as the policing of sex has existed in our society, gay people, particularly gay activists, have speculated about its "cause." The problem up to now has been the inadequacy of our accounts in providing a description of the mediating links between what are ordinarily taken as "cause" and "effect." Historically, these accounts of the relations between gays and the police has not been grounded empirically, but merely "theorized." How, for example, can the actions of the police in regulating sex be seen to be "caused" by the mental state (i.e., homophobia) of individual officers when mental states are not ordinarily evoked as the "cause" of police actions in cases, for example, of robbery or murder. Moreover, when pursued, traditional gay-activist accounts of policing fail to provide a concrete description of how the various critical sites of ruling involved in regulating sex are articulated to each other (e.g., the mini-economy theory). In setting out to investigate the policing of gays, I did not want my conclusions to have this kind of theoretical character. I wanted them, rather, without making any claims for their completeness, to be empirically and therefore scientifically adequate as a description of how the policing of gay men works. This interest, however, required a conceptual shift. Instead of an inquiry into *why* the bath raids took place, our problematic took up the issue of *how* they took place. This shift operated to ground our research in the everyday activities of individuals such as Coulis and Proctor, who on a day-to-day basis accomplish the enterprise of ruling.

In attempting to explain how policing works, gay people, up to this point, have generally not examined in any detail how this process is organized by texts as a documentary mode of action. By substructing the investigative report of Coulis and Proctor's "First Visit" to the Back Door bath, the research focused on the secret penetration of gay men's lives by the police. These investigative activities, however, are not characterized by the physical and psychological abuse typical of a bath raid. In the preliminary investigative work of Coulis and Proctor there is none of the harassment, verbal abuse, beatings, etc. that sometimes characterize gay men's treatment at the hands of the police, yet their textually-mediated actions of inscribing the "facts" of the Back Door case enmesh individuals more securely in this relation than any physical force might. In our society crime and punishment only arise in textually-mediated modes of action. What the analysis of the "First Visit" revealed, consequently, is a world behind a bath raid which turns out to be a lot more determined and determining than a simple face-to-face confrontation between a gay man and an arresting officer. Unfortunately, in their concern over the police, and especially over police violence, gay men have not taken into account how the law provides for and organizes this kind of treatment.

While historically gay politics has attempted to solve the problem of police harassment, etc., by calling for the administering of psychological tests to weed out homophobic recruits, the organizing of gay–police liaison committees, etc., it has failed to understand what this research has underlined: the central mechanism organizing the policing of gays is the Criminal Code. Consequently, getting the police off our backs is not, in the first instance, a matter of developing better public relations with police departments, etc., but of changing the law. This is not to call for reform, but for revolution. After all, the purpose of a revolution is to change the law. While legal reform might be a first and necessary condition, it is not, however, a sufficient one for improving the treatment of gay people in society.

NOTES

1 This paper is dedicated to John DOE, friend, fellow activist, and former housemate. I would also like to thank my colleagues at the Ontario Institute for Studies in Education and a number of activists in Toronto's gay community for reading and commenting on earlier drafts of the manuscript.

2 [*Editors' note*: According to Sears (2011), 306 people were arrested in the raids. The Canadian record for mass arrests was recently broken at the G20 summit in Toronto in 2010.]

3 [*Editors' note*: *The Body Politic*, in print from 1971–87, was Canada's first gay magazine and was the forerunner of *Xtra!* magazine. Archives for *The Body Politic* are available through the Canadian Lesbian and Gay Archives (CGLA), at www.clga.ca/Material/Records/inven/tbp/tbpint.htm.]

4 It has not been uncommon, historically, for the Toronto police to charge a gay man with an "indecent act" and "gross indecency" for allegedly committing

a sexual act "in public." Through a system of plea bargaining, the gay man's lawyer pleads him guilty to the lesser charge – in this case, the "indecent act."

5 Following Marx's social ontology, artifacts can be said to "express," "bear," or "crystalize" a social relation (Rubin 1973). What this language intends is that these artifacts not be taken as "referencing" the social relations in which they arise, but as constitutive of and constituted by these relations.

6 Another way of putting this is to say that this relation is not structured as a series of conceptually bounded phenomena such as variables in traditional social science research that are simply related contingently to one another.

7 A discursive object is a thing which only exists on paper and which is brought into being using documentary procedures for classifying the practices and activities of people, e.g., "crime."

8 In developing the analysis of the ideological circle, Smith acknowledges her indebtedness to Garfinkel's description of the documentary method of interpretation, particularly where he analyses events treated as documents of the schemata of a textual discourse (Garfinkel 1967: 78–9). Smith's account of the ideological circle can be found in (Smith 1982).

9 This relation is not structured as two independent activities: investigating crime and then writing a report. Rather, the report is part of the investigation in that the investigation is not complete until the report is written. This is, in other words, an internal relation.

10 The purpose of the law was underscored when the Ontario Court of Appeal in 1982 extended the definition of a bawdy-house to cover a parking lot where prostitutes and their clients resort to having sex in the clients' cars. *R. v. Pierce and Golloher* (1982), 66 C.C.C. (2d) 388, 37 O.R. (2d) 721 (C.A.).

2 Regulating the Alternative: Certifying Organic Farming on Vancouver Island, British Columbia

KATHERINE WAGNER

Katherine Wagner works closely with extracts from in-depth interviews to identify the essentials of a regulated process that links the text-mediated work of two farmers who have applied for organic certification for their products and the work of the official who evaluates the work they do. The official assesses if the farmers' work – in both their operations and their textual recording of their operations – meets the requirements and criteria in the provincial regulations that will enable the official to recommend certification of their operations as "organic." We see just how having their operations assessed shapes the farmers' daily work, imposes an order on it that creates additional work and takes additional time in their already long work days, all of which the farmers find difficult. Wagner also tracks specific texts that carry organic standards into the work of each of the informants, showing how standards provide one side of a text–reader conversation in which the farmers and the official, in dialogue, each attempt to bring his or her consciousness and reflections on day-to-day work activities into alignment with the text.

Wagner illustrates the embodied work with texts – reading, writing, interpreting in action and talk – done by these key individuals engaged in the process, highlighting the work they must do together in constructing an assessment of a farm's operations. Her account begins at the farm gate, at the farmer's dining-room table, watching the farmer sort through papers he'll have to submit. Accounts of the farmers' embodied work – John's dealing with an infestation of crane-fly larvae, Karen's account of reorganizing her record keeping and filing – puts us into their boots, showing us their work reorganization with all its frustrations, sophistication, and its ground in everyday living and working.

The analysis moves to the inspector's textual work. The "verification officer" is trained by an international body to assess the farm's, and the farmer's, "compliance" to its standards and to properly document what is visible to him and reported to him in his auditing or inspection visit to the farm. Wagner shows how the standardized texts operate between them, connect their work directly and at the regulatory level, coordinate each one's consciousness and activities. The inspector's account of his work shows us just how he fixes on the texts, constrains his actions and talk while doing inspecting, documenting, and writing up a report. We see how he does so, in order, himself, to be seen to "comply" with what he has been trained to do in evaluation and with the ethical standards held for him in the texts he puts on the table before Wagner to illustrate what it is all about for him. Part of the inspector's account shows how his questions to farmers aim at locating farm operations' "non-compliance." The illustration serves, Wagner points out, to show just how the textual work of the inspection is geared to compare what the farmer said on the application with what can be observed on the ground, with a built-in bias to detecting doubtful textual work or operations as "non-compliance" across a set of abstract categories, and filtering out or ignoring the rich, complex experiential knowledge and methods of the organic small-scale farmer.

In buying and eating food produced and distributed within our contemporary food system, people place trust in what Dorothy Smith (1987, 2001) has called "ruling relations." The abstracted relations associated with conventional food production and distribution, in turn, rely on texts essential to the organization of social life across geographic sites. Turning to small-scale farmers who are trying to work with the ecological system, trying to localize food production and distribution to make social relations just and known to people, we are looking at a way of farming that exists within the contemporary global capitalist system and that is challenging and vulnerable to its organization and change. The work of small-scale organic farmers is altered as it becomes subject to social organization that is conducive to industrial food production. From the standpoint of the small-scale, locally oriented, organic farmers in British Columbia (BC), Canada, I investigate the process involving people in organic farm certification. In this process, the farmer is situated in actuality, actively interpreting and acting on texts such as BC's certified organic farming standards that enter the local and mediate reality.

I draw on data from three open-ended interviews with small-scale organic farmer John, in which he identifies four active texts: the Certified Organic Association of British Columbia (COABC) Organic Standards (COABC 2007), a regulating text, read, interpreted and enacted by John; the Islands Organic Producers Association (IOPA) certification application, a form filled out annually by John to retain his organic certification; farm records, created by John and mediated by his interpretation of the standards; and a letter to John from the certifying body, granting conditional certification of his farm. Second, I draw on data from an open-ended interview with small-scale organic farmer Karen, in which she speaks of the organic standards and, more prominently, the records she produces for her annual certification inspections. Third, I draw on two open-ended interviews with Mack, a third-party organic verification officer. Mack's work is central to the certification process. His account delineates how it is that texts coordinate the work of people throughout the institutionalized certification process, and in turn how the coordination of a verification officer's work affects the work of an organic farmer. Mack engages with the farmers' applications and records to produce another active text, a report for the certifying body. This report represents the work of the inspected organic farmer and is used to ascertain or verify her certification. Aside from organic standards, Mack's account reveals two regulatory texts that mediate his work: the International Organic Inspectors Association (IOIA) inspector's manual, and the IOIA inspector's Code of Ethics. Both of these texts were made available to him during a now mandatory, standardized inspector's training course coordinated by the IOIA.

The label "organic" has now generally become associated with the institutionalized programs for certified organic farming that are increasingly centrally organized to facilitate trade on national and international levels. When thinking of grass-roots ambitions for sustainable food systems, it is no longer appropriate to speak of a homogeneous organic farming movement. Organic farming standards as the basis for "certified organic" are often promoted as a much needed "level playing field," in which one set of rules defines how to farm organically and dictates what food can be described as organic. As I began to speak with small-scale organic biodiversity farmers, to listen at their meetings and participate in their conferences, I began to wonder what the "levelling" achieves, who or what drives it and who benefits. How does a standardized quantifiable list of third-party verified certified organic farming practices affect a small-scale organic biodiversity farmer who is trying to forge an alternative food system? More concretely, how is it that the institutionalized program for certified organic farming in BC enters into and reconstitutes the everyday work of small-scale, locally oriented organic farmers on Vancouver Island?

Organic Certification – Delineating the Process

It was sunny but cool. The ground was wet as it always is here on our island in December, but otherwise it was the sort of day we West Coasters take for granted mid-winter when most of Canada is knee-deep in snow. My car sloshed through deep potholes along the chicken-scattered driveway to the farmhouse where I would interview John. This interview would take place during a textually-mediated process, as John worked to complete his annual organic certification application.

Upon arrival John ushered me into his dining room. A long rectangular table filled the centre of the room with space enough for six chairs to tuck around it. The entire table was strewn with papers. Small and large piles alongside open exercise books, receipt books, and ripped loose-leaf with pencilled jottings. John gestured to a chair and I sat, cautiously shifting a few papers aside to make room for my recorder. I apologized, worried I was putting John's work out of order. He responded: "That's just the thing, there is no organization yet."

John's certification application was part of the annual certified organic farm verification process. All certified organic farmers in BC received an application in the mail each year to fill out, copy three times and submit to their certifying body, affiliated with the COABC. For both John and Karen the certifying body was the IOPA. John explains the work process:

> JOHN: In IOPA, [the administrator] does all the coordinating, like he sends out all the application forms, he receives them, puts them in order ... He'll get like ten farms near each other and hire the same inspector who's totally independent, a contractor right? To do the ten farms. So the inspector would get one copy [of the application]. The other two copies would go to the certification committee. So ... then the certification committee would go over the application before [the inspector] gets it. And like if it was a new applicant and there wasn't enough information there, then they wouldn't put [the application] through. And in a lot of cases, they do the same with me, they'll say they can't process it because you're missing this piece of paper. But I try to make sure I've got everything that they say they want! So then the application, you know, goes before the committee on which there are seven or eight people. So they go through – not necessarily every person on the committee would go through every single one, because that would be impossible, right?

There might be 70 or 80 applicants, so for you, one person [it] would take a hell of a long time. So what they do is they divide them up randomly and everybody would get three or four or five or whatever. So you know, they have to say that the application is OK. And then they forward it back to the administrator, and then he'd put them together in the [regional] groupings that I'm saying, to make it easier for the inspector and cheaper. And then he'd pass them on to the inspector, eight or ten or whatever, and he'd take them. The inspector probably reads them before he goes to the farm, then he goes to the farm and he sees what you're doing ... I have to walk him around and show him what's going on, and he'll ask about this or that.

Having been an organic farmer for many years, John competently describes the paper trail that leads to his yearly certification verification. Mack, an "inspector" or, formally, verification officer, describes the process:

MACK: So certifying agencies send applications to the farms and then it goes back to me, and then I get these applications ... and the farmer says OK my name is so and so and my certification number, if they're already certified, is, you know, 125, and here's a farm map of my farm and there's details on there about all the different crops ... So I go through that and I look for possible inconsistencies with the standards and then I call up the farmer and say, you know, I'm going to be your verification officer for this year, and OK, I've got your farm application in front of me, and if I wanted anything clarified I would ask them at that time. And then I'd set up an appointment to go see them ... Then I go to their farm, and when I get there ... I say, "Hi my name is [Mack]" and then we kind of go through the application and I ask if there has been any changes since they submitted it, and then I note those down, you know, if there have been or if not ...

KATIE: What kind of things – changes – are you looking for? ...

MACK: Ah, like if they've decided instead of putting peas in over here they put in carrots instead, or if they're not going to plant this field and instead are going to leave it fallow. Yeah, things like that. Or they got a new neighbour.

KATIE: So you need all the details!

MACK: Oh, we need to know everything. Everything that they're doing, like what they're growing and where they're selling it to, if they have labels, everything. So then I'll usually do a farm tour where we walk around the farm and I go and look at the fields, inspect the soil, look at the weed count, look at the crops in the ground, and I look at the plants, you know and kind of assess their health ...

KATIE: What do you base all these assessments on?

MACK: I base the assessment of the farm on, basically what it said in their applications ... then I'm worried about like, for example, if there's a field that is totally devoid of weeds, then it's like sort of questionable [both laugh]. Like did they spend the money on weeding that, or? And you always have to keep in mind organic control points, which are places where there could be possibility of the organic integrity being compromised. So things like, illegal inputs, like [inaudible chemical names] and stuff like that ... Then I do the exit interview, I say ok, these are my concerns, and they're A, B, and C, and here's the standards that they refer to, and the farmer signs that to acknowledge that they have seen my concerns ... [Then I write] my report, and I sign it and I send it back to the certifying body. And then the certifying committee of that association can take that report and use it to then decide whether or not they want to certify that operation. Or if they want to put conditions on it.

The application process John and Mack depict is an active text-work sequence. A text (the application) is sent to a reader (the farmer) who interprets and works on the text (fills out the application); which is then sent to another reader (certification committee member, via administrative officer). This reader in turn interprets and acts on the text (deciding whether it is complete, presumably based on whether the farmer has filled out all categories delineated on the form). Then, if the text is deemed ready to continue on in the process, it is sent (via the administrative officer) to the next reader (the verification officer), who engages with the text and, in conjunction with a farm tour, works to produce another active text (the narrative report). Both active texts (the farmer's application and verification officer's report) are then returned to the initiators of the text/reader sequence (the certification body and, in turn, the certification committee). Here the texts are engaged with by readers, and thus activated (in the decision as to whether certification will be granted). The committee then works to produce another text (the letter of certification), which is returned to the original reader (the farmer), read, interpreted, and worked on to gain certification for the following year. The entire active sequence – text reader/work text reader/work text reader/work text/text reader/work text reader/ work – is mediated by the central regulating text (the BC Certified Organic Farming Standards), and further mediated by two regulating texts that specifically guide the verification officer's work (the IOIA manual and IOIA code of ethics).

The BC Certified Organic Farming Standards text serves as a regulating text that mediates the work of the farmer, verification officer, and certification committee. It is the farmer's responsibility to learn the standards – an ongoing process as they are revised each year – then to enact the standards through farm practices and prove their enactment and complete compliance annually to the verification officer during inspection:

> KATIE: But [the inspection is] not like a test, I mean there's not any surprises then are there?
>
> JOHN: Well, usually, but the standards get revised every year and admittedly I don't always read the updates, you know. I usually glance through them and if I see something to do with chickens or strawberries, then I'll look at it. But if it's some general thing then sometimes I'll miss it. But then that's what they'll come looking for.
>
> KATIE: They look for the newest thing?
>
> JOHN: Yeah, and if you've picked up on it then you can answer the question, but if you haven't then you may have gone and done something that – and it won't necessarily be something that's prohibited because they don't generally change it from allowed to prohibited unless they, unless something really happens, and they'll alert everybody with emails. But they're not out to catch you in that sense ... But of course they always presume that you read your email ...

Forms of textual mediation are increasingly computerized. In this case, the Internet allows annual changes to be made to the regulating text, easily interjected into the standardized form and technologically distributed through ungrounded space to the requisite population. Thus, John's work in learning and enacting the organic standards involves not only reading and interpreting the standardized text, but attaining access to the text via the technology that makes updates available to him.

When asked similarly about the "work process involved in keeping up with changing standards," Karen too spoke of the role of computers and Internet access, with particular reference to her use of the certifying body's email listserv as an active text:

> KAREN: [IOPA] runs a listserv so we get this listserv and when issues come up, IOPA takes action, like about the gypsy moth spraying and this issue

of fly ash from incinerators that's going into the soil. So we keep up with things that are going on and things that will affect other farmers as well as when new standards come in, or when people have new ideas, like one time it was the source of woodchips. People were putting wood-chips on their paths and they were getting mixed in with treated wood chips and they found out so it's usually somebody that figures something out, then writes it to the listserv and then everyone says, "Yeah, this is an issue and let's make a rule so it doesn't happen to somebody else."

Using the Internet as a communicative tool, members of the certifying body are in contact with farmers on an almost constant basis. Through the listserv, as Karen describes it, farmers post problems they encounter and through authoritative written responses, they are guided through dealing with issues as they occur. In using the listserv, farmers interact with texts in a dynamic form; more consistently and with rapid response in an exchange that mimics conversation while the properties of the text (static, physically present, and materially replicable) remain. Activity is coordinated from one locale to the other via these texts; yet because emails elicit specific, individually tailored written responses, the textualized coordination of the farmers' work becomes more efficient, site-specific, and more continually invasive in the everyday world. Emails have become yet another text through which ruling relations coordinate local sites and bring about particular courses of action. These Internet-enabled authority–text / reader–actor conversations increasingly replace conversations that might previously have occurred over the telephone, in person, or not at all. These conversation takes on a textual form, physically present in the everyday, replicable and retrievable for reinterpretation. The farmer is "agent" (Smith 2005) for texts that are both non-responsive or regulatory (such as the organic standards) and for email texts with the unique property that, while they themselves do not change in response to the readers' interpretation, they elicit text conversations with institutional authorities, increasing the frequency of interactions with these authorities. As such, the listserv allows farmers access to clarification of their interpretation of texts and specifically tailored instructions on a frequent basis.

I have read the COABC organic standards myself, even researching the updates via the Internet, yet I cannot comprehend their organizational function – how they coordinate a farmer's work – simply through my own engagement with them. While I may read for content,

I am concerned here with process: the text does not stand alone "inert, without impetus or power" (Smith 1990c: 122) and "cannot be read in detachment from other texts that it addresses, reflects, refers to, presupposes, relies on and so on" (Smith 2001: 187). The text operates in place and time, actively interpreted within the local setting in which it is enacted and "necessarily embedded in a complex of texts" (187). John's filled-out application for re-certification plainly depicts this property of the text–reader interchange. It exemplifies John's work in reading, interpreting, and acting on texts in the context of a complex of relevant, influential texts. John's own reading of the regulatory text – IOPA's version of the COABC organic standards – and his interpretation of the layout and purpose of the application within the administrative process, guide his work in filling out the form.

JOHN: You know they're always asking you for tips in IOPA through this [application]. It actually asks you, now let's see if I can find the section. Yeah, here you go. "Have you successfully used any new techniques for weed, insect pest or disease control? And eh, any information that you'd like to share with other IOPA people." See, I said about the crane fly larvae. They just were eating the heck out of one greenhouse. They just literally destroyed it, three of the beds out of six were demolished. And we tried BT, we tried beneficial nematodes and none of it worked. And then we put the chickens in there for a week and they just sort of demolished them. We went up and down with the rotor-tiller and as we turned them over the chickens were following the rotor-tiller and eating the larvae.

KATIE: Perfect! And you thought of doing that yourself? You hadn't read that somewhere?

JOHN: No. Like, I called and talkèd to [name], at the bug place. He's an entomologist ... so I brought the larvae up the road to him. They were actually all in there, they were having a meeting including [name] the boss. So they passed the little thing around that I had the worms in and they said, "Yeah, yeah that's crane fly." And they said there's a nematode for it, I think it's spiderama? So I phoned the bug factory up in [place name] and they sent me down 6 million of these things, which is a little packet about this big [*holds fingers about four inches apart*]. And so we used them, and it didn't do anything ... T[he crane fly are] just too tough. And then I talked to a guy who supplies this kind of stuff and he said to try the BT, that that might work, and just put it on the lettuce and when they eat it, it might kill them, and it didn't.

KATIE: So you were pretty stuck on what to do there?

JOHN: Yeah and by that time the whole greenhouse is shot right? So we've
    lost the whole crop in the greenhouse. So we thought, well the chickens
    will eat just about anything that moves, so let's just put chickens in there
    and see what happens, so we took about thirty chickens and put them in
    there …

KATIE: Oh, so you had the solution the whole time, eh?

JOHN: Yeah, but then you see it causes a problem.

KATIE: Because of the manure?

JOHN: Yeah, so you can't grow a food crop on it.

KATIE: Oh, so that's why you put here that you had to sow the buckwheat
    in there.

JOHN: Yeah … if you put chickens in there because of the crane fly … then
    you have to put a cover crop in after that. I germinated the buckwheat
    until it got up to three or four inches and then we just tilled it in.

A section within the IOPA application asks farmers to document helpful tips to pass on to their colleagues in the organic community. In response, John documented his story of a crane fly infestation. Speaking
with John about his "tip" with the filled-out application in front of us, it
became apparent that the tip itself involved allowing "30 laying hens"
access to an infested crop "for one week" to rid a field of crane-fly larvae.
This was a particularly good tip – John was visibly pleased with it – as
two different methods suggested by professionals in the field did not
eliminate the infestation. Yet while John's chickens "took care of the problem," he follows the suggestion with: "We then sowed buckwheat and
later tilled it in." The sowing of the buckwheat is extraneous to the tip;
it is not the innovative information that would be helpful to other farmers looking for a solution to a crane-fly infestation. Rather, this sentence
is included by John to demonstrate his compliance with the standards,
which prohibit the growing of a food crop on soil with raw manure. John
has read and interpreted the standards, enacted them on his farm, and
in turn has read and understood the purpose of the application form as
a text that must demonstrate his compliance with the standards. He has
created this text to represent his work in the institutional process and has
thus documented his compliance with the organic standards.

Demonstrating compliance with the regulating text is a common
theme in John and Karen's descriptions of the annual certification verification process. A typical inspection as described by Karen also involves
a farm tour in which the verification officer knows which things to look

for and what questions to ask in order to potentially reveal a farmer's non-compliance with the standards. Armed with her own interpretation of the organic standards, the farmer knows what will be looked for, anticipates the kinds of questions that will be asked and the kinds of answers the inspector will need to hear and document to reveal the farmer's compliance or non-compliance to certifying board members.

> KAREN: You're kind of just going around and showing them everything. And then they want to look in your shed to see what amendments you have there. They want to see the whole farm, so they walk everywhere on the farm. I had an old fridge one time and they opened it to see, they just want to make sure you're not hiding anything, even though you totally could [*laughing*] because you could just bring it somewhere else.

Karen explains how – whether or not, for example, a fertilizer bag is ever found on the farm – sales receipts can be used to indicate whether farmers could be using "disallowed" fertilizers. She explains: "The producers [who] use alfalfa meal, which is a fertilizer, if they're producing tons and tons and tons of greens then they better have tons and tons and tons of alfalfa meal [receipts], otherwise they're using some other fertilizer." It is the constant collection, retention and organization of these receipts along with the written, dated records of farm work that constitutes the certified organic farmer's record keeping.

Record Keeping and the Time It Takes

The first text John produced for me on my second visit to his farm was a letter from the certification committee last year, certifying his farm on a conditional basis. The letter stated that John was "not taking record keeping seriously." This statement was followed by a referral to "COABC Standard 3.2: Record Keeping Audit Trail." John showed me the applicable standard in one of his many copies of the BC organic standards, which he appeared to keep throughout his home. The standard reads as follows:

3.2.1 Required

1. An Organic Land and Resource Crop Management Register kept in an orderly and auditable form which includes at least the following information pertaining to each production unit. This information will provide a

complete audit trail from farm to final sale (final sale means when the product in question leaves possession of the producer):

a. Input records
b. Crop yields
c. Receipts for purchases and sales

. Copies of valid certified organic certificates from all sources of organic products. (COABC 2007)

A farmer can be decertified for non-compliance with any standard, and John had risked decertification for poor or incomplete record keeping. The institutionalized program for organic certification relies heavily on this complex, detailed form of record keeping. While John does not always keep records in a way he suspects is required, this text (the letter) altered his interpretation of the standards and spurred work processes aimed at satisfying the following year's verification officer and certification committee. John hoped his efforts would be "good enough."

When asked about preparing for the next inspection, John surprisingly did not mention record keeping as a central concern. In preparation for an inspection, he would attempt to pull his paperwork together to create a semblance of organization, which he perceived was expected by the verification officer. The text (letter) / text (standards) reader / work text (records) process involves John's interpretation of last year's certification letter, which alters his interpretation of the organic standards and in turn mediates his production of this year's records.

Like John, Karen emphasized the centrality of record keeping to successful organic certification; and she too recalled a letter she received in which "they basically said next year better go better." Initially Karen was taught how to keep her records through a "workshop that IOPA did on certification papers." This formal learning, along with her interpretation of the purpose for the audits, has guided her record-keeping work. She explains the audits, as she came to understand them, and in turn the work she did to demonstrate her "competence":

KAREN: Basically what they want for certification is for you to prove that
   you are growing everything that you are selling so that you're not running a laundering process through your farm. And that's interesting to
   think about. And part of it is also a test of your competence, so they want

to know your management practices, what you've done when you've had problems, just so they can be sure you know what you're doing. So if a big problem comes up, like my club root ... I would just document those things as happening.

Karen described the annual re-certification inspection as a two-part process beginning with the farm tour that is "usually fun" and "kind of like show and tell where you just go around and show them what you're doing and they'll ask questions," followed by the audit, which is "always a lot of paper everywhere, which gives me anxiety." She explains the audit process, or "scary part" as follows:

KAREN: Well basically they do this audit – that's the scary part, but it's kind of cool when it works. [*laughing*] I always think it's magic when it works. So you're supposed to keep all of your receipts, and then you have a journal and then you have a sales book. And then the verification officer will go down and say, oh so you sold fifty pounds of spinach on August 28th so tell me about that spinach. So you go, ok, in my journal, oh look I planted it on May 4th and they you can say how much seed you put down, what you amended the bed with, how much compost you put in, where you got that compost from. And they just ask about all these things, so you flip to your seed receipts and you can say ok, I got the seeds from here. So you trace it all back for them.

Yet since the "audit that didn't go well," Karen altered her record-keeping habits to suit the verification process. Her opinion of record keeping in general also changed:

KAREN: It's good to have all those records done, and you totally wouldn't do them if you weren't scared of the audit. It makes you keep records. It really makes us think "oh, you have to write down when you planted that spinach," and then if that spinach is awesome, we can look back at when we planted it and say "hey, that's the right time or the right way to plant it." ... It's really hard. And there's a lot of paperwork. But at the same time, I wouldn't do the paperwork if it wasn't for the certification, and it's totally helped me with my business. If I wasn't forced to keep all those receipts they'd probably fly out the window as I'm driving [*laughing*]. And that's what happened in the first years. I just didn't – I couldn't – until I said, "if I'm going to farm this way I need all these papers and so I'm going to get a book and put them all in and file them."

To verify their certification, Karen and John must keep written records pertaining to each crop variety, all compost, every animal, and
all animal feed. They must save every seed packet, every receipt for
grain or inputs, document where they bought their stock, record every
compost rotation, every egg, every input, and retain receipts from every sale. Each component of the farm involves its own paperwork, so
it follows that more components mean more work. Verification officer
Mack emphasized the centrality of a farmer's complete record keeping
to the verification process. Comprehensive farm records presented in
an organized fashion are absolutely integral to his ability to do carry
out his work. Mack explains as follows:

> MACK: I don't believe everything [farmers] say, I only believe what I observe
> myself. Like I snoop into everything … They have to have very compre-
> hensive records … Basically I should be able to go into their records and
> do an audit and track, you know, a carrot that I have in front of me from
> the time they bought the seed until it was delivered wherever else. So
> everything that happened to it, where it came from as seed, any inputs,
> where it was planted …
>
> KATIE: The farmer keeps all these records herself?
>
> MACK: Yeah the farmer keeps the records … Any inputs, labour. Any kind
> of activity done on the crop like weeding, or planting or harvesting or
> whatever … Like the big operations, like at grain farms, for example,
> they have like giant bins of grain that all have lot numbers, and then
> they're shipped by lot number. Stuff like that.
>
> KATIE: And they produce these kinds of things for you to look at then?
>
> MACK: Yeah, ideally yes. [laughs]
>
> KATIE: Not always?
>
> MACK: Yeah, well it's kind of like the weakest part because farmers are not
> usually good with the record keeping … But they should. They should
> have a record of any time they do anything, which is pretty extreme I
> know …

During an inspection Mack states that he should only believe, and
moreover record, what he has observed himself. This facet of his work –
or action – stems from his reading and interpretation of standardized
IOIA coursework, his reading and interpretation of the regulatory
IOIA manual, and his reading and interpretation the IOIA code of ethics. Moreover, as the farm inspection and audit combined are to last a
maximum of two hours, it is important to Mack that farmers quickly

and efficiently produce organized, comprehensive written documentation detailing all farm components, work processes, transactions. From these records Mack can create the requisite report that in turn allows the certification committee to assess his documented version of the reality of the farm, in relation to the regulatory BC organic standards.

Mack's experiences indicate that farm size and biodiversity can be related to the farmer's capabilities in regards to good record keeping. He finds it is the farm operations at each end of the spectrum – the very large farm and very small – that keep the best records:

> MACK: I think that some of the bigger operations might be better at record keeping just because of the nature of their operations and because of other requirements they might have. Like if they're supplying to processors who want their product to be certified organic, then they would require records because they have to show that all the product was certified organic and, I don't know, maybe the government might have stringent tracking requirements for big operations ... Like the big operations, like grain farms, for example, they have giant bins of grain and they're shipped by lot number. Stuff like that ... But I've also seen very small operations where the guy has like only one field of crop, so that makes everything very easy for him.

Considering the complexity of the record-keeping process – involving separate records for each livestock category, for crops, for on-farm seeding and composting procedures, and so forth – the farmers that must keep the most extensive records, and thus might have the most difficulty with record keeping, are those with intricate, self-sufficient, biodiversity systems. While John's farm – in which pigs consume waste and chickens heat the greenhouse and "make litter" for compost for an abundance of various crops – may be held up as a model for sustainable agriculture, it may also be the most complicated sort of farm to textually record. Specifically in regards to time – which Smith explains "is not considered as an abstract property but rather as "the time it takes" ... a dimension central to our generous conception of work" (Smith 1987: 65) – the extended time it takes to create adequate records for a small-scale, full-time, year-round biodiversity farm may mean that the organic "playing field" is neither standardized nor levelled in that it elicits various experiences and various outcomes based on who farms and how they farm.

While Karen does suggest that her record keeping serves a self-educational purpose that aids her in running a successful business, record keeping itself does not of course serve a function in regards to sustainable agriculture; rather, it serves administrative purposes and fits with the business of producing and selling food in a contemporary capitalist society. The work of a verification officer is centred on the production of both the certification application and comprehensive farm records, and in turn records become central to the work of the organic farmer. Mack explains the role of record keeping in reference to how his work is evaluated:

> KATIE: OK. And then I wondered how your work is evaluated. How they know if you're doing a good job.
>
> MACK: … [M]y assumption is that they would keep a file on every inspection. I think how they evaluate the work is that my report should tell them everything they want to know about the operation. They shouldn't have to call me up and say well what about this or that. So if that were the case, if the report was not meeting their needs, then that would be unsatisfactory work … I never have been sent back, but they have the possibility of doing that. It's very thorough. Basically I have to be the eyes for the certification association, so everything that is applicable to them is important.

Importantly, Mack identifies his role as "eyes for the certification association" rather than, for example, as a voice for organic farmers within the system. Asking Mack about evaluation practices revealed that the "thoroughness" of his work is key to doing a good job, to producing a document for the certification body that successfully fits with and contributes to the administrative organization of organic farming. To achieve necessary "thoroughness" Mack has to rely on the work of farmers, in their creation of comprehensive farm records and their presentation of those records in an organized and timely manner. The farmer's work in record keeping is central to Mack's job, and more generally to the institutional process. It is a process that characteristically relies on texts to mediate and regulate daily life. The function of records is to allow for social organization, for the extra-local coordination of activity that makes an institutionalized program for organic farming possible. Texts, activated via the work of both farmers and verification officers, come into play in extended sequences of text-reader action, which facilitate centralized organization of certified organic farming programs.

Officers and Audits

Mack's account helps to explain the increases in daily record-keeping work Karen and John undertook as a result of the inspections they experienced on their farms. Verification officer Mack was trained through the standardized IOIA course, and his account confirms the changes John had noted in inspection procedures over his twenty years of farming organically and reflected a recent administrative change involving an international approach to third-party-verified organic farming. That is, the training of verification officers via the internationally standardized IOIA course. As Mack explains, farm inspection procedure no longer involves the verification officer "writing himself into the report." A verification officer is neither to draw on his own opinion of a farmer nor to try to forge a trusting interpersonal relationship with the farmer:

> MACK: Well, when they first started [organic farming] it was all based on trust.
>
> KATIE: Yeah, and I gather they didn't have any guidelines.
>
> MACK: That's right. But now it's not based on trust at all. There's no trust ...
>
> KATIE: Is there then any way that you would indicate to a certifying body that you thought a guy wasn't trustworthy? Because as I understand it, you're saying that you wouldn't indicate that you thought he was, for example, a "trustworthy kind of guy." That's not going to get portrayed in the report?
>
> MACK: No.

Mack explains further that he does not attempt to develop relationships with the farmers he inspects and asserts that the inspection entails only "objective" observation. The verification officers trained by the IOIA are to become third-party, detached, objective contractors. In speaking about his work, Mack reveals that his interpretation and enactment of the IOIA inspector's code of ethics guides his "objective" focus and in turn mediates his relationship with both the certification body and the farmer:

> MACK: I don't believe I am supposed to [make recommendations to the certification body] ... I don't feel that I should be doing that really. I feel that I should just be saying this is the situation and make up your mind. I can't certify and I make it really clear to them that I'm not certifying them, and I'm not allowed to give them advice. So, for example, if they

have a problem with a particular crop and they need to figure out how they can grow it in a better manner then I can say, you know, go to this web site and they have good advice, but I can't tell you how to do it.

KATIE: Why do you feel that? Why can't you?

MACK: Because then that's breaching, as something against the ethical code of conduct. [*Gestures to "code of ethics" on table in front of him.*]

KATIE: Why would that be?

MACK: Because – you know I'm not really sure why [*laughs*]. I think it's because it could be seen that I'm saying if you do this, then you will meet the requirement and you will be certified. Or something along those lines ... Like – it has to be like pretty far apart – like I can't inspect – I wouldn't and I shouldn't – inspect someone that I'm friends with, for example, or that I've had financial dealings, or I can't work with someone within the next two years of inspecting them ...

Beyond the organic standards, two texts specifically mediate the work of an IOIA verification officer: the giant course manual produced by the IOIA and the IOIA code of ethics. Mack showed me his copies. These texts regulate the relationship between farmer and verification officer, the COABC administration "reaches down into and, by transforming the organizational texts" (Smith 2001: 171–3) – the implementation of the standardized IOIA training, its manual and its code of ethics – extra-locally transforms the immediate actual relationship between farmer and verification officer, altering the work and experience of organic farming and certification.

The Narrative Report – Observation and "Fact"

Using the farmer's certification application and records, the verification officer tours the farm and audits the paperwork, then constructs a report that the certification committee uses to assess a farmer's certification status. Mack describes the work he does to ensure a good evaluation from the committee and no farmer complaints:

MACK: Write a really thorough report. Be as professional as I can with the farmer. And explain to them exactly what's happening and what my role is ...

KATIE: Then by being "as professional as you can" you just mean?

Mack I mean being thorough, not wasting their time, talking about relevant things, Also sometimes farmers get a little bit chatty [*laughing*] – so you have to remind them that [the certifying body is] actually paying for you by the hour.

As the "eyes for the certifying body" through farm inspections, Mack must be able to determine what information or which observations are applicable to the committee and then compose a "thorough" narrative report to meet their needs. This is work in the service of social organization. As "everything that is applicable to [the certifying committee] is important," Mack must learn to recognize and bypass extraneous information provided by "chatty" farmers – information that is potentially important to the farmers themselves but not relevant to the institutionalized certification process.

While the organic standards serve as a multidimensional regulatory text, delineating what is applicable to the certifying body and guiding the work of farmers and verification officers, the IOIA manual and code of ethics further serve as regulatory texts that specifically mediate the verification officer's work in conducting a farm inspection and writing a narrative report. To learn how to inspect, a future verification officer must take the Organic Inspector Training Course offered by the IOIA. This course does not provide the verification officer with knowledge of organic farming; rather, such knowledge is a tested requirement prior to taking the course, meaning that most inspectors are or have been organic farmers themselves. Thus, instead of "how-to" farming knowledge, the mandatory IOIA course teaches verification officers how to conduct themselves and how to document the inspection itself. The IOIA aims to "promote consistency in the inspection process and serves to provide inspectors with good field techniques and uniform reporting methods" (Salmins 1999: 1). Verification officers are taught what to look for, how to look, and the importance of making accurate observations relevant to a report.

Certifying bodies require objectively written reports by an IOIA trained verification officer to annually verify the certification of every farmer under their jurisdiction. IOPA provides the verification officer with a list of headings to construct a narrative report. Selecting the heading "3.5 Buffer Zones," I asked Mack to explain the work he would do to create this section of the report:

KATIE: So maybe just take for example "buffer zones." What would you do for buffer zones?

MACK: So for buffer zones I would look at all sides of the farm ... Basically you have to control the possibility of contamination from outside. And then COABC standards have specified a minimum of 25 feet, so you look at stuff like, OK there's a road right next door and its lots and lots of traffic so would 25 feet really be good, you know? They're encouraged to plant trap crops like a big row of trees so the contamination will get stuck in the trees. Or you look at stuff like, so the neighbour next door is a conventional orchardist and, there's always these high winds that blow in this direction [*gesturing with hands*] and you know …

KATIE: Wow, you have to know a huge amount of stuff …

MACK: Oh yeah! Like you know, if buddy next door has … some kind of conventional operation and there could be a lot of run-off because it's up hill, we have to look at like, are the chemicals gonna be coming down onto the property? Is there water, is there a river coming through his property that comes onto this property? That could be contaminated by conventional livestock or by some kind of giant sewage leaking into it from his big pig operation or whatever.

KATIE: So do you walk the perimeter then? How do you even know?

MACK: You look on their map. And you ask them questions about their neighbour. And then you actually go out and say, next door I can see a forest, or whatever.

Due to his prior knowledge of organic farming techniques, Mack understands the practical use of buffer zones to prevent contamination. In an inspection, however, "buffer zones" becomes a concept in relation to the organic standards, coinciding with a particular codified measurement. Mack's work procedure during an inspection – walking the farm perimeter, measuring the distance between a road and crop, looking at the farm map and asking questions – is indicative of his IOIA training that is mediated by the course manual.

Mack describes his work process in terms of asking questions that pertain specifically to standards, then documenting verbatim the pertinent information provided by the farmer, verbally and through the records. Pertinent information generally relates to specific standards. Information that might not directly coincide with a standard, however, could become part of a report through the recording of discrepancies in a neutral "this is how it was manner." Mack explains, "I'm basically just there to assess the situation, and compare the application to the actual realities of their operation." The report devised by the verification officer makes use of the application paper in comparison with what is observed during the two-hour farm visit. Through the officer's practice of noting any discrepancy between what a farmer says and what the inspector "objectively" observes, the certification committee could become aware of discrepancies between application and the account of what was observed and neutrally recorded. At the same time, only in this way might Mack's report portray the farmer's degree of personal commitment to organic farming. His actions, textually-mediated by training and readings of the IOIA manual and code of ethics, are shaped just so that Mack would never directly include his subjective assessment of the farmer's "organic integrity."

The IOIA code of ethics restricts Mack from making recommendations to the certifying committee in his report: "I should just be saying this is the situation and make up your mind." He explains:

> MACK: Like if [the farmer] tell[s] me something and I can't back it up – like if they tell me … "I have this harvesting equipment that I share with Bob who's a conventional farmer," then what they should have is a letter from Bob saying, you know, "this is the clean out procedure." Like an affidavit saying that he's cleaned it out before they used it. If they don't have a letter, then I say that they've used this equipment and they "tell me" that they cleaned it out before using it. But I didn't see it, so I can't say it like "it's a fact" because basically, it's just something that they told me, not something that I can verify.
>
> KATIE: So what would you write down then?
>
> MACK: I would just say that producer stated that this equipment was cleaned out before he used it.
>
> KATIE: So then you just leave it up to the board to figure out whether that's good enough or not.
>
> MACK: Yeah, exactly.

A farmer must provide textual evidence of his work to back up a claim. It is the very presence of a text – in this case a letter from conventional farmer "Bob" – that allows Mack to document "fact" in his report. Short of the requisite text, Mack does not document "a fact" because verbal explanations are not deemed verifiable within the text-based process. Instead, Mack states what the farmer told him in a precise and neutral manner, leaving judgment to the higher-ranking administration.

The verification officer's account of the farm – his work – serves to arrange the actual system of the farm – the actual work of the farmer – into a particular account that is useful for the purposes of the certification committee. Mack produces a selective, objectified, and partial depiction of the farmer based only on textually-mediated "relevant" information in the interests of organization. Through the report – an active text in the institutional process – this particularized objectified version of the farmer goes on through the sequential certification process to represent the farmer's actual subject being and farming experiences. In this way, the farmer's work enters into an abstracted system, beyond the local and particular, where it serves a function within the ruling relations.

To portray the "objective" stance that is expected of him, Mack takes care to use neutral language in his report and to refer only to what he has observed:

KATIE: And then, so you said you try to use pretty neutral language?

MACK: Yeah. Like I would say, for example, if they were doing something that did not meet the standards – so for example say they put in a new treated post – OK. [*Opens standards, Mack and Katie are both looking at them.*] So I would say, "farmer tells me that they've installed a new fence, for pasture using treated posts. This is in contradiction of 3.6.41," for example.

Mack's impartial and detached writing style – organized by the regulatory texts – mediates the semblance of an undifferentiated individual reporter. This reporter is not to be gendered, racialized, or classed, but impossibly disembodied, capable of recording the truth as it occurred. In confining his communication to such neutral language and thoroughly reporting only what he has observed, Mack's report conveys to the certification committee that he has correctly adopted a "professional" role, allowing them to read and work from the report that acts as the defining word regarding the farm. This narrative report becomes the documented fact from which the committee can then approach the more subjective – yet still textually-mediated and categorically restricted – application provided by the farmer. By Mack removing himself from the narrative report, his report appears as fact that can be objectively known, observable as such by anyone. The way Mack structures his narrative report is indicative of the organizational interests – the ruling interests of the IOIA within the industrialized food system – that coordinate the creation of this text within sequential relations of textually-mediated human activity for a particular purpose.

While the farmer is the author of answers to questions put forth on the application form (a painstaking work process itself), the certification committee does not simply use this application to represent the farmer's work. Rather, the primary purpose of the farmer-authored application is as a reference point from which the work of the verification officer can begin to expose discrepancies. Discrepancies between the verification officer's observations of the farm and the organic standards or discrepancies between the farmer's application and the verification officer's observations act as triggers that can indicate to the certification board a farmer's non-compliance with the organic standards.

The verification officer's report represents the work of the farmer for her certification assessment through "reported speech." What the farmer actually says is located inside professionally "predetermined schema" in a properly prepared, professional document (Smith 1990b: 93–100). In this way, the farmer loses subjectivity in the process. The abundance of information supplied to Mack by "chatty" farmers, sifted through by a verification officer during an inspection, is a rich body of information filtered out of the certification process, left out of official documents, and rendered inconsequential to the certification of the farm. In turn, each certified organic farm is presented to consumers as equivalent to any other certified operation, equally represented by one homogeneous "organic" label.

3 Negotiating UN Policy: Activating Texts in Policy Deliberations

LAUREN E. EASTWOOD

Lauren Eastwood's chapter describes textual practices that were integral to processes of formulating a "high level" governing institutional text. Eastwood draws on her own participation in this process when she worked with the non-governmental organizations (NGOs) involved. The chapter shows us a way to look at the textual practices of negotiating language – in an actual local setting and over an actual period of time – in a document that is in the making and on its way to becoming part of a UN agreement and, potentially, a governing text in institutional processes regulating forest uses in the signatory nations.

The chapter includes versions of the text as they are changed, following particular contentious wording revisions over the course of days, as the highly political negotiations are carried on among government and non-government delegates to the UN meetings. These meetings will produce the wording of one section of "Category III" text. That text, and the section on which Eastwood focuses, was being reworked in the last round of negotiations. The final wording would be central to the organization of future UN and environmental NGO activities; it will be the international text that NGO negotiators and others will have to draw on to call signing governments to account for their actions regarding forest preservation.

Eastwood describes the text–reader relation and work of activating wordings and sections of texts as a taken-for-granted practice hooked into pre-structured UN sequences. She illustrates reading and inscription techniques used by experienced delegates. Reading, marking up, and talking about texts in times and places, including corridors, make up the sensuous mechanics and politics of negotiating the text under scrutiny at these meetings. She shows how the text and specific concepts held in it, located in this sequence, constrain what can be said and "negotiated." UN agreement negotiations become visible as the building up of concepts and wordings in successive versions of the text so that they attain currency in negotiating contexts. The very repetition of these negotiation meetings and UN processes year after year, decade after decade, allows negotiators on all sides to cite, rely on, orient themselves to, and work with language and wordings in familiar ways with familiar textual formats. Experienced negotiators can spot "missing" key phrases such as "review and report" – a future desired institutional action NGOs want inscribed that has been left out of the text. Eastwood's ethnography contributes to an explication of what is presupposed in George W. Smith's and Katherine Wagner's studies, namely, how governing texts are brought into being. Her study opens up to view the variously coordinated practices that enter into the wording of a governing text. We learn from Eastwood's ethnography of the importance of institutional work processes and relations in establishing the language that will govern the workings of an institutional circuit.

Introduction: Analysis of UN Texts in Action

As institutional ethnographers have become interested in investigating the ways in which texts organize institutional actions, a fruitful point of analysis becomes the moment when texts are activated within an organizational setting. As practitioners engage with texts in work settings, researchers can gain insights into how it is that texts work within organizations. This chapter describes a particular sort of text–reader interaction, one in which policy texts are generated and worked on by knowledgeable practitioners. DeVault (2008) writes that institutional ethnographers "follow texts in order to explore and analyse the social relations that connect people across the myriad sites of action in contemporary societies" (7). As, in the case of policymaking, texts are generated as part of institutional processes, this chapter is focused on investigating the moments when policymakers are doing the work of creating and modifying a policy text in order to influence the outcomes it may have if and when the policy is implemented.

Text–reader interactions take place as policymakers debate and negotiate policy, strategically deploying the conceptual currency relevant to the organization and leveraging points of contention between governments in order to influence policy documents. Environmental policy texts within the UN system are negotiated over several days within the context of structured meetings. There are multiple moments of text–reader interactions when practitioners are assessing the current state of the documents and strategizing about how to influence the next iteration of the text. Within policy negotiations, effective practitioners are savvy about how to deploy the conceptual currency, or strategic language, relevant to the particular negotiations in which they are engaging. These are often politicized processes for, as DeVault (2008) argues, the "moment of textualization, for each actor, is one moment in an extended course of action; people anticipate textualization, and, when it is completed, they expect to use its product elsewhere" (7). This is particularly true at the stage when policy texts are in the making. Practitioners' investment in the process lies in the expectation that the texts produced and finalized will be taken up elsewhere.

The focus of this chapter is on several "moments" in the policy process that exemplify what DeVault describes (2008) as textualization, showing these moments as part of extended courses of action. These instances of textualization described here show how members of Civil Society Organizations (CSOs) engaged in the generation of UN policy documents. The analysis is based on my observations of practitioners as they participated in UN-based forest-policy processes. The emphasis on the actual activity of practitioners as they go about their work provides a point of departure for institutional ethnographers, and is informed by Marx and Engels's assertion that, in understanding what has come to be known as social organization, the "premises from which we begin are not arbitrary ones, not dogmas, but real premises from which abstraction can only be made in the imagination. They are the real individuals, their activity and the material conditions of their life, both those which they find already existing and those produced by their activity" (1998: 36–7).

The specific moments examined in this chapter were observed in February of 2000 while I was gathering data at UN headquarters in New York at the final meeting of the Intergovernmental Forum on Forests (IFF). I had been working closely with CSOs in UN forest policy for two years at that point, and had developed an insider's knowledge of some of the key policy dynamics. Framing my analysis at the time was George Smith's (1990) understanding that one should not only "start from the actual lives of people and undertake an analysis of a world (known reflexively)," but one must also "stake out an ontological commitment to a social order constituted in the practices and activities of people" (629) when analysing textually-mediated social organizations. In addition, I relied on Dorothy Smith's assertion that, in understanding how texts work in organizations, the "text is analyzed for its characteristically textual form of participation in social relations ... The text enters the laboratory then, so to speak, carrying the threads and shreds of relations it is organized by and organizes. The text before the analyst, then, is not used as a specimen or sample, but as a means of access, a direct line to the relations it organizes" (D.E. Smith 1990b: 4).

Based on this particular treatment of texts and work in organizational settings, I framed my observations of the work of policymakers around capturing and analysing specific instances that bring into view the text–reader dynamics and moments of textualization within the context of UN policy negotiation took place at the last meeting of the IFF. However, the mode of working with texts, of strategically deploying conceptual currency, and of leveraging points of disagreement between governments is generally relevant within current UN policy processes. I have witnessed similar moments at myriad UN-based policy negotiations since I began this sort of research in 1998. For example, I observed similar dynamics during recent negotiations related to policies on biofuels under the United Nations Convention on Biological Diversity (UNCBD) (in Nagoya, Japan, in October of 2010), and related to forest valuation under the United Nations Framework Convention on Climate Change (UNFCCC) (in Bangkok and Copenhagen in 2009 and Cancun in 2010). During the IFF meeting in New York in 2000, however, I worked with members of CSOs as they participated in the making of forest policy and thus had had access to the behind-the-scenes discussions of texts and their significance. Institutional ethnography allows for a concrete elaboration of the "process of making policy" – a sequence of events that often gets conflated with "outcomes" or "results." My aim here is to make visible how policy "work" gets done by focusing on specific moments of text–reader interaction during the final meeting of the IFF.

How Policy Negotiation Works: UN Forest Policy – Past and Present

The late 1990s was a significant period for UN-based environmental policy. The 1992 "Earth Summit," or United Nations Conference on Environment and Development (UNCED), which had taken place in Rio de Janeiro, Brazil, established an important institutional framework for policy negotiations related to environmental issues. UNCED produced three legally binding environmental agreements, concerning climate, biological diversity, and desertification. While it failed to produce a legally binding agreement on forests, UNCED negotiations established a documentary basis for future forest-policy deliberations.

Clearly, policy texts are negotiated in specific locations by specific individuals. But the complexity of that negotiation process is tied in to the multi-sited and trans-local relations of contemporary textually-mediated organizations such as the United Nations. For example, all the documents negotiated (or signed) at the UNCED meetings in Rio had gone through extensive preparatory stages in meetings in a variety of locations. In addition, issues discussed at Rio had been raised in one way or another in scientific and advocacy arenas for a considerable time prior to the meetings. A policy, once formally established, creates an institutional framework of principles, concepts, and categories that organize implementation and how it gets interpreted. The UN forest policy set up soon after UNCED established two sequential intergovernmental negotiating bodies, each with a two-year mandate. The first UN-based forest-policy deliberations after Rio took place under a body called the "Intergovernmental Panel on Forests" (IPF) from 1995 to 1997. Those were followed up in the "Intergovernmental Forum on Forests" (IFF) which began negotiations in 1997, and held its final meeting, IFF IV, at UN headquarters from 31 January to 11 February 2000. It was during IFF IV that the organizational structure for ensuing forest-policy negotiations was being debated. As a result, participants were not only invested in the policy documents that would come out of the IFF process in terms of substantive issues and the implications for forest degradation. They were equally invested in the outcomes of the policy process regarding the institutional framework under which the subsequent forest deliberations would be organized. For CSO participants who were present at IFF IV, it seemed clear that many issues would not be resolved in this forum. Therefore, they were invested in the decisions that would be made regarding the constitution of the subsequent body, where it would be situated under the UN system, and what substantive issues it would be mandated to take up. UNCED is widely recognized as having been an important event for the institutionalization of non-governmental participation in the environmental policy-making processes. However, the substance of that participation is still being worked out, with some post-UNCED deliberations being known for having better access for members of CSOs than others. The forest-policymaking body that followed the IFF, which came to be known as the United Nations Forum on Forests (UNFF), is the current institutional body under which most forest policy is negotiated through the UN system. The negotiations that took place during the last meeting of the IFF were marked by CSO investment in maintaining access to subsequent forest-policy negotiating bodies. Therefore, CSO participation at IFF IV was organized around both the substance of the negotiations as well as the potential changes that might preclude or limit future participation.

Under the United Nations, CSOs must be accredited through the UN Economic and Social Council (ECOSOC) in order to participate in bodies subsidiary to ECOSOC. Regarding non-governmental participation, the IFF operated under the post-Rio framework of "Major Groups," a term used to designate accredited CSOs and indigenous peoples organizations. Members of ECOSOC-accredited Major Groups could apply to attend IFF meetings and participate in policy negotiations. However, as the United Nations is an intergovernmental organization, the ways in which non-governmental actors participate is organized by particular rules and regulations. Government delegates have access to "closed" or "informal" negotiations, whereas individuals who are not on government delegations generally do not. While some of the specificities related to access are up to the discretion of the chair of a given meeting, within meeting rooms there is often designated space for members of Major Groups, and opportunities to weigh in on texts are limited.

Negotiations themselves are fundamentally text-based. A "Chair's draft text," for example, may be produced and disseminated at the start of a given meeting (such as IFF IV). In the case of the IFF, meetings lasted for two weeks, with specific agenda items based upon a predetermined "programme of work." During the two-week period, different agenda items were negotiated concurrently in separate locations under "working groups." Typically, participants chose to follow a specific working group and report back to colleagues about what took place in those negotiations. In some cases, a text in UN deliberations may be carried over from one meeting to the next (e.g., from IFF III to IFF IV), but the general goal is typically to achieve a "clean" text during a particular meeting so that the chairs and the secretariat can prepare final reports for that meeting that reflect "consensus." In consensus texts, individual authorship of specific language is rendered untraceable to actual individuals; the finalized text represents collaborative authorship of the governments involved.

Operating within the framework of consensus is challenging in an organization that has close to two hundred members. As governments have widely divergent political positions, many participants have come to view "the consensus text" as the "least common denominator." It carries the weight of having been agreed upon by all participants, but may not reflect any one participant's ideal policy formulation. Negotiations may become heated and drawn out in the final hours when points on which particular delegations are not authorized (by their governments) to budge remain contested in the final text. That text then remains in square brackets ("bracketed text") and is therefore not considered to be "clean text." During the early days of the meetings, government delegates tend to intervene in negotiations to raise broader points of concern about the chair's or other draft texts. As negotiations reach the end of the designated meeting time, it is this bracketed text that becomes the primary focus of deliberation, in order for delegates to hash out the issues and generate a consensus document.

In addition to deliberations in working groups, some negotiations take place in larger plenary format, in rooms that have become somewhat iconographic of UN meetings. In these cases, the members of the secretariat staff and the chair(s) are seated at the front of the room, and government negotiators are located in alphabetical order (by country) in rows facing the front. Glass booths for interpreters are located around the perimeter, and participants have access to microphones and earpieces connected to channels for translation of the deliberations into official UN languages. There is often designated space for Major Groups at the side or the back of the room. If government negotiators are interested in speaking, they can signal their desire to make an "intervention" with their government placard. The chair then takes note of all government negotiators who express an interest in speaking and invites them to make their intervention. As negotiations move into the working groups and away from the plenary meeting, government negotiators' interventions are often framed in the diplomatic style that is characteristic of UN interventions, but will generally contain more substantive content regarding their points of contention with particular segments of the text.

In working groups, government negotiators have the opportunity to intervene on specific paragraphs while members of the secretariat staff take note of the interventions. The subsequent draft of the chair's text, often released after each round of deliberation, is intended to reflect the scope of governments' interventions. At various points during the process, Major Groups are given the opportunity to intervene. Generally, at the end of plenary sessions, for example, time is allotted for at least one representative of a Major Group to make a statement. In these cases, Major Groups will have met before the plenary to prepare a statement that captures the interests of Major Groups present. Working group negotiations are less open to Major Groups' participation, as governments have the right to the floor, and negotiations are notorious for running beyond the allotted time. When meetings reconvene, the topic of interest to Major Groups may have been displaced by the next item on the agenda. In addition, if issues become particularly contentious among specific governments and progress is not being made in plenary or working group meetings, "closed" meetings will often be held to hash out the differences, limiting or precluding official access by Major Groups. When chairs perceive a level of intransigence on the part of particular governments, "contact groups" are typically organized in order to provide spaces to work through specific sticking points. Government negotiators are often reluctant to include Major Groups in these contact groups, as this would compromise frank discussion among UN Member States.

Major Groups that engage in these deliberative processes understand this terrain and organize their work around ways of influencing the texts as they are negotiated. In what took place in the meetings at IFF IV (February 2000), I focused on the work of Major Groups as specific texts were being negotiated by government delegates over a series of days in the type of format I describe above. Given the structural advantages for Member States, Major Groups participating in UN policymaking know that it is imperative to keep track of specific texts throughout the process as they are being transformed. They recognize that when "bracketed" text has become "clean" text, it is essentially no longer up for discussion. During the early stages of the negotiations, part of Major Groups' strategy is typically to get government negotiators to voice concerns during deliberations about chairs' draft texts so that problematic language can be bracketed and later debated. Likewise, Major Groups leverage points of contention between governments by identifying which governments have raised concerns about text during the early stages of negotiations. They then use these disagreements evidenced by the bracketed text to lobby sympathetic governments regarding issues that are of importance to them.

Another strategy that is used to influence the outcome is to encourage government delegates to make interventions in the policy deliberations that contain language that Major Groups find to be important. This strategy gets the language into the texts, as government interventions are supposed to be taken into account by the chairs. While the substance of government interventions does not always show up in the next iteration of a chair's draft, the procedural space is there for government negotiators to point out to the chair that elements of their prior interventions were not incorporated. Major Groups carefully observe the negotiations to see if the government negotiators actually raise the issues that they want to see in the documents, and subsequently review the chairs' summary documents to see if the issues have been transcribed into the actual texts themselves. If the language is not represented in the text, Major Groups can return to government negotiators and suggest that they pressure the chairs to include the substance of their intervention in the next version of the text.

During this process of reviewing various iterations of the policy documents as they are negotiated over several days, the policy text is activated by practitioners through the strategic use of the conceptual currency that is relevant to the given negotiating arena. McCoy (1995) points out that text-mediated relations "rely on individual moments of interpretation, where texts are activated within discourse by competent users through the employment of known-in-common interpretive schemes" (182). The work of participants and the "moments of interpretation" that activate the text as it is being negotiated constitute an extended course of action that is largely invisible in the final policy document itself. Furthermore, the explicit origins or definitions of conceptual currency are not explicated in the documents themselves. Becoming knowledgeable about the politicized meanings of language and strategic discourse of policy is an important part of becoming an effective participant in the process. As concepts get imbued with politicized meaning, a disconnect occurs. This disconnect depends upon forms of social organization in which a concept and the practices it regulates and reflects can be taken apart. "Concepts thus become a kind of 'currency' – a medium of exchange among ideologists and a way of thinking about the world that stands between the thinker and the object" (Smith 1990b: 42). While "speaking to the text," as policymakers say, that is being negotiated requires a particular level of "working within the system" rather than fundamentally challenging the discourse of policy, effective negotiators and participants skilfully tap into the known-in-common interpretive schemes to deploy conceptual currency and strategically influence the policy process. As participants come together to produce the policy text, they deliberately engage with the textualizaton process in order to influence the outcome.

Making Conceptual Currency Visible:
Documenting Text–Reader Interactions

Throughout my participation in the IFF negotiations as a member of a Major Group, I engaged in multiple moments of textualization and textual activation. Through my involvement in these deliberations, I gained a sense of the work that participants do that is not apparent in the final UN official documents. The text–reader relationship is rendered invisible in most of the documents and texts that are produced within the context of intergovernmental negotiations through the United Nations. However, this text–reader relationship is very visible when texts are being activated within the context of the actual negotiations. Much of the work of practitioners within the negotiations involves engaging with the texts as they are produced. This work takes place during negotiations, as delegates migrate around the room and have discussions with each other as interventions are being made. Texts are also taken up "in the corridors" outside of meeting rooms and in smaller meeting spaces and cafeterias as participants cluster around a particular version of a text and carefully go through it to see how they need to approach the next stage of negotiations.

During my participation in UN meetings, I regularly witnessed these sites and moments of textual activation. Methodologically, unlike formal interviews with practitioners about the policy process, this sort of observation allowed me to see how the texts organized the actual work of participants. While in some cases, as I observed instances of textualization, I was able to ask practitioners about the details of the work that they were doing, I often had to rely on my own understanding of the interpretive schemes and conceptual currency in order to understand the intent behind participants' commitment to particular language in the documents. By IFF IV, with a solid sense of the history of UN forest-policy negotiations, I was fairly comfortable with decoding and interpreting conceptual currency, and could participate in and observe the regular textual work of IFF policymaking.

"Category III": Activating Specific Text

A number of documents were worked up within the period of the IFF negotiations. In order to demonstrate the processes of textualization and text–reader interactions, I am focusing here on the text of an agenda item labelled as "Category III." The extended title of the agenda item was: "International arrangements and mechanisms to promote the management, conservation and sustainable development of all types of forests." The mandate for policymakers as they approached Category III was to "identify possible elements, work towards consensus, and engage in further action." The wording of this mandate is, like many UN-based mandates, nebulous and broad. What it meant in the context of the IFF process was that delegates were tasked with identifying existing international arrangements (institutions, organizations, or agreements) that were relevant to the work of the IFF. In addition, delegates were tasked with working to come to some kind of consensus regarding the scope and structure of future international forest debates, an issue that presented concerns for Major Groups due to the potential implications for access to future deliberations.

Category III was first discussed during a plenary session at IFF II in 1998 in Geneva, where general background information was given regarding existing international arrangements on forests. Several broad statements were made during the IFF II plenary sessions by government delegates and also by Major Groups. Then, at IFF III and IV, the substance of the text on Category III was negotiated in greater detail. At the end of each segment of negotiation, the co-chairs drafted a new text that was intended to capture governments' interests and concerns, and work towards a consensus text.

The document that I have chosen to analyse is one that was drawn up by the facilitator of a contact group during IFF IV. As was noted in my description of how UN policy negotiation works, contact groups are formed when contentious issues appear to be taking up more time than is allotted to them during the plenary or working group meetings. In the case of IFF IV, while the formation of contact groups had the effect of marginalizing some of the less involved government delegates as well as the Major Groups, the secretariat's objective was to get the most highly invested government delegates together to hash out the most contentious issues. It was within this context that the text for Category III was negotiated during the final days of IFF IV in February of 2000. As the group of active negotiators became more select and honed down to those with the greatest stake in a particular outcome, Major Groups increased their lobbying efforts and active participation in the process. Given the contentious nature of the negotiations, part of Major Groups' work involved accessing the texts under discussion. The various drafts negotiated by members of the contact group were not widely available – at times the drafts were disseminated only to particular government delegations. More often than not, Major Groups had to rely on some previously established connection with a government delegation in order to obtain the most up-to-date version of the text.

The document on which analysis focuses was negotiated by the contact group convened to discuss Category III on the evening of 10 February 2000. The facilitator of the contact group compiled the text after the contact group had disbanded at midnight. The text was then faxed to the government delegations who were most involved in the process, and who would need to prepare positions on the text before the next round of deliberations. Major Groups were able to obtain the text in time for their morning meeting before scheduled events on the next day through a Major Group representative with contacts to government delegations. On the morning of 11 February, upon convening in the NGO room, where Major Groups were given space to work and meet, copies of the text were distributed to participants, who immediately went to work assessing the changes that had been made from the previous draft.

This type of activity is a standard manner of dealing with the changes in the texts, as individuals are often not involved in some of the segments of the actual negotiations. Practitioners are either told by other participants what types of interventions were made, or they surmise from the most recent version of the text where the discussion is most likely headed. The more experienced participants are able to recognize particular interests imbedded in fairly opaque text. A seasoned participant in negotiations has the ability to recognize, amid the UN-ese, the intricacies of the debates, the history of the negotiations, and the multiple vested interests.

On a tangible level, the complexity of the interpretive schemes excludes all but the most informed participants. In addition, the opacity of the terminology indicates how conceptual currency shifts as some terms gain traction and as deliberations take place in parallel arenas, including other policymaking forums. The text for Category III (proposed by the facilitator of the contact group on Category III) evidences several dynamics that were important for Major Groups.

For the purposes of this analysis, the document that was disseminated in the early hours of 11 February will be referred to as "the Text." It is reproduced, interspersed with analysis and description, below – much as it looked in the original before being worked over by participants (including the typographical errors that existed in the original document – see note 1).

The Text, Bracketed Text, "Clean" Text, and Problematic Language

When participants of the Major Groups obtained a copy of the Text on the morning of 11 February, they immediately went to work on it, knowing that their influence on the future negotiations was primarily based on their ability to participate in the specific changes that were being made on this particular version of the text. The Text being viewed by Major Groups on 11 February still contained bracketed text. In addition, it contained governments' proposed changes in language that would substitute for the bracketed text. Knowing that "clean" (un-bracketed) text was generally not up for discussion, Major Groups focused on the points of contention in the document in front of them. Upon receiving the Text and circulating copies of the document to representatives who were present in the room, Major Groups began to discuss the text methodically. Page one of the Text is reproduced as it appeared on 11 February in figure 3.1. I was asked to take notes that would capture participants' comments. These notes were to then provide a basis on which to debrief members of Major Groups who were not present at that specific meeting. The notes would also provide specific points for a coherent and consistent Major Group position to be used for lobbying government delegates.

Before beginning a discussion of the substance of the Text, Major Groups had a brief discussion of concerns about the fact that they were not given a copy of the Text by the co-chairs or the contact group facilitator, and had to obtain a copy by somewhat nefarious means. Frustrations regarding the lack of ability to participate in negotiations without access to texts were raised. These frustrations were tied to long-standing concerns about what it means for international governance to be participatory and transparent. The first substantive issue related to the Text that was raised was that the proposed changes in its first sentence shifted the language of the Text in a direction that Major Groups considered to be problematic. The significance of the italicized text in that sentence (see figure 3.1) is rooted in the work that was done by participants at the UNCED conference in 1992. One of the options, based on the bold text that was proposed by some governments as alternative language in the first paragraph, was to replace the phrase "the management, conservation, and sustainable development of all types of forests" with simply the "sustainable management of all types of forests."

10 February 2000/12 am
CONTACT GROUP
TEXT PROPOSED BY THE FACILITATOR
International arrangements and mechanisms to promote the management, conservation
and
Sustainable development of all types of forests (Category III)

INTERNATIONAL ARRANGEMENT ON FORESTS

I. OBJECTIVE
1.   The main objective of this international arrangement on forests is to
promote the **sustainable** *management,* **management, conservation and sustainable**
development of all types of forests and to strengthen long-term political
commitment **[and establish a legal framework]** to this end. The purpose of such an
international arrangement would be to promote the implementation of
internationally agreed actions on forests, at the national, regional and global
levels, to provide a coherent, transparent and participatory global framework for
policy implementation and development, and to carry out the
principal functions, based on the Rio Declaration, the Forest Principles, chapter
11 of Agenda 21 and the outcomes of the IPF/IFF process, in a manner consistent
with and complementary to existing international legally binding instruments
relevant to forests.

II. PRINCIPAL FUNCTIONS
2.   To achieve the objective, this interna6tional arrangement on forests will
perform the following functions:
        a)   Facilitate and promote the implementation of IPF/IFF
    proposals for action as well as other actions, which may be agreed upon,
    including through national forest programmes and other Integrated programmes
    relevant to forests; catalyse, mobilise, and generate financial resources and
    mobilise and channel technical and scientific resources to this end, including
    by taking steps towards the broadening and development of mechanisms and
    future initiatives, in order to support implementation through enhanced
    international cooperation;

        b)   monitor progress at national, regional and international levels on
                the basis of **[voluntary]** reporting by countries, as well as by
                reporting by regional and international organizations,
                institutions and conventions;
        c)   enhance international and regional cooperation and policy and
                programme coordination on forest related issues among **[the**
                secretariats of] international and regional organisations,
                institutions and conventions, as well as to contribute to
                synergies among them; including coordination among donors;
        d)   foster international cooperation including North-South and public-
                private partnerships, as well as cross-sectoral cooperation at the
                national, regional and global levels;
                                        1

Figure 3.1 Document from Intergovernmental Forum on Forests, January–
February 2000 (IFF IV), 1/4.

Upon viewing this proposed change, Major Groups immediately stated
that the "language of Rio" ("the management, conservation, and sustainable development of all types of forests") should be retained in the
Text.

Negotiating "Problematic Language"

"The Language of Rio"

The "language of Rio" that Major Groups had a commitment to retaining represented a wider range of Major Groups' interests, including
conservation and sustainable development rather than simply "sustainable management," which is considered to be more nebulous and
ambiguous, and therefore weaker. As Major Groups were discussing
the changes in the Text, they expressed concern that the attempt to
change the language was simultaneously an attempt to weaken whatever institutional (organizational) arrangement would result from the
negotiations. They recognized also that within the UN system there is
significant documentary momentum assigned to previously negotiated text. Therefore, Major Groups' use of the phrase "the language
of Rio" as they engaged with the text was invoking the power of the
codification of language within a system based on consensus through
deliberation.

  This case exemplifies the fact that decisions within the UN system are
based in part on a stream of documentary precedents. While such repetition may seem excessive to those not involved in the UN system, it is
the basis of "soft law" agreements. Participants recognize that reitera-
tion may occur in the same body, especially the UN General Assembly.
The intent is the same – to build up a cumulative record of norms or
standard assertions to be read as evidence of the existence of customary
law or international public policy (Finkelstein 1988: 18).

  In this vein, some of the documentary resources available to Major
Groups as they approached the Text involved codification of language
in official documents within the UN system. Conceptual currency is, in
part, generated through the repeated inclusion of particular terms or
phrases in successive documents. This was very much the case with the
"language of Rio." Major Groups were reticent to see the phrasing of
particular key elements change from the language that was codified in
the documents that came out of UNCED, and they had recourse to the
documentary stream of texts which used UNCED agreed-upon terminology to make their case.

"Monitor" versus "Review, Monitor, and Report"

The next point of interest for Major Groups in the Text showed up
in the second section of the document, under the heading "Principle

Functions." Major Groups very quickly saw that paragraph "(b)" was missing some of the key language that was established during the IPF (Intergovernmental Panel on Forests) process – the predecessor process to the IFF. Whereas the Text stated that one of the functions was to "monitor progress at national, regional, and international levels," Major Groups noted that the IPF language had included the words "review and report" after the word "monitor." This was an issue for Major Groups due to the lack of progress made on *implementing* the IPF Proposals for Action. Major Groups were adamant about retaining the IPF wording in order to make sure that progress on implementation was not only *monitored* – but that it was also *reviewed* and *reported on*. A significant part of Major Groups' work was organized around concern regarding the potential for policy processes to weaken prior commitments. This was a regular point of contention for Major Groups. While they were not enthusiastic about the IPF Proposals for Action, they realized that the agreed-upon Proposals for Action could be further weakened throughout the IFF process if key elements of the language were left out of IFF documents. Again, as with the "language of Rio," participants explicitly used the term "the language of IPF" to indicate that they were relying on the currency of previously negotiated terminology. Getting language "into the text" was often an arduous process. Interventions might be made using specific terminology with the hope that it would be reflected in a chair's summary or draft text. If the language was contentious, it was either not written into the documents (perhaps due to a chair's judgment that it would create unproductive debate) or was contested by other delegates who insisted that the language remain in brackets. In this way, particular phrases could be introduced into the negotiations yet remain absent from the final documents. Major Groups were concerned about the relative ease with which things could be dropped from IFF texts, anticipating the struggles that would ensue to get the language back into subsequent documents.

"Voluntary"

While Major Groups were clear about what they wanted to see in the final report of IFF IV, they were also willing to make some concessions in order to lobby more effectively for the points they deemed most critical. As they assessed the Text, some participants suggested they might have more leverage in lobbying governments if they could identify elements that Major Groups would be willing to let go in order to convince governments to support other key issues. To underscore the importance of reintroducing the "IPF language," Major Groups were willing to make the concession to the term "voluntary" remaining in the final text for Category III. This was not ideal, as "voluntary" reporting and monitoring of the implementation of the IPF Proposals for Action weakened the strength of the policy. However, Major Groups were aware that governments often do not agree to a final text that does not include the word "voluntary" in relation to virtually everything that they are agreeing to do. Therefore, Major Groups had a good sense that the term "voluntary" would probably find its way back into the text regardless of their efforts to the contrary. Governments expect Major Groups to contest this term, as Major Groups would clearly prefer that the policies delineate obligatory actions on the part of governments. So in being willing to tell governments that they would not fight the inclusion of the word "voluntary," Major Groups were engaging in the kind of strategy work that is regularly done by participants during the textual negotiations. Realistically, Major Groups were lacking the official means to modify text at this late stage in the negotiations. However, they could invoke the power of previously agreed-upon text such as the "language of Rio" or the "IPF language" in order to influence the final outcome as much as possible. They could likewise invoke the larger discourse of Member States' accountability to civil society in policy processes.

Thus, at the morning meeting, participants discussed the importance of various proposed textual changes and decided on what they "could live with" and what they were more reluctant to accept. They were well aware that they would be able to make a stronger case if they were able to point to trade-offs in demands and concerns. Such strategizing regularly took place with both governmental and non-governmental participants. In the case of Major Groups, the larger bargaining chip was the somewhat nebulous concept of "government accountability to civil society" and the more specific argument regarding accountability to powerful constituencies of large NGOs. However, in cases where government delegates were unwilling to budge on their choice of language, or when the government blocks were engaged in contentious battles among themselves, the "accountability to civil society" argument was unlikely to carry much weight. Particularly towards the end of the negotiations, Major Groups recognized that their influence on the process was limited. The structural dynamics of negotiating texts in contact groups reinforced this by minimizing the number of participants with access to the actual negotiations. Some government delegates were beginning to realize that they were either going to have to defy consensus on particular texts or go "back to capital" – having agreed to something that they were explicitly directed (by their government) *not* to agree to, as government delegations are sent to negotiations with specific instructions regarding policy positions, and they must report back with results.

Towards the end of UN-based negotiations, the vested interests become more apparent as particular governments become more intransigent. Deals tended to be made among government delegates, rather than with the input of Major Groups. Part of being savvy about the various processes involves knowing how to strategize to maintain foothold in the process. In the case of the IFF deliberations by 11 February, Major Groups knew that they were structurally disadvantaged, yet they strategized around the actual language in the Text in relation to the negotiations in order to maximize their influence.

"… and Establish a Legal Framework …"

After discussing the "language of IPF," the discussion of Major Groups turned back to the first paragraph of the Text (reproduced in figure 3.1). Some commented that they were pleased to see that the phrase "and establish a legal framework" was still in brackets. The debate over a whether to negotiate a legally binding instrument (LBI) was a major point of contention during the IPF/IFF process, for Member State and non-governmental participants alike. Surprisingly, by the end of the IPF meetings, Major Groups were opposed to a legally binding instrument on forests. They had participated in the Rio negotiations with the intent of establishing an LBI, but had developed some serious concerns about how the language of the legally binding instrument was being articulated. A key issue for Major Groups involved the fact that "forest" policy was largely being negotiated by people with an expertise in forestry, rather than by a range of stakeholders with varying views on the importance of forests – regarding the dynamics involving complex ecosystems and land tenure rights, for example. Leading up to and including UNCED deliberations, forest policy quickly picked up the tenor of "forestry" policy, according to Major Groups. The very focus on "sustainably managing" forests that was written into the UN forest-policy negotiations set the terrain as being relevant to people with forestry expertise. In addition, it became clear during the deliberations that trade issues were going to have to be addressed. As a result, the framework for a legally binding instrument that was being negotiated throughout the UNCED and into the IPF process included significant trade-related elements, as timber and managing forests for their wood-product outputs has long been a central aspect of Western forestry. Major Groups began to lobby against a legally binding instrument on forests, as they became concerned that the policy was essentially shaping up to be a trade policy – one that would facilitate and potentially streamline timber trade, or one that would focus on the "sustainable management" of forests, but not one that would reflect the broader range of concerns that Major Groups had about forest degradation, such as land tenure rights for indigenous peoples.

Therefore, during the IFF meetings, Major Groups were keeping a close watch on whether openings were being made for discussions related to a legally binding instrument on forests, as they felt that that would revive prior deliberations that they had found so problematic. Throughout the IFF IV meeting, Major Groups attempted to assess whether or not the negotiations would result in an LBI on forests, a possibility that was still on the table at IFF IV. Meanwhile, government delegates were grappling with this issue, which is evidenced by bracketed text in the 10 February version of the document, indicating a last-ditch effort on behalf of governments in support of an LBI. However, the existence of brackets signalled that this would not be an easy issue to transform into consensus text. Brackets also opened up space for Major Group input, as they began to focus more explicitly on lobbying sympathetic governments. Some of the text that exemplifies this tension is reproduced in figure 3.2.[1]

During the morning meeting of Major Groups as they assessed the Text, paragraph 2 (f) (see figure 3.2) was immediately seen by Major Groups' representatives as taking a strong pro-LBI stance due to its reference to an Intergovernmental Negotiating Committee (INC). According to Major Groups present at the meeting, advocating for an Intergovernmental Negotiating Committee would allow the forest debates to follow the precedents set by the United Nations Framework Convention on Climate Change (UNFCCC) and the Convention on Biodiversity (CBD) – both of which are legally binding agreements. For those opposed to an LBI, any mention of an INC needed to remain in brackets and eventually be eliminated from the final text so as to avoid setting up the institutional framework consistent with a legally binding agreement.

e) provide a forum for continued policy dialogue and development among governments, which would include international organizations, and other interested parties, including major groups, to foster a common understanding on sustainable forest management and to address [international] forest issues and emerging areas of priority concern in a holistic, comprehensive and integrated manner;

f) strengthen political commitment **[inter-alia]/[especially]** through

- ministerial engagement;
- developing ways to liaise with the governing bodies of international and regional organizations, institutions and instruments;
- promotion of action-oriented dialogue and policy formulation related to forests;

[the formulation, through an intergovernmental negotiating committee (INC) with a time-bound mandate, of a legally binding instrument on the management, conservation and sustainable development of all types of forests, providing for financial support to implement the commitments contained therein; and with provisions for regional and thematic protocols; and taking into account existing instruments, processes and regional agreements;]

III. STRUCTURE

3.To achieve the objective and carry out the functions outlined above the **[GA or ECOSOC]** would:

a) *(new formulation)* **[establish a standing intergovernmental body which may be called the United Nations Forum on Forests (UNFF)1 , which would serve as a central reference on forest-related issues to governments, international and regional organisations, institutions and instruments relevant to forests, as well as to major groups;]**

b) *(new formulation)* invite the executive heads of organizations of the United Nations system and heads of other relevant international and regional organisations, institutions and instruments to form a collaborative partnership on forests to support the work of the UNFF and to enhance cooperation and co-ordination among participants. Such a partnership should build on the high-level, informal Inter-agency Task Force on Forests (ITFF), which would translate guidance from and recommendations of the UNFF into coordinated action, including joint programming and submissions of coordinated proposals to their respective governing bodies; and facilitate donor coordination. The ITFF will submit coordinated inputs and progress reports to the UNFF. The ITFF should take into account the role of FAO as task manager for chapter 11 and Agenda 21, and operate in and open and transparent manner:

c) *(new formulation)* **[initiate urgently an intergovernmental negotiation process on a legally binding instrument on all types of forests, providing for financial support to implement**

Figure 3.2 Document from IFF IV, 2/4.

"Providing Financial Support"

At this point in our meeting, another issue was raised in reference to paragraphs 2 (f) and 3 (c), where there is mention of "providing financial support." The issue of financing is regularly a sticking point in UN-based environmental negotiations. Typically, countries from the Global North argue against the inclusion of language that speaks to "new and additional financial resources," while Member States from the Global South advocate for such language. Many Northern delegations (the United States in particular, and the European Union less so, for example) were clearly directed not to agree to commit "new and additional" funds during the IFF process. However, not surprisingly, the issue of resources and funding was raised in an overwhelming majority of interventions made by delegates from the Global South during the IFF process. Given developed countries' intransigence on providing "new and additional" funds, the presence in the text of references to providing financial support signalled an alliance between Northern pro-LBI countries and Southern countries. Major Groups assumed that if language referencing financial support existed in the Text, then there must have been some backroom deals among Global North governments such as Canada, a pro-LBI country with significant influence in the process. In other words, Major Groups surmised that Northern pro-LBI governments were willing to accept the language of financial resources in exchange for support from Southern governments regarding the legally binding instrument. The language on page 3 of the Text (reproduced in figure 3.3) likewise demonstrates contention over issues of funding. Significantly, the only part of paragraph 3 (which begins on page 2 and continues on page 3) that is not in brackets is segment (b). The remaining segments, (a), (c), (d), and (e), are left bracketed due to their associations with legally binding agreements, funding, or both contentious issues.

As Major Groups discussed the Text, there was agreement among most of the participants present that another bullet should be added on page 2, under paragraph 2 (f) (see figure 3.2). They wanted the paragraph to read "strengthen political commitment through ... multistakeholder participation including representatives of major groups as defined in Agenda 21 in the formulation and implementation of forest policy." Clearly, this was an attempt on the part of Major Groups to keep a foot in the door of whatever process followed the IFF meetings. This was not a random request, though, firmly caged as it was in the language of the IFF process. So, while Major Groups knew that they couldn't introduce new language, and there was a good chance that Member States would be unwilling to do so at this stage in the process, they felt it important to highlight previously agreed-upon language that they considered to be stronger than that represented in the document under negotiation. Throughout UNCED and subsequent processes, the participation of Major Groups was referenced in multiple documents. Using the UNCED documents (and particularly "Agenda 21")

...Commitments contained therein, allowing for regional and thematic protocols, by setting up an INC with a time-bound mandate.]

d) *(new formulation)* [establish a forest fund through the consolidation of existing and the generation of additional funds, for the implementation of actions derived from the IPF/IFF proposals for action, as well as those taken by this arrangement;]

e) [take steps toward the establishment of a global mechanism to promote the transfer of environmentally sound technologies in support of sustainable forest management to developing countries.]

IV. PROGRAMME OF WORK

4. The UNFF would work on the basis of a multi-year programme of work, drawing on the elements reflected in the Rio Declaration, the Forest Principles, chapter 11 of Agenda 21 and the IPF/IFF Proposals for action.

5. **[The programme and methods of work for the intergovernmental negotiation process would be determined by the INC, and draw on, as appropriate, the elements reflected in the Rio Declaration, the Forest Principles, chapter 11 of Agenda 21 and the IPF/IFF proposals for action.]**

WORKING MODALITIES

6. The UNFF **[and the INC]** should be open to all states, and operate in a transparent and participatory manner. Relevant to international and regional organisations, including regional economic integration organisations, institutions and instruments, as well as major groups, as identified in the Agenda 21, should also be involved.

7. The UNFF may recommend the convening of ad-hoc expert groups of limited duration, involving experts from developed and developing countries, for scientific and technical advice, as well as to consider mechanisms for finance and transfer of environmentally sound technologies and encourage country sponsored initiatives, such as international expert meetings.

8. The UNFF would initially meet annually, for a period of up to two weeks, subject to the review referred to below. The UNFF would have a high-level ministerial segment for two to three days, as required. The high-level segment could include a one-day policy dialogue with the heads of organisations participating in the collaborative partnership, as well as other forest-related international and regional organisations, institutions and instruments. The UNFF should ensure the opportunity to receive inputs from representatives of major groups as identified in Agenda 21, in particular through the organisation of multi-stakeholder dialogues.

Figure 3.3 Document from IFF IV, 2/3.

as documentary anchors for the definition of the term "Major Groups" allowed non-governmental organization participants to argue for the agreed-upon value of their continued input in the UN processes.

"Intergovernmental"

Major Groups, as they reviewed the third page of the Text (see figure 3.3), argued that the word "intergovernmental" should be removed from paragraph 3 (a) due to the fact that if it were to be "intergovernmental" the new body would represent a continuation of the institutional structure of both the IPF and IFF processes, both of which were problematic to Major Groups in that they were discouraged with what they saw as a lack of progress in the negotiations through both post-UNCED forest-policy negotiating bodies. While they were reluctant to endorse a move towards a legally binding agreement, they did not want the "talk shop" to continue in another forum that would merely reproduce the failings of the old ones. Instead, Major Groups wanted to make sure that the institutional framework for the new forum was most amenable to the possibility of actually implementing the Proposals for Action that had been produced in the IPF process. Furthermore, Major Groups wanted to see the section which stated that the new body, called the UNFF, "which would serve as a central reference on forest-related issues," be replaced with "which would serve to promote dialogue and action on forest-related issues" (see figure 3.3). For Major Groups, the underlying causes of forest degradation had been identified, and Proposals for Action had been agreed upon, but governments were not willing to actually take action to implement the policy recommendations. Merely having a "central reference" body in the form of the UNFF would preclude opportunities for action regarding stemming actual forest degradation.

As is typical of such text–reader interactions, there was a fair amount of skipping around the text as Major Groups read through the document and went back to points that they felt they had neglected to address earlier. For example, one participant suggested that people return to page 2 (reproduced in figure 3.2). She was concerned that, while paragraph 3 was not bracketed, 3 (b) appeared to be somewhat problematic. This tied page 2 into the discussion regarding the structure of future forest negotiations. It was apparent that governments were supportive of the UNFF as a proposed standing body. This proposal, if it were agreed upon by governments at IFF IV, would be sent for approval to the Commission on Sustainable Development (CSD) and, from there, on to ECOSOC. Provided that the proposal for a standing body passed the approval of both tiers of decision making, it would become institutionalized. Major Groups and government delegates alike were concerned about getting language into the proposal that would allow for the standing body, should it be approved, to have the components, terms of reference, and mandate which reflected their interests. For Major Groups, a large part of this involved making sure that the subsequent body was organized institutionally to allow for nongovernmental organization participation.[2]

The Un-bracketed Text of Paragraph 3 (b): "A Standing Body"

The point of contention that the Major Groups had with the Text in paragraph 3 (b) was that it indicated that the powers of the Interagency Task Force on Forests (ITFF) should be enhanced. The ITFF, composed of eight private and intergovernmental organizations, was not seen to be sufficiently participatory and transparent for Major Groups. Furthermore, they were not entirely supportive of the role of the Food and Agriculture Organization of the United Nations (FAO) during the IPF/IFF process. The FAO was not only one of the members of the ITFF, but it was also the task manager for the forest-related chapter of UNCED's "Agenda 21" document, which gave it a prominent role in the forest-policy process. The fact that paragraph 3 (b) was not in brackets meant that Major Groups had to find other ways of lobbying government delegates about their concerns in reference to the ITFF.

As I attempted to capture all of these issues in notes in the margin of the document, Major Groups were able to use the marked-up version of

---

VI.   SECRETARIAT

9.   *(New formulation)* A compact secretariat, constituted in accordance with agreed rules and procedures of the United Nations, and strengthened through secondments from international and regional organizations, institutions and instruments, as well as voluntary contributions from governments and other donors, should be established to support the work described above.

VII.   FINANCIAL SUPPORT

10.   *(new formulation)* The work of the ITFF would, to the extent possible, build upon the work undertaken and resources already available in existing institutions and organisations.

11.   *(new formulation)* The meetings of the UNFF and of the secretariat would require funding from the regular budget of the United Nations to be mobilised, to the maximum extent possible, through reallocation of resources and supported through voluntary contributions from governments, organisations, and other donors to a trust fund, as well as through in-kind contributions.

12.   [Funding for the INC should be provided along similar lines].

VII.   REVIEW

13.   *(new formulation)* The international arrangement of forest should be dynamic and adapt to evolving conditions. Accordingly, the effectiveness of this arrangement would be reviewed every *(number of years)* in order to determine necessary changes in its structure and modalities of work, as well as the need for its continuation.

4

Figure 3.4 Document from IFF IV, 4/4.

the Text to create lobbying points and to circulate to other Major Group participants who were unable to attend the morning meeting, yet who were interested in continuing to have an impact on the policy outcomes of IFF IV.

Participation as Strategy and the Shifting Nature of Policy Processes

I was able to see, in the meeting that was held on the morning of 11 February, how the Text played its part in Major Groups' "negotiation" of specific textual elements and how they brought their experienced reading abilities to the documents they encountered. Members of Major Groups were able to anticipate what openings would allow them to influence the process of negotiation and outcomes in future settings. While none of the participants who were present in the room that morning saw the document as being the best possible policy related to forests, Major Groups' attention to the Text reflected their understanding of how to work within the institutional constraints and framework of the UN policymaking system. The work that they engaged in, in bringing their insider knowledge to the version of the Text that was disseminated towards the end of IFF IV, represents the sort of strategy work that individuals in textually-mediated organizations regularly deploy. In the United Nations, non-governmental participants and government delegates alike are savvy as to the possible points of leverage that are available to them at any given point in the policymaking process. The examples described in this chapter highlight what it means for invested participants to engage in policymaking in attempting to ensure that their interests are reflected in a process that is ultimately ambiguous.

Indeed, the examples in this chapter give a picture of the larger, as well as the "micro," textual dynamics associated with one aspect of what happens inside institutions of global governance. While the participation of Civil Society Organizations has become quite institutionalized within the organizations that are currently positioned to have very powerful global effects, the ways in which participation really works in actual settings continues to be contested terrain. Participants in policymaking processes are well aware that the nature of engagement in these arenas is constantly shifting and transforming. In some ways, these changes relate to literal access to negotiations. In other ways, however, the culture or standards of participation may shift, or the level of engagement may change in a more nuanced and subtle manner. As the twenty-year anniversary of UNCED negotiations was marked by additional high-level meetings in

2012 (Rio+20), questions related to the substance of non-governmental organization participation in environmental policymaking are still front and centre. These questions are all the more important given the recent shifts in UN-based policy discourses to include a substantial rhetoric related to the privatization of development and environment programs. The Rio+20 theme of a "green economy" exemplifies this shift, which effectively brings elements of environmental policy under the purview of the market. Within this largely neoliberal framework, access to knowledge and capacity to influence policy become topical questions for members of CSOs who are interested in engaging with the policymaking processes. As a result, the strategy work that members of CSOs currently engage in is related to the opportunities to define the conceptual terrain of the term "green economy." In the lead-up to Rio+20, some of the key ways that CSOs engaged with documents involved the kinds of dynamics I have outlined in this chapter. Members of Civil Society organizations engaged with the texts that were negotiated by governments prior to Rio+20 meetings, and they looked for strategic points of entry as the language of Rio+20 began to be codified with implications for future policy processes. While this highly text-based policy-oriented process is often frustrating for members involved, practitioners understand the importance of engaging with the texts – in addition to doing work in other locations outside of the policy realm – in order to keep important language in the texts and to continue to influence future policy outcomes.

NOTES

1 The text itself had many typographical errors in the original draft form. I reproduced the text with the errors so as to maintain a sense of what the text looked like when the delegates received it. For example, in part III ("Structure"), paragraph 3 (b), the last sentence should read: "The ITFF should take into account the role of FAO as task manager for chapter 11 of Agenda 21, and operate in an open and transparent manner." There are also two sections labelled "VII."

2 These spaces for participation shift, however, with structural changes in terms of where negotiations are located in the UN apparatus. One such structural change occurred when the UNFF was created. Rather than operating under the auspices of the Commission on Sustainable Development (CSD), as its predecessor organizations (the IPF and IFF) had, the UNFF is located directly under ECOSOC, a shift which had consequential implications for NGO participation in the deliberations. These are described in Eastwood (2005), chapter 7.

PART 2

Diverse Textual Technologies

4 Producing "What the Deans Know": Cost Accounting and the Restructuring of Post-Secondary Education[1]

LIZA MCCOY[2]

Liza McCoy's chapter introduces us to the distinctive textual technologies of financial and managerial accounting. With research done in the early 1990s, while some of the details of her account of college and university practice may not apply today, the forms of inquiry and explication of public-sector reorganization offer a powerful model for examining how new managerial technologies of accounting are applied in local sites. McCoy shows how, in a college reorganization, the work of instructors that fitted no ordinary scheme of measurement was made calculable. She shows us how two texts operate in its accomplishment. She instructs the reader on new accounting practices and technologies as they are brought into play in college processes to enable costs of programs and courses to be measured and compared with one another when decisions are to be made about allocating funds. Administrators confronted the problem that evaluating the costs of faculty work did not fit straightforwardly into the accounting framework. The chapter shows us how the textual work resolves faculty work into an accounting format and makes it possible for financial managers to make comparisons between programs, departments, and faculties in accounting terms and to evaluate their relative merits.

McCoy's two texts are charts drawn from original texts so that the reader can see what the cost/contribution comparisons look like in accounting terms. Accountancy is a technical field with which most of us are unfamiliar. In preparation for her research, McCoy took courses in financial and management accounting. She takes us on a tour of the circuit from financial planning and policies of financial management to the regulation of the front line of departmental programs in relation to overall college financial benefit. Interviews with those in various positions – the financial accountant, the dean, and the department chair – in the college managerial circuit enable her to describe how their work is coordinated through the texts and the new accounting practices that now subordinate department practices to the newly empowered financial management of the college.

McCoy's piece shows via use of interview extracts how different actors, whose work is coordinated in university administrative accounting processes, practise and implement the discourse of organizational restructuring locally. Zeroing in on accounting procedures, McCoy, again via interview extracts, also makes visible the power of the text – as one side of the text–reader conversation – to regulate and coordinate different actors' readings and what is said in the negotiations regarding the text's future use in accounting for and organizing instructors' work. She emphasizes throughout her study how incorporating the texts coordinating people's work in her ethnography makes visible the actual ways in which people's work is being reorganized by introducing and requiring the application of specialized modes of textual representation.

Accounting as a Textual Practice of Ruling

The centrality of documentary forms of knowledge in contemporary relations of ruling is a major theme in the work of Dorothy Smith (1987, 1990). Smith uses the term in a broad way, a way that encompasses the varied and interconnected practices of management, administration, government, law, finance, education, business, and the professions (1987: 3). Smith invites us to see these practices of ruling as the coordinated actions of large numbers of people spread across diverse sites and to recognize the prominent role played by texts in this coordination (think of case files, report cards, labour force statistics, international trade agreements, medical records, financial statements ... the list is endless). Smith argues that understanding the organization of power in contemporary society requires attention to the textual practices through which the social and physical world is represented as the object of administrative and professional action. Contemporary ruling, Smith claims, depends heavily on objectified forms of knowledge and apparently neutral, subject-less accounts of people and situations: "A mode of ruling has become dominant that involves a continual transcription of the local and particular activities of our lives into abstracted and generalized forms ... It involves the construction of the world as texts, whether on paper or in computer, and the creation of a world in texts as a site of action" (ibid.). Of increasing currency are representational strategies that measure and quantify (Porter 1992), converting local particularities into standardized, calculable units that enable quantifiable comparisons among different sites and activities.

One of the most widespread of these quantifying textual practices is accounting, which has two main forms, financial accounting and managerial accounting. Both involve combinatory and analytic procedures that work with numerical data constructed through the categories of double-entry bookkeeping. This is an inscription practice that represents people's activities and the products of those activities in the "abstracted and generalized" form of monetary units. Financial accounting is the term for procedures performed in fulfilment of legislated reporting requirements, such as the production of financial statements circulated to shareholders, lenders, and government agencies. Managerial or cost accounting is not a legislated requirement, and when performed, does not need to follow any legislated guidelines, although there are standard techniques known to trained accountants. As the name indicates, it is produced primarily to provide information to managers, and is rarely published outside the organization. In addition to using bookkeeping data, it may use other quantifiable data generated within the organization as well, such as hours of work, numbers of units produced, or numbers of students enrolled.

Recognizing the prevalence of accounting in contemporary relations of ruling suggests the usefulness of taking a closer look at the ways that accounting texts are produced and used and shape, albeit indirectly, many of the daily circumstances of our lives. Accounting, rather than being a simple matter of neutral record keeping after the fact, plays an active conceptual role in setting the terms in which organizational activities can be thought, discussed, and evaluated. At the interface between organizations, accounting categories work to align one organization's work processes with those of others (funders, creditors, customers). This is especially prevalent in relations of accountability, where grant recipients, state-funded agencies, and company subsidiaries report on their activities through documents prepared using accounting categories and procedures imposed by the more powerful organization.

Critical accounting theorists (Hopwood 1990; Miller 1994) describe accounting as a calculative practice that constructs a particular form of visibility: "Accounting practices create the costs and the returns whose reality actors and agents are asked to acknowledge and respond to" (Miller 1994: 3). Related to this notion of accounting as a form of textual visibility is the theme of accounting as a form of social control

(Hoskin & Macve 1994; Miller & O'Leary 1987; Hopper & Armstrong 1991; Hopwood 1989; Robson 1992). Although individual people and their actions are absent from accounting documents, controlling and shaping what people do is one of the main uses of managerial accounting. Accounting as visibility enables a form of management that works through evaluations based in comparisons among individuals or divisions. Accounting visibility sets the terms in which activities can be authoritatively known and evaluated, and it does so in ways that intend managerial relevances and realize, at the local level, abstract concepts (such as "efficiency") drawn from the theories of neo-classical economics. The result is an instance of what Smith calls the closed loop of an "ideological circle":

> The categories structuring data collection are already organized by a preordained schema; the data produced becomes the reality intended by the schema; the schema interprets the data ... Issues, questions, and experiences that do not fit the framework and the intercalated relation of categories and schemata simply do not get entry to the process, do not become part of the textual realities governing decision-making processes. (1990: 93–4)

The managerial and discursive weight placed on accounting representations as displaying relevant, authoritative truths structures the ways that organizational situations can be conceived and solutions proposed. Accounting teaches the people whose work is therein represented to compare what they do (abstractly counted up as productivity, costs, sales, etc.) with established standards; accounting is most effective as a form of social control when people learn to carry out their activities with reference to the accounting representations that will be made of them, and when they learn to understand an organizational situation in the terms provided by the accounting visibility – or when, regardless of how they prefer to view the situation, they are constrained to adopt the accounting categories and the schema that operates them in order to influence organizational decision making, thereby limiting the scope of any real alternative.

Hopwood (1990) has proposed that organizational change, particularly in the public sector, be investigated through attention to changes in the pattern of visibility constructed through the accounting system. Changing the visibility provided by accounting – what is identified, measured, compared; and what staff can be held accountable for – is one of the most powerful ways to refashion an organization from within, in ways that articulate its many work processes to the market, or that import, with pressing urgency, hitherto unconsidered relevances. This sort of change is an important dimension of public-sector restructuring designed to reduce the role of government and promote the distribution of public resources through quasi- or actual market relations (Walsh 1995).

I have been studying these aspects of accounting as a textual practice of ruling (visibility, social control, organizational restructuring), using an investigative approach proposed by Smith (1987), which she calls institutional ethnography. In Smith's usage, the term institution has the specialized meaning of a complex of relations forming part of the ruling apparatus, organized around a distinctive function such as post-secondary education, bond markets, or health care. This notion of institution directs the researcher's attention to the way the activities of numerous agencies, organizations, professional associations, and individuals are coordinated into a "functional complex." Here are work routines, especially text-mediated ones, and a conceptual order that enables the "interchange between different specialized parts of the complex" (Smith 1988: 60).

The term "ethnography" signals a focus on the actual practices of people, which is intended to lead to an understanding of how those practices, coordinated textually across multiple sites, constitute the particular institutional relations addressed by the research. Research strategies employed by researchers doing institutional ethnographies have included in-depth interviews (Mykhalovskiy & Smith 1994), participant observation (Ng 1996; Reimer 1995; Diamond 1992), the collection of naturally occurring talk (Jackson 1995; Turner 1995), and textual analysis and archival research.

My study looks at the introduction of a form of managerial accounting in an Ontario community college. Like many parts of the public sector in Canada, post-secondary education is undergoing a process of restructuring driven by reduced operating grants and shaped by government policies designed to expose the delivery of public services to the discipline of the market. Faced with this situation, and conscious of their organizations' role as tools of state policy, college administrators have responded by seeking new ways, often borrowed from the private sector, of successfully accomplishing their new entrepreneurial obligations. Colleges, like other public-sector organizations, have long performed rudimentary forms of cost accounting, but in the new context their managers have identified the need for more rigorous forms of cost accounting typically used in the private sector. One such is called program costing. This is an analytic exercise that produces unit costs for the college's educational "products," allowing administrators to say, for example, that a program training dental technicians costs $46.64 per student per day to run. This is a form of managerial information not hitherto produced with any regularity or precision in the colleges.

I learned about this new practice during the course of another research project[3] that looked more generally at the relations of funding and accountability in the college system. Intrigued by what I was hearing about program costing, I decided to focus on one particular college where program costing had been introduced the previous year. I will call this college Fulton College. My research involved a series of in-depth interviews with administrative and teaching staff at Fulton in the early 1990s. I also took courses in both managerial and financial accounting in order to develop at least a first-stage practitioner's knowledge. This allowed me to talk knowledgeably with informants and to read accounting texts according to the standardized interpretive schema they intend.

In this chapter, I focus on a description of program costing as a documentary form of knowledge that constructs a specific visibility. In taking up the notion of visibility, I want to avoid discovering visibility through a practice of analytic abstraction. Instead, I want to investigate accounting visibility as it is intersubjectively produced by members in the setting. This directs attention not only to the text and its elements but also to the practices of interpretation and use that activate and accomplish the text's potential visibility. Accounting texts make use of standardized techniques, so that anyone trained in accounting should be able to read an accounting text at the level of identifying the type of analysis it performs. It is actual users of the text who read it for its significance in making visible relevant features of their actual setting. That is what I explore here.

The discussion that follows is built around the descriptions and explanations offered by informants in their conversations with me. In these conversations I was interested in finding out how managers identified the situation they were in as one that called for a new (to the colleges) practice of cost accounting; how they went about developing and implementing the work processes – of data collection, sorting, analysis – that produce the new representation; how the new documentary practice is articulated to pre-existing documentary practices, especially ones that hook the college into wider institutional relations with state agencies, clients, and other colleges; and, what will be my main focus here, how people in the colleges read and use the new texts and how they orient to the new objects of knowledge the texts produce. To begin, I will sketch in very briefly some aspects of Fulton College and the college system, the type of restructuring under way, and the new relations within which the need for program costing was identified.

Restructuring in Ontario Colleges

There are over twenty Ontario Colleges of Applied Arts and Technology (CAATs), which are similar to community colleges elsewhere in Canada and in the United States. They are semi-autonomous non-profit organizations integrated into a centralized system funded and administered through the provincial Ministry of Education and Training. The college system was set up in the 1960s to handle the baby boom demand for post-secondary education as well as to meet employers' demand for skilled labour (Dennison & Gallagher 1986). Established through an act of the provincial legislature, the college system is designed to provide a level of vocationally oriented education distinct from the elite university system;[4] unlike community colleges elsewhere, Ontario CAATs do not function as an alternative route to university, and college students cannot easily transfer into a three- or four-year degree program (although this is starting to change).

Fulton College, like other Ontario colleges, offers two- and three-year post-secondary diploma programs, short training programs (under a year in length), apprenticeship training, skills upgrading, and continuing education courses; it also provides training services on contract to government and local employers. Programs are geared to specific occupations or occupational clusters. The title of the program indicates the sort of job the student will be prepared for: for example, office administration, stationary engineer, small engine repair, dental assistant. Programs consist of a prescribed sequence of courses and must be approved by the Ministry of Education and Training that governs and funds the college system. Students admitted to the program move in a cohort through the set sequence; in longer diploma programs they may have the choice of elective courses chosen from a pre-established pool of options.

The teaching work of the college is divided into divisions corresponding to broad occupational fields (e.g., business, fine arts and design, health sciences, technology). Each division is headed by a dean, who is accountable to the vice-president of academic affairs. Within the divisions, the various programs come under the direct management of chairpersons who are accountable to the dean of their division. (In colleges, the position of chair is a non-rotating managerial appointment.) Any one chair will be responsible for a cluster of related programs: for example, in the business division, one chair will handle all the programs dealing with office administration, secretarial skills, and word processing; a different chair handles business management, marketing, and accounting programs. The actual teaching work is performed by salaried full- and part-time teachers; however, as in the university sector, in many divisions there is an increasing administrative reliance on temporary employment, which is cheaper and more "flexible." Salaried teaching staff is unionized. A single collective agreement is negotiated for the entire Ontario college system, although individual colleges may negotiate additional agreements with their local unions in a range of areas.

At the time of my research, the provincial operating grant to the college system had been cut, but government policy documents explicitly instructed colleges not to respond by reducing their operations and thereby restricting access to college programs. It was in this context that administrators at many colleges were redoubling their efforts to develop a strong entrepreneurial division that could engage successfully with the burgeoning competitive market in contract training for employers. However, contract training still provided only a small portion of most colleges' overall revenue. Post-secondary diploma programs made up the largest chunk of activity, and here there was no possibility of going out and drumming up business in the private sector; all the colleges could do was try to teach as many students as possible with the government funding they were given (since future funding depended on current enrolment levels).

Here is how an administrator at Aldrich College (also a pseudonym) described the need for program costing. This was the first time I heard about the practice being used in the colleges.

I mentioned to you our dilemma of survival. You know, not having enough money and – we've got to look for ways of deciding where we get our biggest bang for the buck. And we have to think more of that now. In the past it was more community service. Now we've got to think, how can we provide the maximum bang for the buck in the community?

It's getting to that. So we have to know a little bit more about program costs – internally. So we have to make a hard decision: yes, that's important, that program for the community. But this one is more important, we can do more of this. And maybe they're of equal importance to the community, but we can do more of it here because it is more efficient than it is here. So if we have costing information, we can say, well, it's a hard decision, but this one's got to go. And we're going to have to do more and more of that. It's a sign of the times. And that's what's been happening in the world.

Here we have a description of an accounting procedure in terms of what it makes visible (bang for buck, efficiency) and how it will figure in the justificatory framework that the speaker, as a manager, can employ in producing the accountability of the decisions he makes; notice his reference to what "we can say." Note also that the speaker is describing a transition between interpretive/justificatory frames – from "community service" in the past to "maximum bang for the buck in the community" now. Obliquely referenced by these terms is a whole set of relations and procedures – for developing new programs, proposing them to the board, applying for ministerial approval, as well as explaining to staff, students, and local employers why certain programs have been eliminated. Colleges have a legislated mandate to develop and offer educational services identifiably of service to "the community." Whatever programming choices college managers make have to be accounted for in those terms, and colleges have mechanisms and procedures, such as program advisory committees, for accountably identifying "community needs." The change this manager is describing is one that adds another dimension of evaluation/justification, that of "efficiency," or, more colloquially, getting the "maximum bang for the buck." As he describes it, college managers now need a way of evaluating college programs along that dimension as well: "deciding where we get our biggest bang for the buck." This involves not just finding and measuring efficiency, but comparing efficiency across programs ("we can do more of it here"). Program costing as a documentary practice offers a way to do that.

At Fulton College, managers spoke about similar pressures and needs to know more about costs. But from the perspective of the administrator in charge of developing program costing there, the issue wasn't just one of providing new information to senior managers. He identified a situation where exogenously imposed changes demanded internal readjustment, not only in administrative procedures, but in the thinking and practice of college employees:

> Academics are peculiar beasts. They live in a world of, let me get on with doing my job, and don't bother me with dollars and cents. Unfortunately the current system is putting us in a position of being a business. Okay? We're a business. And we have to very carefully balance the humanistic side of our aspect against the bottom line.

He spoke of "a major culture change that has to be born and nurtured within the college":

> It has to permeate right through the organization, right from top to bottom. Everybody has to be thinking about ways and methods of working in a more efficient manner with the idea that that more efficient manner isn't going to create redundancy in jobs, it's going to allow us as an educational institute to do more with the resources that we have.

Administrators at Fulton were working to effect this "major culture change" through a range of policies and activities, most of which relied on or appealed to accounting representations that could be read as giving an objective picture of the college's financial squeeze. They had adopted a policy of allowing representatives of the union local to see their accounting records; they held seminars to teach faculty and support staff how college funding was organized. They set up a budget committee where deans and chairs had to account for their budget forecasts and respond to requests that they seek a "more efficient manner" of running their programs. And they introduced program costing.

Program Costing at Fulton College

The program costing at Fulton was designed to calculate, for each program, the cost per day and per classroom hour, and to set program costs against the program's "revenue" in order to calculate the program's contribution to the overall operating expenses of the college. A representation of the program costing appears in figures 4.1 and 4.2. This is a condensed excerpt from the program costing for one academic division. For clarity, I will begin with an explanatory reading of these texts.[5] The reading offered here is shaped by my training in accounting as well as by what I was told by people in the college.

Costing documents of this kind work through and visually display an analytic exercise. They are constructed to be read from left to right, and from top to bottom, working in a movement that starts at top left and finishes bottom right. A reading following this temporal and spatial organization allows the reader to follow the working out of the analysis. The chart and the analysis begin with amounts that are taken from previously worked up accounting representations (we will have occasion to take a closer look at this aspect of the process in the next section). Then, basic mathematical operations of addition, subtraction, and division are performed, using the given figures.

At Fulton, program costing takes the form of a computer printout several pages in length. It has two parts to it. The first (see figure 4.1) lists all the programs and shorter courses offered by the division in a list down the left side of the page. The first column of figures ("Training Days") represents the work of the department converted into measurable units of activity.[6] Then, going across the page are the costs associated with each program, by category: direct costs (materials, equipment), allocated salaries (teachers), and an allocated portion of the salaries paid to the dean and other departmental staff (chairpersons, secretaries). A share of the overhead costs for the college as a whole is also allocated. The different costs are totalled for each program, and then at the far right, there is one column showing the cost per day for each program, and another showing the cost per student contact hour, which means scheduled classroom time for which a teacher is officially present. These last figures divide the total cost by the measured units of activity, in order to discover unit costs for the department's saleable "product."

The second part of the printout (see figure 4.2) again lists all the department's programs down the left side of the page. The first column of numbers (1) lists the revenue for each program. This might be student fees and a portion of the operating grant based on enrolment, or the price paid by the federal government for the training courses it sponsors at the college. Right next to the revenue column come two columns showing the total expenses of the program, taken from the previous page (Figure 4.1). The first expense figure (2) includes the allocated portion of institutional overhead. The second, lower figure (3), includes only those costs associated with the department (materials, teacher salaries, and dean's and chair's salaries, etc.). Right after these two columns comes an amount (4) arrived at by subtracting the first expense figure (2) from the total program revenue (1). This shows the program's

Fulton College -- XYZ Division								
Program Name	Training Days	Direct Cost	Allocated Salaries	Dean & Staff	Overhead	Total Cost	Cost Per Day	Cost per SCH
A	61545	60,037	1,065,281	225,927	747,156	2,098,402	34.10	5.68
B	19805	76,365	153,138	72,703	240,433	542,638	27.40	4.57
C	15300	32,715	257,067	56,165	185,742	531,689	34.75	5.79
D	28900	113,758	322,200	106,090	350,846	892,893	30.90	5.15
E	35615	83,506	641,719	130,740	432,366	1,288,331	36.17	6.03
F	4845	37,602	78,420	17,786	58,818	192,626	39.76	6.63
G	12835	97,650	179,184	47,116	155,817	479,767	37.38	6.23
	178845	501,633	2,697,009	656,527	2,171,178	6,026,346	33.70	

Figure 4.1 Fulton College program costing document, 1/2.

"contribution" to the college as what is left after departmental costs and allocated overhead are covered. Most of these figures are negative. In the next column (5), contribution is expressed as a percentage of expenses (contribution divided by expenses). In the last two columns, the same calculation of contribution as a figure (6) and then as a percentage (7) is performed, this time using the expense figure that does not include overhead (3). Each column of figures is totalled. Percentages for these totals are calculated using the same procedure as above.

The columns on the far right occupy a privileged position in the spatial layout, since they are both the end point in the reading process and the first figures the eye falls on in a casual glance. This is the important information, the analytic "news." Notice that the contribution rate without overhead has been placed in this last space, and that the percentage showing the aggregate contribution rate without overhead for the entire division appears in the ultimate analytic position at the bottom right.

The managerial significance of expressing contribution as a percentage or rate is that this additional move permits (invites) efficiency comparisons among programs and across divisions. Contribution figures will necessarily vary widely among programs, which all have different costs. By using contribution as a percentage, quite different monetary figures can be compared and found to be instances of the same contribution rate. Or a small program, in financial terms, can be discovered to be outperforming a larger program that brings in more revenue and has proportionally higher costs. (E.g., in figure 4.2, Program B brings in less revenue than Program A, but has a much higher contribution rate.)

At Fulton, the previous year was the first time such information about departmental activities had been assembled. This form of analysis intends the kinds of "hard decisions" mentioned by the Aldrich

Fulton College -- XYZ Divison								
						Revenue Over/-Under		
Program	Revenue	Expenses w/Overhead	w/o O/H	Contribution w/Overhead	%	w/o O/H	%
A	2,017,238	2,098,402	1,351,246	-81,164	-3.87	665,992	49.29
B	652,462	542,638	302,205	109,824	20.24	350,257	115.90
C	470,038	531,689	345,947	-59,651	-11.22	126,091	36.45
D	969,090	892,893	542,047	76,197	8.53	427,043	78.78
E	902,792	1,288,331	855,965	-385,539	-29.93	46,827	5.47
F	170,876	192,626	133,808	-21,750	-11.29	37,068	27.70
G	317,096	479,767	323,950	-162,671	-33.91	-6,854	-2.12
	5,499,592	6,026,346	3,855,168	-526.754	-8.74	1,644,424	42.65
	(1)	(2)	(3)	(4)	(5)	(6)	(7)

Figure 4.2 Fulton College program costing document, 2/2.

administrator, or, in the Fulton administrator's terms, the balancing of the "humanistic aspect" against "the bottom line."[7] In making visible what can be interpreted as an indication of program efficiency, the program costing can be used to make and justify decisions about which courses to drop, in the event such decisions become necessary. But that is a relatively infrequent event at a college. The pressing, ongoing need identified by college administrators is to cut the costs and increase the "efficiency" of all their operations, even the ones they choose to keep. Here is how that works. Placing the contribution-without-overhead rate in the final right-hand column highlights a reading of "contribution" as arising out of the managerial work of the division's dean and chairpersons. Only those costs incurred in the department have been included in the calculation. College overhead, which represents an arbitrary allocation of costs incurred elsewhere in the college, is left out of the figure that offers a measure of program or divisional efficiency. This kind of representation is a technique of managerial accounting called "responsibility accounting" in the accounting literature – a way of sifting out those revenues, costs, profits, or losses that can be attributed to the managerial purview of specific positions, and for which the incumbents can be held accountable as a feature of their job performance. Here is the cost accountant at Fulton College:

> ACC: ... Um, in the old system, the president had control over everything.
>   We try to make the deans responsible for the operations.
> LM: Of their divisions?
> ACC: Yes. Right, so the only way we could make them responsible is to tell
>   them, okay, this is what you're bringing in, this is what it's costing you,
>   right? So the only way we could do that is to go through the costing
>   exercise across the board and so, okay – short programs are not making
>   money, post-secondary programs are making money, the division as a
>   whole is looking good, but you have certain programs that are being car-
>   ried by other programs. This is the reason for doing this kind of exercise
>   at this stage.

Here we see the powerful organizing potential of the document. The accountant describes the way the program costing document is being used by him and the administrator in charge to "make the deans responsible for the operations." He describes this making responsible dialogically (Bakhtin 1981), enacting[8] as direct speech what he and the administrator can tell the deans. And what he is enacting is talk that has as its warrant and referent the program costing document ("this is what you're bringing in"). He is enacting the situation of showing a dean how to read the program costing as an evaluative representation of her or his division, in the context of implementing a new system of responsibility.

Elsewhere the same orientation to the new accountability is visible in the accountant's description:

> LM: Um, so for your own internal use prior to what you're trying to develop now, what kind of internal information about costs ... were you generating?
>
> ACC: Okay. What the deans knew before is what the ministry was paying on the SCH [student contact hour].

Here is an interesting shift in the accountant's answer. Whereas my question includes the accountant among the users as well as the generators of accounting information, his answer does not include himself and was, on first hearing, frustratingly elliptical. The technicality of "what the ministry was paying on the SCH" need not concern us here; my revelation concerned the accountant's focus on "what the deans knew." After studying the transcript, I came to see that the accountant speaks of his work as producing knowledge for others that will be acted upon in specific ways. The "internal use" that matters is not what he might know, but the production of knowledge for which deans can be held accountable in the new relations of managerial accountability his work is helping to put in place.

> Acc [describing the old system]: No, they had no responsibility [LM: For?] the operations. All we give them is a statement saying this is your expenses, they say that's okay ... Then at the end of the year we say, the college is showing a loss, why? This is why we have a loss: you're running too many programs that are not bringing any mark-up. Like, our operating overhead is between 26 and 30 per cent. Now we're trying to tell them, bring in your programs at 26 to 30 per cent. Anything under that is a risk. So we're trying to feed that into them right now.

Notice that, again, the accountant is talking about accounting documents as constructing a particular visibility that warrants claims in the context of managing the managers. He sets up a contrast between two forms of cost documentation in terms of what they show and, most particularly, what response they can evoke from the deans, what next phase of action they can intend. The old form of cost documentation, a simple statement of expenses, is described as evoking nothing more than acknowledgment from the deans ("that's okay"). There's nothing the deans need to do with that information. The new program costing is described as answering the question about why the college is "showing a loss" (an expression that is also a reference to the accounting representations that discover and make losses visible). College accountants have calculated that overhead costs as a percentage of total college costs usually run between 26 per cent and 30 per cent. The percentage contribution rate worked out in the program costing repeats that form of calculation at the level of the program. This visibility, when interpreted for them by the accountant, sets the deans a clear task: in the case of under-contributing programs, they are to find ways to "bring in" their programs at the specified contribution range. The deans must be taught this new knowledge and its implication for their work: "We're trying to feed that into them right now."

The reluctance or incompetence of the deans was a steady theme among the top administrators who decreed and the support staff who produced what the deans should now "know" about their programs. One administrator leaned across his desk to cover my microphone with his hand and stage-whisper that some of the deans couldn't even balance a chequebook. The accountant talked about how at first the deans had a hard time reading the program costing documents ("They had the same trouble you're having," he said); now, however:

> ACC: ... the deans and them, they're showing a lot of interest in the papers, so they support this method better than they had last year when we asked them for the first time to [participate in] this exercise.

As a powerful reshaper of organizational accountability, the program costing catches the deans up in a new set of relations. As well as supplying knowledge about the profitability of their programs that they may have to use in justifying their actions to senior administrators, the program costing is also a picture of their effectiveness as managers. Small wonder they start "showing a lot of interest in the papers."

Not only deans show an interest; accountable to the deans, and actually doing the day-to-day work of managing the programs whose costs and contributions are represented in the program costing are the department chairs. Although the program costing is worked out for the division as a whole and as the responsibility of the dean, the line-by-line calculation of each different program's costs and contribution permits cost responsibilities to be assigned within the division, where each chair is responsible for certain programs. Chairs too are thereby pulled into the new relations, and orient to the new visibility. Here is what one chair had to say about one of the more contentious aspects of program costing:

> Last year they did a flat 30 per cent overhead ... they're now saying, okay, we'll look at adjustable overheads, not flat overhead. So one of the things we were going to immediately argue for is that we have several programs in this division where our students have field placement, concurrently with ... that means we have one set of classrooms in use, but in practice we have, in actuality we have two groups of students ... So we say, you can't charge us 30 per cent, if you're charging those programs with students in five days a week 30 per cent overhead, because we're in fact getting double use out of the classrooms ... We're saying, here are some things we're doing where we run very economically and that's fine if that gets reflected back in the program costing.

This chair and her dean are taking an active interest in the program costing, for they are seeking to influence its further development as a representation. The chair talks about (enacts as direct speech) a plan to try to negotiate a variable overhead rate in the calculation of program cost. The current system of program costing involves the application of overhead cost as a flat percentage – that is, overhead is not calculated as a function of specific departmental activities. But, as this chair rehearses her argument, certain of her department's programs use space – and heat and light – economically because one set of classrooms serves two groups of students, since they take turns being off-campus at field placements. The chair talks about advocating to have the program-costing process further elaborated to make visible that kind of "economy." Notice also that she describes the program costing as a process whereby the central administration "charges" her programs for resources and services; here we see the textual establishment of quasi-market relations inside the organization.

As managers perceive the consequences of the new visibility – the indications of their managerial effectiveness, the potential for comparisons among programs and divisions, the opportunity to make the better-resourced divisions "pay" for their bigger offices and classrooms – some managers (the administratively adept, perhaps) seek to influence or benefit from that visibility. In fact, the accountant spoke about plans to look into a general overhead costing process that would be based on square footage used in classrooms and office space. As the program costing is developed and extended, more and more aspects of college activities come to be representable as having financial value and being measurable in financial terms.

In addition to advocating for program costing refinements, deans and chairs also orient to the new visibility by trying to find ways of improving the recordable efficiencies of their programs. Since departments do not have any control over revenue for most types of program, improving efficiency is mainly a matter of finding ways to reduce program costs. Teaching is labour-intensive activity, and by far the largest cost item in the calculation of program costs is teacher salaries. The program-costing representation makes teacher salaries visible as a drain on contribution. So one big effect of the program costing is to focus managerial attention on teacher salaries and teachers' work, with the aim of finding ways to lower teaching costs while still teaching the same number of, if not more, students (since revenue is linked to enrolment). To see in more detail how this is happening, it is useful to begin with a look at a documentary practice behind the program costing.

Calculating Teachers' Work

The program costing process at Fulton makes use of existing documents that are gleaned for data on costs and revenue; it depends on a range of prior documentary practices that work up textual versions of college activities in numerical and financial terms (student registration, accounts payable, etc.). One such, and an important one, is the documentary practice known in the college system as "SWF" (pronounced "swif"), an acronym for the Standard Workload Form. The SWF is used to calculate the workload of college teachers each semester. It functions to bring the terms of the collective agreement into each department of every college, and has been in place since the mid-1980s when teachers went on strike over excessive workloads. Although they had a collective agreement which set out the maximum hours teachers could be asked to teach, these were frequently disregarded by college administrators trying to increase enrolment while holding staff salaries down. One outcome of the strike settlement was the development of a standard formula for calculating teacher "workload."

The SWF is a method and a textual process that relies on objectively knowable and officially documented aspects of the teacher's work – number of students registered, number of scheduled class hours, type of evaluation to be performed (e.g., essay tests or multiple choice) – in order to arrive at an attributed number of average work hours per week. The application of the formula involves multiplying scheduled class hours and numbers of students by factors representing evaluation method and preparation requirements as set out in the collective agreement. Teacher "workload" is therefore not determined by teachers figuring out how much they work, but is rather determined independently of their experience of doing the work. It is the work of the department chair to fill out (or cause to be filled out) and approve SWFs for all the teachers in the department. This is not a representation after the fact. SWFs are filled out in the process of determining what courses a teacher will teach in the upcoming semester and what other work will be expected of her or him, such as developing curricula or going to speak in high schools. The process of SWF thus applies the terms of the collective agreement to the work any one teacher is being asked to do, and by calculating workload by means of the formula, it can be seen whether this proposed set of tasks fits or contravenes the terms of the agreement. Adjustments can then be made in the planned work so that it does conform. Adjustments can also be made in the representation, so that conformity is a textual accomplishment alone.

As a standardizing system it is not inflexible. There are open categories that allow for the teacher's manager – the department chair – to include any type of work the teacher might do and to attribute hours to that work. This part, however, is discretionary, whereas the application of the formula to the scheduled teaching is obligatory. It then arises in this relation that there are points of contention around the representations of teachers' work on the SWF. Some teachers are reportedly impatient with the SWF process because it can prevent them from taking a workload they feel they can handle. So they might collaborate with their chair in adjusting the form to show conformity with the contract while leaving them free to teach a schedule that might otherwise be calculable as going over the weekly maximum. Other teachers are frustrated that, because of the chair's discretionary power, much work they do is rendered invisible because it does not enter into the workload calculation;[9] the result is that they are working more hours a week than they would like, or the contract allows.

For the department chair, the SWF process puts constraints on the deployment of teaching staff. The chair is accountable for getting the teaching needs of the department filled while assuring that the work being done is in conformity with the collective agreement. The filling out of the SWF is both the means of figuring out how to do this with the available staff as well as a record that it has been properly done.

Pulling SWF into Program Costing

The SWF is being taken up in the work of program costing as the means for allocating portions of teacher salaries to the various programs in a division. Any one teacher assigned to a division might teach in several of that division's programs; some teachers in service departments like social sciences, math, and English teach courses to students in all the other divisions. In order to come up with the individual costs of programs, the main cost item, teacher salaries, has to be sorted out from the general bookkeeping account in which all teacher salaries are recorded. The document currently available in the system for doing this is the SWF, and it is with recourse to the SWFs in their files that deans can tell the accounting department what percentage of each teacher's salary should be allocated as a cost to which courses and programs.

The SWF, which in its original field of use intends a future actuality (the upcoming semester), is now being taken up in a course of action in which it is read as a historical record of what work the teacher did for the purpose of allocating that work as a cost item. Hence, the accuracy of the SWF representation comes to matter in a new way. At Fulton College, a review of all the college's SWFs was undertaken as part of the development of the program costing. And there, SWFs were not being read as evidence of proper conformity with the collective agreement, but as potential source material for the program costing and as indicators of efficiency in the deployment of human resources. The accountant again:

ACC: Like meeting with them [the deans] this year, we realize that it had certain errors last year.
LM: The SWF system?
ACC: Yeah.
LM: What kind of errors?
ACC: Well, we have teachers here who aren't doing the full number of teaching hours, right? Yet they have to be allocated somehow, so what they

say is, this guy only taught 13 hours per week, but we paid him for 18, so what happened to the other five hours? So the explanation there was, you have to charge this guy for 18 hours not 13 hours. His salary is based on an 18-hour week. So these are the kind of errors we found last year and we're trying to correct them this year.

Here the accountant displays the new reading and the problems or "errors" that become visible with it: some ways of filling out SWFs result in gaps that make it hard to use the SWF information to allocate costs. It can then appear, as the accountant's description suggests, that some teachers are not doing as much work as they are being paid for, and that divisions are negligent in allowing this to happen. In fact, the collective agreement does not stipulate that full-time post-secondary teachers must do 18 hours of classroom teaching a week; it establishes 18 hours as a maximum. But the new use of SWFs in cost allocation, and their scrutiny by the administrator in charge of program costing, results in pressure on chairs to avoid the appearance of missing hours, and to find ways of "maximizing" teachers – having them teach a full 18 hours in the classroom without going over the allowable weekly maximum of 44 hours, arrived at by multiplying class hours by number of students by factors for preparation and evaluation.

A department chair described how she was orienting to the situation that her SWFs were now being read outside the department, and in a new way. She told how previously, the coordination work[10] performed by teachers was not represented on the SWFs in her department. The teachers doing this work taught fewer courses to give them the time to do coordination, but no attempt was made to attribute hours to the coordination and include that in the calculation of "workload." It wasn't a problem, she said, because "everyone knew" how much work the teacher was really doing. But now the chair has devised a way of quantifying coordination work on the SWF:

> CH: So then their total workload now resembles the workload of a faculty who's teaching 18 hours in the classroom, as it should. So from their standpoint I've been trying to make it a historical document that will more accurately reflect what faculty have in fact been doing. But since nobody paid much attention to it, nobody cared that they be particularly accurate. But now they are paying more attention to that, and I'm paying more attention to it because, from my perspective, we have very hard-working, dedicated people in the division and I don't want it to look as

though their workload is less than the workload of people elsewhere in the college who are less careful about the SWF. At the same time, I realize that as I do that and everybody else presumably does the same thing, what that results in is the SWF being taken much more seriously and ultimately reflecting if not reality, at least a different reality than before. So I'm feeding that process, but if I don't feed that process that's to the detriment, or could be to the detriment, of the faculty in my area and I don't want to do that.

This chair is very careful to present her new SWF strategy as something she has developed to protect and benefit the faculty in her department. The managerial work she is describing in this account is both proactive and imposed; it is a kind of inter-divisional competition, an escalating process "fed" by the efforts of others such as herself who actually do the work of managing teachers and accomplishing the textual representation of teachers' work. Her account highlights the experience of seeing how her own actions contribute to a process of questionable change rippling through the college, while at the same time knowing that she cannot opt out of the process without jeopardizing her staff and (this is only implied) her own reputation as an effective manager.

But the SWF does more than provide the necessary information for cost allocation purposes; as a quantified representation of teachers' work, it figures in efforts to improve program efficiency by "maximizing" teachers. The program costing process directs attention to teacher salaries as a cost item, and provides the warrant for administrative requests that deans and chairs do something to lower teacher costs. The accountant:

This is the type of thing we have to show the chairs and the deans and say it's costing you too much to operate these programs and this is the challenge, they have to come back and say, okay, we could do the same programs cutting back ... The equipment and supplies are a very small part of the expense. Could you do the same programs with less teachers? Could you get teachers that teach 18 hours, which is what their contracts call for, rather than the 15 hours they're teaching now, because of the way the programs are set up. So these are the challenges that deans and chairs will have to face based on this kind of exercise.

Here the accountant, again enacting a conversation, shows how the visibility constructed in program costing can be interpreted as suggesting the need to reduce the number of teachers, or to find ways of getting more teaching work out of the teachers available. Here the reference is to the managerial work of chairs: "because of the way the programs are set up," some teachers are underutilized even within the constraints of the collective agreement. The "challenge" now is for deans and chairs to reconfigure or reschedule their courses and sections of courses so that, as much as possible, each teacher is teaching the maximum number of hours, as calculated according to the workload formula and represented on the SWF. This leads to increased administrative interest in new forms of curriculum and new teaching devices, such as computer-marking and self-directed learning, that would justify lower evaluation factors[11] in the workload formula. This would then permit a teacher to teach more students or more courses, and still be shown on the SWF to be carrying a workload in conformity with the collective agreement.

"Doing the programs with less teachers" implies an overall decrease in the numbers of teachers employed, and despite college administrators' stated reluctance to lay off teachers, layoffs were happening. The president of the union local at Fulton was trying to keep as many full-time jobs as possible. She described a plan to negotiate a local agreement with the college administration that would give full-time day faculty access to part-time, continuing education ("Con Ed") night school courses. She was considering what she could offer the college administrators in return for that access. One plan depended on and took up the visibility produced through the SWF system.

> You could maximize our teaching by filling in two hours at night .... Unless you've got a full class you can't maximize us. You need 25 for – you need 35 actually in every class, so unless you get the economy of scale in all your classes, we're not maximized ... If I say to you, if you let me do that and give me the access to Con Ed, I will talk to my faculty about do we really need point three, you've been doing that for the last ten years, can you find a better way of that? You've been, uh, when you made the agreement for that course on the faculty evaluation factor you didn't use the computer to mark papers, your students didn't in some programs, some of the business programs, the test is done right on the computer. You know, you actually sit down and do the test on the computer, it's not pegs. or things, the answers are in and the computer marks them. Um, I could encourage my faculty to do more of that and reduce the factor, reduce their work. It's a smarter way of working.

The union president's argument, as she rehearses it, begins by representing what the union wants as consistent with, and in fact, furthering the goal of management to maximize teachers. She goes on to detail how she will ask faculty to agree to lower evaluation factors, in recognition of changes they may already have made that take advantage of computer possibilities. She will also encourage faculty to look for ways of reducing the time they spend at evaluation, so that they can reduce the factor through which evaluation work is textually represented in calculable terms. Thus, the union president, in planning what she hoped would be a viable negotiating strategy designed to save full-time jobs, was taking up managerial relevances and the documentary forms that concretize them, and in so doing, was helping to bring these relevances even further into the day-to-day organization of teachers' work. (Not surprisingly, at the same time, college management at the provincial level was trying to get the union to agree to renegotiate the SWF factors in the next round of collective bargaining.)

Concluding Comments

We hear a great deal about restructuring in the public sector – massive budget cuts, privatization, outsourcing, the shift to non-standard forms of employment, the increased reliance on market relations as a mechanism for the distribution of resources. Critical perspectives on these projects often focus on the effects, since those are most easily visible. What I have wanted to do with this study of program costing is to take a close look at how the elements of change that add up to "restructuring" actually come about. Dorothy Smith's notion of text-mediated relations of ruling and the investigative approach of institutional ethnography offer a way to examine restructuring as it occurs through the coordinated practices of actual people. When we look in this way, texts and representational practices come into view as key constituents of the restructuring of institutional relations. Since contemporary ruling depends in a large way on documentary forms of knowledge that construct in texts the objects of managerial or professional decision making, changes in relations of ruling are likely to be evoked and driven through changes in the kind of documentary knowledge produced and the uses to which it is put. We have seen that this is the case in the colleges, where changes in the pattern of government funding (a text-mediated relation) place new demands on colleges and pull them into competitive market relations (also text mediated). College administrators try to position their colleges to flourish in these new relations through a cluster of changes designed, in their words, to make colleges more entrepreneurial, more customer-oriented, and more efficient. We have seen how some of their efforts in this direction depend on the kind of visibility that program costing constructs. And we have seen how restructuring ripples through the college as managerial staff orient to the new visibility, adjusting their work routines and divisional procedures with reference to the new forms of representation.

NOTES

1 *Editors' note*: this chapter is a revised version of L. McCoy, "Producing 'What the Deans Know': Cost-accounting and the Restructuring of Post-secondary Education," *Human Studies* 21(1998): 395–418. Note that some of the accounts of college and university procedures and funding McCoy describes refer to the early 1990s and no longer apply in 2012.

2 I am grateful to Eric Mykhalovskiy and Dorothy Smith for their comments on this paper. I would also like to acknowledge the debt this research owes to George Smith, who died in 1994.

3 George Smith and I conducted an institutional ethnography exploring the organization of the Ontario college system with respect to the management of the delivery of job training (Smith & McCoy 1991). This research consisted of in-depth interviews with college managers, ministry officials, training managers in private industry, and union officials.

4 In Canada, the term "college" is not generally used to describe four-year degree-granting institutes; those are "universities."

5 Readers without a background in accounting, or without experience of administrative work processes mediated by this sort of representation, may find the description of program costing hard going. Or else, excruciatingly boring. I invite such readers to consider their experience – of confusion, glazed eyes, irritation – to be a recreation of what many Fulton deans and chairs felt when they faced program costing for the first time. I would also add that making sense of the rest of the article does not require the reader to have fully digested the workings of program costing as a form of analysis.

6 A "training day" is a textual category supposed to stand for one day in which the department's teaching resources were available to one registered, full-time student. This is a measure that already exists in the college system, since it is used in calculating the provincial operating grant and

government training purchase. Using it in the program costing articulates the costing visibility to the funding process that results in program revenue. In this quantifying procedure, which is given to all the colleges by their government funders, one training day is assumed to comprise at least six "student contact hours" of officially scheduled classroom tuition. Actual individual students are in this figure only in an indirect and concealed way. There is no exact correlation between one training day – a measure of departmental resource availability – and one registered student – a quantification supplied by the registrar's office. This is because part-time students and full-time students are counted up in the same stream of data by converting part-time students into portions of training days. Therefore, one training day can also represent departmental resources available to two registered part-time students.

7 The term "bottom line" draws its sense from accounting documents such as the one presented here, where the final figures in any analytic display come at the bottom of a column of figures. It is customary in accounting to draw two parallel lines under final totals, to mark the end of an analysis or mathematical operation. The "bottom line" – the "reality" that must be considered or appealed to in understanding a situation or making a decision – is represented in the figures that appear at the bottom of the document.

8 A striking feature of the explanations collected in the interviews is the extent to which these explanations are formulated as accounts of speech: the informant describes the work process or situation by enacting the direct speech of her- or himself and others. Sometimes this is presented as the narrative of a past event, reporting on what was said; often it is presented as an argument the speaker is planning to make in the future; sometimes a routine activity is verbally illustrated by acting out a typical conversation through which the activity is accomplished (for example, an informant asked to explain what a "promotion meeting" is responds by acting out a typical discussion characteristic of such meetings). It is not to be supposed that these enactments exactly match what was said or what will be said; their usefulness as data in this kind of study lies in what they suggest about what can possibly or appropriately be said, and especially how what can be said depends on and is oriented to the textual forms through which events and activities are known in authoritative ways.

9 Teachers have the right to refuse SWF allocations they consider to be unfair, and there is a committee that hears SWF complaints. The loophole for management, however, is that only tasks officially assigned by the chairperson need be represented in addition to the standard attributed hours

for teaching, preparation, basic administrative work, and meeting with students. Because teachers are considered to be professionals who determine the best way to carry out their professional duties, the unrepresented work they claim to do can be argued by the chair to fall within the territory of their professional choice.

10 Coordination work provides a link between the administration of a program and the teachers who teach courses in it. Often this work has a textual element – distributing and collecting final grade lists, giving room request information to the scheduling office, etc.

11 Attributed weekly hours for evaluation are worked out on the SWF for each course by multiplying the number of students by a factor such as 0.2 or 0.3. What determines the factor is the type and frequency of evaluation to be performed. At the time of my research there were three possible factors. The highest factor went to forms of evaluation that are the most time-consuming, such as marking essay tests and written assignments. The lowest factor was assigned to courses where evaluation is done during class time, such as when a teacher in a technical class grades students by observing their work during class hours. The middle factor was assigned to courses where evaluation takes place outside of class time but is less time-consuming than marking essays (e.g., marking multiple choice or true/false tests). New forms of curriculum are assumed to shift evaluation work to the student or to a computer, thus supporting arguments to lower the evaluation factor assigned to a course.

5 Text in Performance: The Making of a Haydn Concerto

LEANNE D. WARREN

Leanne Warren explicates the score as "musical text" and its role in organizing musical creation. She uses video, observation, interviews, and the texts of the score of an amateur orchestra's rehearsal of a Haydn cello concerto to show how the text brings musical creation into dialogue with a relevant tradition of musical interpretation. McCoy introduced us to specialized textual formats to be read in accountancy terms. Warren instructs us in how a musical score is written to identify notes, variations in pace and sound and how it is assembled to be read by musicians. With scores inherited from the past, there is minimum direction about how what is written should be taken up in the act of playing. Warren shows us intersecting discourses (music not language) that enter into the interpretive practice that is the music as it is played at the moment of performance. She describes embodied practices for a musician playing in an orchestra. Reading a score is only a first moment in articulating an interpretation that coordinates with others reading and contributing their part in the same composition.

The text of the score is the focus. We are shown what is given visually and we are told how it is to be read. Warren then describes discourses that enter the score's interpretation into complex historical traditions. She shows that the direct coordinating of the musical work of an orchestra member through the mediating score of the concerto also ties that musical work into a complex of historical and contemporary traditions of interpretation. We can begin to see a relational process analogous to what literary theorists have described as "intertextuality" (see D.E. Smith's chapter in this book). This is how the text "selects" from the reader's resources what is relevant and applicable to the text being read. But here we are talking about patterns of sounds held in memory. Warren opens up that which is examined in institutional ethnography as a "text–reader conversation" (see part 4) in which the reader, in activating the text, takes it on as given and as governing, while at the same time responding and going beyond.

Warren draws on interviews with the soloist, the conductor, and a member of the orchestra to tell how individual players bridge in performance the distinctive ways each takes up the text within well-understood conventions. We see how Mikhail Bakhtin's notion (1981) of an utterance – a resource for institutional ethnographers – can be applied to music; every utterance as dialogic, both drawing on and shaped by what is historically given and as renewing, creating, and projecting into the future. We learn here new ways of understanding how the musical text brings the past into the present and becomes the organizer of an ongoing collective creative work.

This is a study of the work of an amateur orchestra creating a concert performance of Haydn's Concerto in C Major for Violoncello and Orchestra (Hob. VIIb:1). It considers how that work is organized by the text that is the centrepiece of collective effort, the musical score. By this I do not mean that the score is an authoritative statement of the composer's intent which any single performance can only approach. The overriding goal of the method of inquiry which places the text in the centre of our attention is to explore how the surrounding social relations and discourses are carried into an actual work in progress. The score is a link between the macro level of musical discourse embodied in other texts, such as books of musicology, musical ethnography, and performance practice, the related macro level of performance history which is recorded in a discography or passed down aurally and orally, and the micro level of individual performance (Smith 1999: 6–7). It also connects the individual work of composers, in their own social contexts, to the present exposition of their works, and to the accumulated experience of its performers.

The relationships are illustrated in figure 5.1.[1] The score is not a distinct object in the diagram; it is part of all of the processes shown by the lines and arrows. The solid lines represent connections made literally with and through the score. Dotted lines indicate that the score is not part of the interaction, but is a necessary part of it, as when an audience hears a work played. Dashed lines mean the process might be either an aural or written transmission of information. Two-way arrows represent an exchange; that is, the score influences a specific performance, and the performance has an impact on the score, either as it is understood for playing or as it is written about, recorded, or edited. Since the composer in our case has been dead for two hundred years, he is only

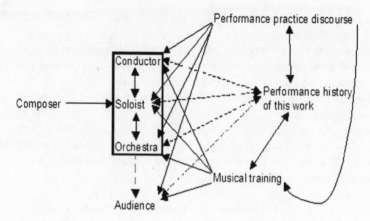

Figure 5.1 Connections between discourses in musical performance.

present in this performance to the extent that the score is able to represent him and his intentions. A composer present for rehearsals or conducting the work would function as part of the performing group, in the sense of being directly involved in interpretation.[2] The box enclosing the conductor, soloist, and orchestra shows the performing group for this concerto.

This study furthers existing ethnomethodological and phenomenological examinations of orchestral performance, which focus mainly on the development of collective understanding of time and other coordinating mechanisms taking place in the performing group, by exposing some of the processes and relations underlying the taken-for-granted "common ground" of the score. Whether we consider the score a repository of musical authority to which performance must conform, or as something "oriented to as a persisting, objective entity … whose specific meaning emerges through interaction" (Weeks 1996: 248), it is a fact of most musical ensemble work that the only person with a complete score is the conductor. Individual players orient themselves to a partial text that is not held in common with players of other instruments; there is no one common ground to be found solely in the parts the players have on their stands as they work. This places participants in a position more like a group of blindfolded people each led to a different part of the proverbial elephant and told to lead it out a door. First each must figure out what the object at hand might be (or at least which end of it goes first) from limited knowledge, then where the group is to lead it, then how to do it together. It is entirely possible for a group to get the elephant out the door without ever arriving at a detailed common understanding of exactly what the animal is, relying instead on knowledge of the surroundings and of the process of leading something, knowledge which is external to both the situation and to specific instructions provided in it. Musical performance has been recognized as this type of process (and as the intersection of the performance history/discography and teaching discourses in figure 5.1) for many years.

> The player approaching a so-called unknown piece of music does so from a historically ... determined situation, determined by his stock of musical experiences at hand ... all his past and present fellow-men whose acts or thoughts have contributed to the building up of his knowledge. This includes what he has learned from his teachers ... what he has taken in from other players' execution; and what he has appropriated from the manifestations of the musical thought of the composer ... [A]nd within this socially derived knowledge there stands out the knowledge transmitted from those upon whom the prestige of authenticity and authority has been bestowed ... the great masters among the composers and the acknowledged interpreters of their work. (Schutz 1964: 168)

In an earlier work Halbwachs places the score as an organizational centre:

> [Musical notation is the] ... means of expressing in a conventional language all the commands which the musician must obey if he wants to reproduce a piece of music properly. The conventional character of the signs of musical notation ... consists in the fact that they have meaning merely by continuous reference to the group which invented and adopted them. (cited in Schutz 1964: 163)

The first difficulty with these interpretations is that there is no one text held in common by all the players in the orchestra. Though individual parts are derived from the conductor's complete score, and for simplicity I refer to "the score" here, it is somewhat misleading to speak of a single textual entity in most ensemble work. The second, implicit, assumption is that there is some ultimately correct performance that musicians work towards. This is certainly not a belief shared by the players I spoke to, and it was not my experience as a player. I am also not entirely convinced that "the incompleteness of musical signs is unavoidable as they are in effect instruction to performers that have to cover a range of unknowable contingencies" (Weeks 1996: 250). It is, of course, true that composers cannot be expected to anticipate all of the local settings or conditions in which their music might be performed. It is also true that "musical notation is only an approximation of the sounds intended by the composer" (ibid.). I would argue that the seeming incompleteness of standard musical notation is not an error, omission, or unavoidable compromise between written and aural media, but a deliberate economy. When we consider music of the Baroque and Classical periods, at least, the understanding of how to bring together the composer's intentions and the particularities of performance context is simply not required to be entirely carried in a musical score. As both Schutz and Weeks have stated, it resides in the surrounding discourses of performance practice, musical instruction, and performance history, and in people's knowledge of the situation in which they work (Schutz 1964: 166; Weeks 1996: 250).

Though classical musical performances usually begin with the score, it is essential not to take its existence, form, or use for granted. All of these aspects must be explained from within the activity it frames.

Texts and Action

A text is "a material object that brings into actual contexts of reading a standardized form of words or images that can be and may be read/seen/heard in many other settings by many others at the same or other times" (Smith 1999: 7). Under this definition, being a text does not depend on physical form or language structure. So long as the object is comprehensible to users and can be reproduced identically in many locations and at different times, it can be a text; the definition is a wide one that relies on action by readers as well as the material properties of the medium. A photograph, for example, may exist specifically to carry a summary of the experience portrayed in it beyond the place and time captured. It can be taken home and put in an album to tell its story without any other content at all, or it may serve as a prompt to a story being told (McCoy 1995). Both connect the viewer to a story beyond the photograph's contents and rely on the viewer's invocation of a set of surrounding references to become meaningful and usable in a particular way. The user and text must be interactive, since neither alone will accomplish the activities we can observe.

To use texts as the basis of exploration beyond the individual, however, we must look further: "The text itself is to be seen as organizing a course of concerted social action" (Smith 1990a: 121). A musical score is written: it carries symbols which have specific meanings for those trained to read them, and does so across time as well as distance, and so it falls within our definition of text. It is an active text with organizational power because it structures a common course of action, beginning with the instrumentation specified and continuing through notes to phrasing, dynamics, and other interpretative markings.[3] Its organizational power is social because it involves the purposeful interaction of groups, including such things as hierarchies of authority and the position of performance arts in other social institutions such as the economy.[4]

The same text can be active in a number of different ways. If we were to make a musical score into a decorative object by framing and hanging it on the wall, it would not become less active. From a musical performance view it is then inert (Smith 1990: 121), since it does not organize coordinated action. Viewers could, however, activate it using the discourses of aesthetic appreciation instead.[5] If it were taken into a classroom it could be used within the discourses of harmonic analysis, with participants leaving notations on it. The reader's understanding of when and how to invoke a particular set of references or discourses arises from the everyday location of the reader as well as the instructions carried in the text itself. Discourses, text, and reader are all interacting to produce what we can see and hear, and take for granted, as everyday work.

It is not necessary for a text to be identically understood by, or even identically available to, everyone working with it. Like emergency call reports generated by 9-1-1 dispatchers, which contain only some of the information given by the caller and a selected history of events which provide a context for action in the current situation (records of previous [domestic violence] events, outstanding warrants, and so on) (Pence 1996: 88), the musical part used by an orchestral player presents only the portion of the whole story of the work that directs the action required by that player. Both 9-1-1 reports and scores are condensed formulations, shorthand renditions of complex events requiring coordinated responses appropriate to a unique situation, and rely on a common understanding of both the language and symbols used to convey meaning and action previously taken in similar situations for "correct" activation. If we consider figure 5.1 and Schutz's outline of musicians' knowledge again, it is the score which carries into the immediate practices of musical performance the intentions of the composer and the accumulated authority of systems of notation, and of structural and interpretative conventions of the musical genre, all occurring at a distance from the specific performance work under way. The roles of notation and structure are examined in the next section.

The Structural Organization of Musical Text

Haydn's Concerto in C Major for Violoncello and Orchestra, Hob. VIIb:1, now a standard work in the cello solo repertoire, has only a brief modern history. Though Haydn listed the work in his notebooks in 1765, it was "lost" until a single set of parts was discovered in 1962, when the archives of the National Museum in Prague were opened for study by western musicologists for the first time since the Second World War (Landon 1983: 5). Both in time of composition and in style, the work can be firmly placed in the European tonal tradition that was established and achieved its cross-cultural, unified character during the Baroque period, developed through the Classical and Romantic periods,[6] and still informs the work of Western composers, though it is no longer hegemonic.

Musical scores are visually complex texts and embody complex organizational ideas that must be understood before the musical idea can be presented. I will describe briefly the conventions of musical writing which underlie this score and what they assume players know, as a reflection of both the musical tradition to which the Haydn concerto belongs and the common practices of Baroque and early Classical performance. The first page of the full score (figure 5.2) is an example of the organizational mechanisms discussed in this section.

In the major/minor tonal tradition, music is written on a "staff" (plural, staves) consisting of five horizontal lines in a group, and placement of notes (circles and short vertical lines, or "stems," of various types) on the staff indicates their pitch and duration. Rests, periods of silence, are indicated by various markings for different lengths (the symbol at the very end of the first line in the oboe part, for example, is an "eighth rest"). Each instrumental section in the orchestra has the notes and rests making up its "part" on a separate line in the score. Where the section

KONZERT in C

Figure 5.2 First page of Haydn concerto score: © 1988 by G. Henle Verlag, München; Bärenreiter-Verlag, Kassel. Used by permission.

is subdivided (Violin I and II, Oboe I and II, for example) and the parts written on separate staves, a curly brace, {, at the extreme left indicates that more than one line is played by the same instrument. Similar instruments' lines are grouped together by a square brace, [, as in the grouping of string parts. Placement of the solo line varies between editions; here it shares the staff with the orchestra cello part, beginning in bar 23 (not shown).

The "time signature," written at the beginning of the movement or points of change within movements, sets limits on two essential characteristics of the music. First of all, it dictates how many "beats" there are in a "bar," which is the horizontal space on the staff bounded by single vertical lines; second, it indicates the type of note that is the reference beat. Reading a notation of "C" ("common time") on the first page, for example, players know that there will be four equal beats in each bar and the reference beat is a quarter note; that is, whatever mathematical subdivisions of the beat are used, there will be a total of four quarter notes in each bar. Bars and time signatures together create a common standard of even and discrete divisions of time, and dictate patterns of emphasis within them (Weeks 1990: 344). In 4/4 time the first beat of the bar generally receives the strongest emphasis, the third beat a lesser stress, and the other beats are unstressed unless an exception is made explicitly by an accent.[7] The conductor knows to use, and the orchestra expects to see, the pattern of baton motions denoting 4/4 time; where the point of the baton "rests" indicates which of the four beats all players should be playing at that instant. From the orchestra, the 4/4 pattern looks something like figure 5.3. Beats 1 and 4 are in front of the conductor, beat 2 is to his/her left, and beat 3 to the right.

Within each complete set of written lines played simultaneously, called a "system," bar lines are aligned vertically. Looking down the

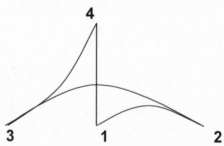

Figure 5.3 Pattern of conducted beats in 4/4 time (orchestra view).

page, a conductor sees the collection of notes which makes up each bar for each instrument or section. Notes written immediately above one another are played together and occupy the same space of time within the bar, even when one player has many notes while another has only one (so, for instance, a quarter note will occupy the same amount of horizontal space as two eighth notes). The same applies to rests. Making sure that forward movement through the notes and rests is simultaneous, as written, is what Weeks (1990) calls "synchrony." Synchrony is vital for the correct production of harmony, as described below.

Two major dimensions on which the role of the score in musical production can be thought of are *vertical* and *horizontal*, and different aspects of music are organized primarily one way or the other. The most important dimension of the score for ensemble work is vertical, as it organizes time and action simultaneously so specific notes are played together to create the harmonic foundation of musical structure. The opening chord of this concerto, for example, is composed (in order from the bass line upward) of the notes C-C-G-E-C-C-E-C-C, which in the work's key of C major is a tonic chord in root position. ("Root position" means the note naming the key, the "tonic," is in the lowest pitch). As is customary in a Classical tonal structure, the opening chord establishes the aural centre of the work and the expected progression of harmony that will define it. Both performers and audience are sensitized from the first notes they hear to expect particular sounds, and combinations of sounds, at specific melodic junctures in the music, especially transition points such as the "cadences" (chord progressions) which mark the end of a thematic exposition or elaboration or the end of a movement. Chords and progressions are the punctuation of music,[8] and a written score ensures the orchestra produces them in the place and form the composer intended.

The aural effect of a specific instrument playing a given note in the chord are also part of the defined intentions of the composer in this period. There is a clear auditory difference between the harmonic third of a C major chord played in the middle of the ensemble pitch range and tone colour (as here, in the second horn and split violin parts), and the same note played at the top of the pitch range with a more penetrating tone colour (e.g., by the oboes). It is central to the tonicity-establishing role of the opening chord that the most obvious notes are C and G, not E, so there are fewer Es in the chord and they are played by instruments in the middle of pitch range and tone colour. Writing the notes explicitly in each instrumental line ensures this effect is realized, while simply indicating "C major" and letting players allocate the notes among themselves would not.[9]

A second aspect of the vertical organization of musical text is the relative duration of notes in different parts, which is also connected to the horizontal dimension. Continuing with the example of the opening chord, we see that the first note has different time values in different lines. Oboes and violins have dotted eighth notes, meaning they are to sustain the note for three-quarters of a beat, while the horns have quarter notes. The sustained Gs and Es emphasize that the key being established is C major rather than C minor, which would have E flat (half a tone lower) as the third of the chord instead of E, or another key altogether (which would have a different 5th note than G). The lower strings (viola, cello, and bass) have the tonic C for one eighth note and then the same note an octave lower for one eighth. The repeated Cs maintain the emphasis on key, while the relatively rapid movement establishes *tempo* (the speed with which beats succeed one another), which might otherwise be unclear in the series of dotted notes.

The second important organizational dimension of a written score is horizontal, taking in foundational ideas such as tempo, *melody* (successive sounds which create a recognizable unity to be stated and elaborated in the piece), and overall *form* (the pattern in which movements, or parts of movements, succeed one another).[10] Subdivisions of the beat are also horizontal constructions; the use of many short notes, for example, can give an impression of an increase, or many long notes a decrease, in speed without a change in overall tempo. *Articulation*, the relative length and emphasis of the sound of different notes, is another horizontal aspect of the passage of musical time which can be manipulated for desired effects. It is, along with tempo and phrasing, the feature which most often distinguishes one interpretation of a work from another. *Dynamics*, changes in sound volume, also operate horizontally, as can be seen easily in the markings for them: *crescendo* (increasing volume from left to right), is denoted <, and *decrescendo* (decreasing volume from left to right), is written as >.

Horizontal and vertical dimensions overlap in harmonic progression, a particular chord series punctuating the horizontal melodic line and providing overall structure. Players move through the notes written in the score as time passes sequentially, whether their parts are melodic or harmonic, and it is this dimension (and only this dimension) which is visible to individuals on their own working parts. Vertical movement, how all the players move forward together, is apparent to players by listening to one another. Only the conductor sees the vertical and horizontal motion of the group simultaneously on the score.

The message encoded in musical texts must be translated to another medium, sound, to be conveyed as intended. Musical literacy includes understanding the meaning not only of notes, bar lines, and so on, but also of interpretative indicators: markings for dynamics, articulation, tempo, and style. In a work of the Classical period, instructions appear as both symbols and words written in Italian, the formal language of classical music, rather than the everyday language of the time and place in which the score is written or read. Both symbols and formal language make up the everyday vocabulary of the working orchestra musician. The question we are considering is not if or how musicians understand the various languages intellectually, but how they use their knowledge that there are instructions, and how they come to read them to produce a coherent performance.

Reading Haydn

In this section, we explore how an amateur orchestra used the score to put together a convincing performance of the Haydn concerto. The orchestra was a fairly standard one for works of the period: five first violins, four second violins, four violas, five celli, one double bass, two French horns, and two oboes. I videotaped and made notes at the first rehearsal of the soloist with the orchestra, and later made notes at the final performance, as well as conducting formal interviews with the conductor ("C"), the soloist ("S"), and one orchestra section leader ("M").

The score was used in two forms. The conductor had a complete score and the soloist and orchestra individual parts. Orchestra section leaders each had a copy of the complete score for reference, but did not play from it.

The process of "reading Haydn" begins when the soloist first takes up her part.

> s: I have to put [this performance] in the context that it's not a new piece; it's a piece where the score and what's there is already out in the aural world in recordings. So long before I started to look at it, it was something I knew, not from the text, exactly ... it was first heard ... I did take this text, which is one of the more pure editions[11] ... and try to come to it new ... despite the interpretations that have gone before that couldn't help but somehow influence me.

The soloist's choice of score was deliberate:

The piece is one I knew in my ear. I know it, I learned it as a student, but I'm looking at it afresh. And I did actually get this particular score, this edition, which is different than the one I first learned, as a way just to come to it completely fresh ... I wanted to have no reminder, because I'm sure even fingerings, bowings, things like that that I had chosen then definitely affected the overall picture, and I wanted to not go to those ... It had been a long enough time that ... I would forget.

The connections to performance history that the soloist took such pains to break are not the notes or markings written by Haydn, but instructions added to a particular edition by the soloist, her teacher, or an editor. Using a different text also weakens the connection to the performance practice discourse prevailing when she first learned the concerto and allows her to reconnect to current understandings.

s: When I first started it as a student it was in a time when the prevalence of early music performances wasn't so strong. There weren't the kind of groups and there weren't the people playing in ways that made the music understandable the way it is now. It was more a Romantic interpretation.

Breaking all these connections, though it creates space for an individual interpretation, does not remove this performance from its discursive context.

s: [A] sense of the final product in my ear ... comes from a conglomeration of performances ... that I'd heard that were moving; not necessarily even of this piece, but of styles of Haydn ... I wanted it to have a certain spirit and a certain tone, a certain pacing.

As Schutz describes:

Even before starting to play or reading the first chord our musician is referred to a ... set of ... previous experiences, which constitute in their totality a kind of preknowledge of the piece of music at hand. To be sure, this ... refers merely to the *type* to which this individual piece of music belongs and not to its particular ... individuality. But the player's general knowledge of its typicality becomes the scheme of reference for his interpretation of its particularity. (1964: 167–8)

The soloist's decision to place her work simultaneously within the general context of other performances of Haydn's works and a specific understanding of performance practices, yet outside her own historical knowledge of this piece, is a conscious one; it is known. The intended relations between players in their work with this score are also known. This is a concerto, and the score reflects the divisions of practice and authority that are required to produce a concerto rather than some other type of work. The title of the work immediately tells musicians that there will be a soloist as well as an orchestra, which means the interactions between conductor and ensemble will be altered by the addition of a second interpretative leader.

> s: Because this is a concerto, the way things are chosen and the course we take is led by how I choose to play, and hopefully I had chosen tastefully with how the music was written … You're allowed to stamp your interpretation on the music really more than in any other situation … There's such a tradition, or just the way the text is set up, that the orchestra is there to be a part of that great music, and it's only enjoyable for them as they work at it with the soloist … You don't negotiate for it, it's just "oh, that's how you want to do it."

The composer's name locates the concerto in a specific time and place where the solo line is predominant. The fundamental character of the performance is based on the soloist's "picture in her ear," even though the conductor has built up another vision of tempo, articulation, phrasing, and so on from his own knowledge, in the same way and from the same discourses as the soloist.

> c: So interpretation is mostly based on tempo … If the conductor and the soloist agree on the basic style, there's really nothing to do ,… [A]s a rule whatever tempo is good for the soloist, that's the tempo because it's their concerto … Sometimes you have to be completely different than what you thought and you have to redo everything in order to put that information in your body language.

If there is a disagreement, the same conventions apply to how it should be resolved, though if the conductor believes the soloist has diverged "too far" from the composer's intentions, there can be conflict. The conductor described a famous example:

> c: [Pianist Glenn] Gould decided to take an overly, overly slow tempo, and [conductor Leonard] Bernstein did an unfathomable thing ... He actually talked to the audience before time and said, "Mr. Gould and I disagree completely, so I want to tell you that I am not responsible for anything in this performance."[12]

It is not surprising that two such powerful characters as Gould and Bernstein should disagree, nor is it unusual that the final performance followed Gould's interpretation. This story is recounted with laughter (and some disapproval) because Bernstein registered his protest with the audience, making visible what is normally resolved out of sight.

Although the soloist's view of the work predominates, by design and by tradition, how that view is communicated to the orchestra must be negotiated between the soloist and the conductor: "I'll give the cue here, you give the cue here; here I follow you, here you'll have to follow me" (C). It is then up to the conductor to make sure that the orchestra understands and follows the soloist's lead.

> s: The conductor['s job] is conceiving of many different things, of an oboist breathing and the timpanist having to hit [the timpani] ... To keep the organized structure everyone in the orchestra has to go through the conductor ... We just have to trust and rely that they are really attuned to the soloist. It was an interesting exercise, how it always has to go through that other person to make it work.

Before the orchestra meets with the soloist for the first time, the text is given another interpretative shape in the discussion of bowings between the string principals and the conductor.

> M: We would get together with the principals before the first rehearsal, work out our bowings, and run them by [the conductor] to see how he feels, if he agrees with it. If he doesn't he'll make changes and then we'll come to the first rehearsal with the bowings and possibly have a couple of bowed parts ... Some of the music ... [the conductor] bows completely himself, and we just copy the bowings and make small changes we feel work better for us as players ... It takes quite a lot of time, there's a lot to go over, you know, the relative merits of how to phrase, how to bow.

The focus on bowing arises from the physical properties of stringed instruments and bows. As the bow is drawn across the strings from left to right ("down bow"), the weight of the player's hand and the heavier end of the bow (the frog) make it easier to generate a stronger tone. The reverse is true when the bow is pushed the other way, from right to left ("up bow"); the tip end of the bow is lighter and likely to move away from the string rather than be pressed down into it, so the tendency is to begin with a lighter sound. Unambiguous ensemble articulation and interpretation require unified bowing, and reproducing a phrase exactly requires exactly the same bowing pattern to be used. Writers on Baroque performance practice stress that "a player must follow the bowings indicated by the composer, for the articulations indicated in the score may be those that 'deviate from the customary manner.' Thus many articulations, *particularly those that indicate the usual or customary manner*, may not be marked at all. They must be added by the performer in accordance with the style and character of the piece" (Cyr 1992: 88, my emphasis). On individual string players' parts, the symbols indicating "up bow" and "down bow" are prominent additions made by hand.

It is clearly not the case that musical notation contains, or is assumed to contain, "all the instructions the musician must follow to reproduce a work properly" (Schutz 1964: 163). On the contrary. Interpretative notation in a Baroque or Classical score expresses what the composer is not willing or able to assume a musician will do without it. An example of performers doing the same thing for themselves is a "tip" marking written in on the viola part.

> M: The reason for that is that it's sort of natural to play it in the middle of the bow and [the concertmaster] decided she wanted them right at the tip there because some of the players were a little bit strong and at the tip you don't have any choice but to stay quiet; you just can't go anywhere.

Exceptions noted in the score are, however, changed as the group works if the composer's rationale is not clear and there is no accepted practice to direct them. In the last bar of the first movement, the final notes in the oboe parts are eighths followed by eighth rests, while all other parts have quarter notes.

> C: Oboes, for some reason you have eighth notes at the end – make it a quarter like everyone else [*beats time and sings, "dee dee deeee."*]

I don't see any reason why we should keep it. [Oboes make note on their parts.]

While orchestra members look to the conductor for direction where there is disagreement or where the score is not clear, leadership in over-all interpretation comes from the soloist, by convention.

M: Mostly it's attacks on notes and so on. A printed note doesn't give you any real idea of how you start or end a note, and what you do is to make the same style of playing as the soloist ... Hopefully you don't have to be told by the conductor; you're responding ... directly to the soloist, her body language and so on ... A great deal of it is in the body language of string playing that you follow ... You see the bow, which is what counts. The bow is out front and you're following that a lot, seeing how it is and responding to it.

When the piece is going according to players' "own understanding of what would have been expected" (M.), listening and watching provide direction to the orchestra. "You're listening. You're watching your score, your part, you're watching the conductor and you're listening to the so-loist, and you're listening to all of the other players too, of course" (M.).

S: Ideally in an orchestra that's what's happening, you're always listening to everyone ... The conductor's role is so paramount, and yet the best conductors are the ones who allow the orchestra to listen to each other and just guide the interpretation most successfully.

Players can take their attention off their parts to watch and listen be-cause they know from experience and convention what is coming next in the harmonic structure and where their part leads into it.

Conductors know that their only means of communicating what is not written is visual.

C: I have to translate as much as possible to visual, to show it visually in my hands, which is the only medium I can use in the concert. As a conductor I try to use that medium throughout, unless at some points it's impossi-ble to explain. If the people don't have all the information or knowledge that I have ... then I have to stop and explain ... For instance, in Haydn's time when you have those three *legatos* in the first bar you don't play "tadadadadadada," but "tada tada tada," you always shorten the last note so you make the definition of those *legatos* ... If you give it to any 19th century, or even any modern, orchestra without so much knowledge of classical style, they [will] probably phrase it as a full *legato*. It's in the classical [style] you feel all those three *legatos* articulated very well, and that will give you extreme clarity ... If you have Brahms, he'll write the same thing, and he won't necessarily make that an issue, but in that case you try to sustain as much as possible.

The misunderstanding the conductor is describing arises when players read the score literally because they lack historical knowledge; they are disconnected from the performance practice discourse that would allow them to just know the different intentions behind Haydn's and Brahms's identical notations.

An example of the conductor's role in balancing the ensemble's interpretation through visual cues occurs at a *tutti* entrance (orchestra and soloist playing together) in the third movement (p. 44, bar 98). The soloist identified this point as problematic in rehearsal; she had felt "run over" by the accompaniment, yet held back by the orchestra's tempo. In the concert, the conductor's time-beating gestures became much larger and more emphatic, which the orchestra player understood as a direction to follow him rather than the soloist.

> M: What's happening is every time the *tutti* comes you're recovering the tempo a little bit. He would have been making sure that his tempo was the one everyone was following, not the tempo that they might think it should be ... Tempos do fluctuate and that's OK ... as long as you come back to the original concept ... With some orchestras and tempos, you know, they see black notes and go faster ... It's really important to hold back ... so [the conductor] was being very precise about it ... It's like holding the reins on a horse.

Another issue that had to be worked out in rehearsal was the relativistic understanding of dynamics appropriate for a concerto rather than an orchestral work without soloist. The imprecision of dynamic notation is well known to musicians; as the conductor Wilhelm Furtwängler said, the score

> cannot give any indication as to the really intended volume of a *forte*, the really intended speed of a *tempo*, since every *forte* and every *tempo* has to be modified in practice in accordance with the place of the performance

and the setting and the strength of the performing group ... The expression marks have intentionally a merely symbolic value with respect to the whole work. (quoted in Schutz 1964: 166)

This edition of the score specifically says: "*f* and *p*, which are often found only in the string parts ... were also used ... to signalize [*sic*] to the orchestral performer when he is to take the lead or to accompany" (Haydn 1989 VI).

> M: The *forte* when she's playing is not a *forte*. When she is playing it's very quiet, and the same dynamic marking when she's not playing is twice as loud, because you're accompanying and when you're accompanying your dynamic changes are all much quieter and more subtle than when you're playing on your own.

Simply knowing this to be the case does not provide any precise indication of the final dynamic level, but it does provide a cue to the conductor that direction may be needed, and to the orchestra to look to the conductor for it.

> C: On request of [the soloist] ... I know in concertos we have to really watch this even more, but the whole area where we play "<u>bee</u> pum pum <u>bee</u> pum pum" [*bowing on his hand for emphasis*], if [the soloist] wants to play *piano* [*soloist demonstrates phrase as conductor talks*], it's a very hard thing to establish, so we really have to be almost nothing. [*Comment from section cellist:*] Yes, Verdi-like – think of Verdi, five *pianos* [*ppppp*], OK? This is around 68. [*Players make a note on their parts.*] (video, 12:10–12:50)

Sometimes the conductor changes his directions:

> C: Now, I would like to go back. When I wrote *mezzo-forte*, sometimes I wrote it in at "bada bada pum pum" ... to increase gear a bit – I'm starting to think it shouldn't be there. Maybe just cross it out, because as you're getting so involved, so enthusiastic about it, that's just a little loud. It's a ... hard thing with concertos, you want to be involved but you have to play under all the time. So what I suggest is just keep those fires inside and when you get to the orchestra parts, just go for it, OK?

An exception to the ensemble's common understanding of time that does not require explanation or negotiation occurs at the *cadenzas* in the first and second movements. (A *cadenza* is an unaccompanied passage, usually an elaboration on the final cadence, where the soloist displays her virtuosity. In this edition the notes of the *cadenza* are given, though they are not original [Haydn 1989: VI].) In sharp contrast to the rest of the work, *cadenzas* have no bar lines. Their absence is a notational convention indicating to the soloist that she is free to deviate from the stress patterns and tempo restrictions of the rest of the movement.

The entry to a *cadenza* is heard as a brief statement of the dominant chord; on the orchestra parts, it is visually differentiated only by a *fermata* (a dot under a curved line above a note or rest). A *fermata* can be interpreted as either doubling the duration of the note or rest or as an indefinite "hold." The conductor indicated the latter and the entry to the *cadenza* by cutting off the orchestra, then lowering his arms and crossing them in front of himself until he heard the soloist approaching the end of the *cadenza*. He then raised his baton and held it until the closing trill of the *cadenza* had been held for two beats of the movement's original time, then conducted a downbeat, saying "3," held the upbeat for "4," and gave an emphatic downbeat with both hands for the first and second beats of bar 129, the return to bar lines and measured 4/4 time (video, 10:48–11:00). I asked M. how he recognized the beginning and end of the *cadenza* without written cues.

> M: I would know that from knowledge of music ... If I was sight-reading this, the progression of notes in the last bar coming into the lead-in to the dominant is the common entry to a *cadenza*, and you would be slowing down before. You see, the wiggly line is slowing down (I put that in) but sight-reading we would be following the conductor.
>
> L: How do you know where to come in?
>
> M: When the conductor makes a downbeat, that's the only way you know. Or the soloist would look back.
>
> L: There's the dominant trill coming off – is that a convention of where to come in?
>
> M: Common in that period, yeah. If you had to guess you'd probably come in there and you'd probably be right, but I personally wouldn't come in unless the soloist gave a good visual link.

Another example of bringing together performance practice and historical knowledge discourses with the circumstances of one performance occurs near the beginning of the third movement. The viola, cello, and bass parts have a series of repeated eighth notes with no phrase or articulation markings, a pattern which recurs throughout the movement and is the foundation of its tempo. The soloist and conductor explained.

s: Pulse was the thing I was the most concerned about, like these, the cellos [*indicates the repeated eighth notes*] ... I tried to just sort of show the intent of the phrase ... They gave a strong beat four times in every bar, but they could actually have a beat by not having any strong beats, like [*sings*] "ta ta ta ta ta ta ta ta"; they could give a four-bar phrase and I'd hear. And I know that in the first rehearsal I actually made a comment about that, but afterward I realized it would be much better if I let [the conductor] do that. It still was a difficult thing to find the right words to explain; repeated eighth notes are a very difficult technique.

c: I remember [the soloist] being frustrated that they [the phrases] didn't take shape. Well, the thing with repeated notes ... any modern player would just try to play them as equal as possible – they don't have the shapes written in the part, there's nothing there. They follow obediently what's written and just try as much as possible to play it equal, and that's just a static, no-feeling phrase ... In a place like that what I will try to show is where the phrase is going.

He demonstrated this in the rehearsal.

c: I'll tell you exactly what happens ... Usually when you go louder, you all play slower – "*pum pum pum pum pum pum pum pum*" [*demonstrates by "bowing" forcefully on his hand with the baton*] and should be "*bom* bi bi bi ..." [*fading out*]. So as you notice I hardly need to do anything once this is established, but it's not "*ta* ta ta ta ta ta ta ta *ta* ta ta ta ta ta ta ta" [*beating with exaggerated emphasis on the underlined beats*]. So if you can stand to do it for a while, count "*one* two three four five [*pause*] one two three." "*One* two three four five, da da da, *dee*" [*leans forward and makes wide sweeping gesture with arm to demonstrate "moving" of last three notes, downbeat with wide motion on "dee," the first beat of the next bar*]. Five *diminuendo* [*makes shape of dynamic marking with fingers*], three *crescendo* [*makes this sign*], a *little* bit of phrasing.

s: Sometimes, though, I hear every bar being stressed, and it should be every two bars [*sketching an arch with hand*] or every four bars [*sketching a wider arch*].

c: Yeah, that's when we know it's in control.

The impact of this conversation was obvious in the final performance.

m: That's where ... you would have heard, all of a sudden, the accents coming every four bars, it's like a bigger motion. But there's nothing in here [the part], and that's one of the things that would have been expected from performance practice of the period … It was part of their musical training.

In all these examples, the role of the score is exactly that of the active text outlined in the introduction. It provides a known, coherent structure for coordinated present action, and signposts to a common frame of reference in particular musical discourses. Every point of difficulty in putting together a convincing, coherent performance of this work arose from too literal a reading of the text, a reading which disconnected the players from their own references. The best description of the role of the score comes from the soloist: "It's the guide, it's what connects us together, gives us the reason to commune, to share … on a very deep level, on a very organized level, something really creative … It's non-chaotic, it's completely the opposite of chaos."

The Road to Chaos

I stated earlier that the score should not necessarily be accepted as the final authoritative statement of the composer's intentions; it is not taken as one by the musicians in this group. Authority resides in the accumulated history of performance and the plausibility of an interpretation.

s: At the core of what we strive for artistically is, "How do I make this meaningful? And what is the meaning, and does it have to be the same meaning exactly?" I think the attempt should be there [to do what] the composer intended, but … is it there that it can only be played one way for it to be art, or for it to be a master work, or is it … already just implicit in the writing of it the capacity for it to be interpreted many different ways? It's still this piece and not something else.

c: Things are changing all the time, interpretations of the same piece by the same composer and by the same interpreter will be different at different times … but you have always to do what's true to you at that moment … When I went to Oregon to study with Rilling[13] and he did the B minor Mass [of J.S. Bach] – I have his recording and listened to it many times; I know exactly what articulation he is doing when – I heard him in [the] first rehearsal and he was doing something *completely* different. Completely different tempo, completely different articulations … A person who has the authority he did with the first recording can do the same work completely differently with the same authority.

A credible position among players and musicologists is that Baroque and Classical period composers wrote into their scores the interpretative markings that they could not assume the musicians would just know, trusting players to use their own knowledge to fill in the outline given in the score. It also appears from the problems encountered in this performance that such common knowledge is no longer to be taken for granted. Changes in musical notation and the structure of scores, beginning in the late Classical period and accelerating during the twentieth century, can be viewed as a change in the ability of composers to assume performers are connected to the discourse the composer intends to reference. While Schutz identified this problem as a reduction in the "general musical culture of performers and of listeners" (1964: 167), it may simply be the result of an expanded definition of musical culture and a corresponding reduction in common history.

Consider the enormous expansion of what orchestra musicians are expected to know. In addition to the formal notation and classical Italian, which are the common historical languages of European tonal music, advanced students and professionals are expected to have a working knowledge of at least German and English, plus Latin for early music and French for opera (A. Dokken, private conversation). Alternative notation systems, which include signs indicating the "shape" of the tone to be produced, for example, rather than a specific note or value, mean performers must also collectively interpret another, much less codified, set of instructions and their surrounding discourses.[14] They must also do so across an ever-expanding repertoire drawn from multiple musical traditions. The loss of harmonic conventions also makes it more difficult for players to use their own ears and their interactions with one another as reliable guides for action.

Expansion of musical notation offers composers a great deal of freedom to widen the range of musical expression. They may also specify ever more exactly what they wish to say and how the performer is to say it. R. Murray Schafer's 1980 work, *Adieu, Robert Schumann*[15] is a conservative example of how detailed instructions, even within the broad structure of tonal notation, narrow the possibilities for performers. On page 35, bar 4, for example, we find the instruction "gradually mute with hand" on the percussion parts, in addition to the *ff>p* markings indicating a dramatic lowering of volume. Similarly, in the next two bars of the string parts, the composer directs "half of each string section sustains tremolo; half take mutes and enter playing a very rapid *pianissimo pizzicato* on the same notes" (original emphasis). On page 36, bar 4, flutes are directed to articulate "flutter tongue," a commonly understood technique, and clarinets "quasi flutter tongue" (which is not). The discursive connections of this score are far more complex than those of Haydn's; it is simultaneously very demanding and highly confining for musicians.

Toru Takemitsu's *I Hear the Water Dreaming* for solo flute and orchestra (1989) is less obviously different from Haydn's score, but careful reading reveals a similar tendency to constrain performers to the composer's intentions. The conductor is specifically told to subdivide 5/8 time as (3+2) and given a metronome marking ($\flat$ = 112) rather than a general range, such as *allegro*, from which to select an exact tempo (1989: 1). String players are not free to subdivide chords in their parts as they like or according to convention; they are told cellists 1–3 are to play particular notes while 4–6 play others (1989: 1, bar 3). Coupled with the very large orchestra specified for this work (71 players), such minute management of effects by the composer must make players more dependent on the score for direction; there is simply too much to take in with a fixed amount of rehearsal time. Performers understand this process and are keenly aware of its implications for them:

> c: Nowadays they put in so much information there's almost no room for interpretation because it [the score] wants so much. They want to make sure that the orchestra will do exactly what they have in mind ... The problem with that is you lose some spontaneity, because you feel you can't really make this new ... I conducted a modern piece ... in which everything was written in, and all I had to do to make it work was to beat time.

> s: The room to try something in a different way or to maybe connect to the music in a certain way so that it becomes a part of your expression isn't there because you're having to fit in so much detail ... You're a mechanical vessel for that sound ... It's not your own pulse that you can connect to that, it has to be just so.

A musical recording, another form of text, contributes both to players' stock of references and to the standardization process.

> c: Of course, now we have audiotapes and performances become generic, and more and more generic, because you hear one and then everybody tries to play the same way, more or less. And then if you have a new

work that nobody ever had before you can immediately put it on a tape, and then if you know the composer was on the recording, everybody tries as much as possible to imitate that because the composer was there, and there's really no room for saying, "Yeah, but it might work differently, a different way."

The difficulties the conductor expresses here may be another part of the "unknowable contingency" Schutz and Weeks referred to – the condition of not being free to use what is known from other sources creating uncertainty that can only be resolved by reference to the text. The impact of the outside discourses in which this condition originates (those which redefine musical notation, for example) is then falsely identified as a property of the texts which convey it; that is, as an essential characteristic of musical notation regardless of the conditions of its use.

Changes in notation, a larger field of required knowledge, and recording technology and distribution all appear to be changing musical scores into less freely active texts. All reduce the connectivity of the text to frames of reference outside themselves, and push towards the literal interpretations these musicians found so limited. Haydn's score, though it represents a more restrictive structure for composers, leaves performers more freedom to define the particular connections that give meaning to their work.

Making the score a question at the centre of inquiry, rather than taking it for granted, allows us to see in practice what Schutz presented in theory. The social processes and relations summarized in the score but residijng outside it appear in what performers just know how to do when they read a score to perform it. We are also able to see the deceptive nature of innovations, such as harmonic change and alternative notations, which promise freedom and deliver only another kind of control.

NOTES

1 Exchanges can take place either at the same time (e.g., between soloist and orchestra) or over time (e.g., between one performance and the collective performance history of the work).
2 The discourses of composition are excluded from this figure.

3 The essential difference between musical scores and other written texts is that their meaning is most definitively realized in *sound*, not the silence of the reader's mind, as is possible for every other textual form. (Few of us, regardless of our training, are able to hear an entire musical work in our heads.) This has implications for judgments of the "rightness" of a performance, which is an assessment of whether a given reading of the text is correct, but need not confuse an exploration of its organizational role in work.

4 Works are often selected for performance based on their ability to draw audiences.

5 My thanks to an anonymous reviewer for this example, and comments that greatly clarified this section.

6 Very approximately, 1600–1900. Haydn's life (1735–1809) spanned the late Baroque and early Classical periods, and his work was a major influence on the forms which came to represent them, especially symphonic and sonata forms (Grout, 1980).

7 The pattern of stresses distinguishes from one another time signatures with the same total number of beats in the bar. 3/4 and 6/8 times, for example, each have six eighth notes in a bar. The totally different effect of the two signatures comes from the stress patterns: **123456** in 3/4 time, **123456** in 6/8.

8 Like punctuation in written language, musical punctuation makes a collection of notes into a specific kind of statement. A progression from dominant to tonic, for example, often serves the function of a period (.) by marking a clear end to a "declarative" statement.

9 Such a procedure, called a "figured bass," *was* common in music for keyboard instruments of Haydn's time, where there was relatively little variability in tone colour across the range of the instrument.

10 Though Malhotra (1981) identifies melody as the most important aspect for individual players, coordination is most evident in harmony. In a work of Haydn's time, harmonic dissonance is rare, and if it happens, players can be reasonably sure a correction is needed.

11 The *Urtext* editions generally contain only what was written on the originals from which they were taken, with some updating of notation for modern users and correction of errors such as missing rests (Haydn 1988: VI). They may be as close as we can expect to come to the intentions of their composers in a written form.

12 This incident is recorded on a CD reissue of Brahms's Piano Concerto no. 1 on Sony SK60675. (Many thanks to an anonymous reviewer for this reference.)

13 Helmuth Rilling, a conductor and noted authority on the choral works of
J.S. Bach.
14 Attempts have been made, unsuccessfully, to standardize modern notations (such as the International Conference on New Musical Notation held
in Ghent in 1974).
15 The Schafer example was reproduced in the original publication of this
paper.

6 "Three in a Bed": Nurses and Technologies of Bed Utilization in a Hospital[1]

JANET RANKIN AND MARIE CAMPBELL

Janet Rankin and Marie Campbell provide an insider look at the organization of hospital care in British Columbia and the power of the particular textual forms of information produced and generated through a computer software system for regulating and organizing multiple levels of work. Their account presents the computerized managerial forms of work that link front-line nursing practices to province-wide hospital restructuring. They begin with brief experiential accounts of nurses' practices to show the "troubling aspects" in two nurses' care of patients. What is done with each patient, uncomfortable and in pain, as they are moved through the nurses' care is readily recognizable as not "optimum care." Nor, the authors point out, were the nurses orienting to two conventional standards for nursing care: (1) *the professional code of ethics, and* (2) *nursing standards of care. The account shows how nurses conform their practices to accomplish the virtual reality of the managerial software.*

The authors track in detail the hospital's Admissions, Discharge and Transfer (ADT) software-system production of specific textual forms for managing the flow of patients into and out of hospital beds, rooms, departments and Operating Rooms (ORs). Several layers of "patient placement" clerks produce "bed maps" and other reports to organize complex hospital work and timed flow of patients. The information generated by the ADT software is produced, continually updated and printed twice per day by clerks, nursing staff, and hospital managers. It tracks and locates patients as they are admitted into, transferred among, and discharged from beds.

The chapter shows how, in the context of scarce bed resources and the high costs of staffing hospitals, the system is designed to "expand" the hospital's bed capacity with a textual "sleight of hand." Fictitious beds are created in the ADT system in which patients can be held in a virtual space at various stages of hospital processes. This production of an in-text space allows the hospital management to manage its workers through timed procedures and make and produce accounts of its good use of resources. What this means for nurses is that they are bringing their nursing practices and interactions with patients into line with the needs of the technology and its textual production and accounting processes. Because nurses are responsible for moving patients and ensuring that beds are available, it speeds up their work and interactions with the patients.

They then track the ADT system information from hospital to a national overseeing organization. They find that how that organization aggregates the data into patient groups according to the hospital resources they consume allows the work of doctors, attending nurses and nurse managers, and directors of services to be monitored, reviewed, and restructured. Their incorporation of texts into ethnography thus makes visible just how the computerized production of a statistical knowledge of appropriate bed utilization and post-surgery care is both consequential for staff and presents issues for patients.

In acute care hospitals there is an inevitable uncertainty about patient admissions, because illness and accidents are unplanned. Emergency admissions account for 50 to 70 per cent of all hospital admissions (Canadian Association of Emergency Physicians 2001) and cannot be booked in advance. This uncertainty complicates the job of hospital administrators and their new public management (NPM) strategies that "re-conceiv[e] and, to some extent reorganiz[e], many if not all organizational activities (support and administration as well as production or service) as work processes involving identifiable inputs, outputs and customers" (McCoy 1999: 9). Managing waiting lists[2] and determining who should be admitted next remain big problems for physicians, hospitals, and health authorities. However, a computer program has managed to tame the movement of designated patients into, through, and out of many hospitals, including the hospital studied by Rankin. In this chapter we consider, from the standpoint of nurses, how admission, discharge, and transfer (ADT) software works as a technology of governance within this hospital. Hospitals must account for and manage carefully all the costs of providing hospital care, including the use of buildings and bed capacity – and the latter is where ADT becomes important. Kerr, Glass, McCallion, & McKillop make this case as follows:

A hospital can only achieve maximum possible efficiency when fixed investments are fully utilized ... If capacity under-utilization exists, fixed costs are higher than necessary and average resource costs of treatment are not being minimized. Therefore, while some degree of spare capacity is essential to meet periods of peak demand ... excessive spare capacity generates inefficiency and needs to be identified. (1999: 640)

Managing bed use and reducing spare capacity become the focus of much of the attention given to effective utilization of the hospital's fixed investments. The area in which the hospital can exercise control is around "patient turnover," the hospital production line. The ADT system supports the expeditious movement of patients in, through the system, and out of hospital beds on the basis of information that relates these activities to costs. Inevitably, nurses are involved in these processes, either directly or indirectly, as we shall see. One of the impacts on nursing is in the emphasis placed on discharging patients, as the observational note below suggests. We show that ADT organizes nurses' attention to particular goals and reorganizes their professional judgment and actions in concert with the accounting logic embedded in the technology. As we go on to argue in this chapter, nurses' consciousness is being restructured within a hospital environment that is more and more viewed, understood, and mobilized in relation to the virtual realities of management-oriented information such as that generated through using ADT.

The Discharge of a Postsurgical Patient: An Account of Routine Nursing

The account that follows comes from Janet Rankin's participant observations during the mid-1990s. As a nursing instructor, Janet was updating her clinical experience by working alongside Linda, a registered nurse (RN) one morning on a busy medical and surgical ward. Linda's assignment, Janet discovered, was to care for "all the patients in eight designated beds," and she was assisted in this work by a licensed practical nurse (LPN). The morning tasks revolved around administering medications, assessing patients, getting patients ready for breakfast, assisting them to get washed, making beds, changing dressings and bandages, monitoring intravenous drips, and helping patients to be mobile, all in addition to responding to phone calls from the families of patients or from physicians and staff in other hospital departments.

Ms Shoulder is one of Linda's assigned patients. An otherwise healthy, middle-aged woman, yesterday she underwent the surgical repair of torn shoulder ligaments (rotator cuff injury). She is to be discharged at 11 a.m. Precise discharge arrangements were made well in advance of the surgical procedure during her appointment in the pre-admission clinic.

Ms Shoulder has spent an uncomfortable post-operative night. She tells Linda that she slept poorly. This morning, her nursing care focuses on the large shoulder immobilizer she is wearing. The shoulder immobilizer is a type of sling that is worn for six weeks following that particular surgery. It prevents the patient from abducting the shoulder joint (the arm is maintained in a snug position, close to the body; any movement away from the body is to be avoided). Having one arm thus disabled makes it difficult for Ms Shoulder to wash and dress herself. Linda places a chair in the bathroom, provides Ms Shoulder with a towel and washcloth, and tells her to wash what she can and that a nurse will be back later to help her dress. When Linda and Janet return twenty minutes later, Ms Shoulder's face is pale and her skin is clammy. She has managed to wash her hands, face, and crotch but is complaining of severe discomfort in her shoulder and that her stomach is "queasy." Linda leaves to get some pain medication, and Janet assists Ms Shoulder back into bed. Linda administers the pain medication (two Tylenol with codeine) and asks Ms Shoulder when her husband will be arriving to take her home. Linda proceeds to do the "discharge teaching" related to the shoulder immobilizer. Before leaving to attend to her other duties, Linda asks Janet to remove the bulky surgical bandage and replace it with a lighter one. Janet is also to assist Ms Shoulder to dress and be ready for discharge. Getting dressed is a complicated process and takes fifteen minutes. Ms Shoulder requires help putting on her underpants, slacks, shoes, and socks. She is unable to wear her bra and needs help to drape her blouse around her operative shoulder and stretch it across her chest to do up the buttons. She requires help with all the buttons. Once dressed, she appears fatigued and very uncomfortable. She continues to complain of nausea, and at one point Janet assists her into the bathroom, where Ms Shoulder experiences a brief spell of the "dry heaves." Janet leaves her resting on her bed and goes to find Linda.

Linda is in the Same-Day Admission Room. There is no bed in this room, and it is not officially part of Linda's assignment. Linda is preparing a newly arrived patient (Ms Leg Wound) to go to the operating room for the surgical procedure of debridement and application of a split thickness skin graft to a large open wound on her leg. Three weeks previously, Ms Leg Wound was hospitalized following a motorcycle accident.

She was discharged into a home care program. Her deep leg wound has not responded to the prescribed wound care regimen at home, and now more aggressive surgical intervention is indicated. Ms Leg Wound is in a wheelchair with her injured leg elevated. Linda is going through her chart, checking for a signed surgical consent, looking at laboratory results for particular blood tests, and reading through the physician's orders. Linda is also conducting a short "pre-op" interview (last time to eat or drink; last time to urinate, etc.) and ticking these details off on a checklist. She takes the woman's vital signs and assists her out of her clothes and into a hospital gown. The physician's orders include directions to "compress the wound preoperatively." Linda unwraps the bandage, assesses the wound, and places a large salt-water compress over it. She will then document a description of both the wound and the treatment. But Janet interrupts Linda to report Ms Shoulder's condition. Linda stops her work with Ms Leg Wound and hurriedly checks Ms Shoulder's chart to see whether she may receive any medications to control her nausea. There is no physician's order authorizing the administration of an anti-nausea medication, and so Linda, glancing at her watch (and seeing that it is close to 11 o'clock, the assigned discharge time), makes the decision to administer an antacid, stating that she "hopes it will help." As she does this Ms Shoulder's husband arrives to drive her home. Ms Shoulder is given a prescription for an analgesic and advised to purchase an over-the-counter anti-nausea drug on the way home. She is given a small cardboard tray in case she vomits in the car. She is then discharged at the required 11:00 a.m. checkout time, looking decidedly unwell.

On the surface, this story about discharging a post-operative patient into the care of her husband is apparently unremarkable. Discharges similar to this happen daily, in hospitals all across Canada. In most hospitals, discharge after rotator-cuff repair happens even sooner after surgery. Indeed, shortly after Janet observed this discharge, the allocated length of stay[3] in this hospital for a patient undergoing a shoulder repair was also shortened, the procedure becoming a "day care" (ambulatory care) treatment, with the patient's discharge slated for the same day as the surgery. But the story about Ms Shoulder has some troubling aspects, including some nursing practice that is unlikely to hold up well to professional scrutiny. We use these observations as an entry point to explore how Linda and Janet's nursing work – not optimal nursing care – happened as it did. We now ask, How is it that two competent and experienced nurses would make these choices about nursing care?

Of possible professional concern would be Linda's breaking of the rule about nurses administering a drug (the antacid) that has not been ordered by a doctor. Linda's administration of an antacid for a patient's complaints of nausea, unrelated to acid reflux disease, did not reflect "competent application of knowledge" (Registered Nurses Association of British Columbia 2003) about pain and nausea. More generally, the ad hoc course of action the two nurses followed does not exactly satisfy expectations of the code of ethics established by the Canadian Nurses Association (CNA) that states that "nurses provide care directed first and foremost towards the health and well-being of the client" (CNA 2002: 4). In this situation, nursing actions that demonstrate compliance with professional codes and standards would have seen Linda or Janet phoning the physician to obtain an order for an anti-nausea medication. After the medication had had time to work, the patient would have been assessed to ensure that both the pain and the anti-nausea medications were effective. Also, after an uncomfortable night, Ms Shoulder might have been allowed more time to sleep and her breakfast offered later, at which time her discharge teaching could have been given. This course of nursing intervention would have increased Ms Shoulder's ability to be receptive to the important instructions about her shoulder immobilizer, not to mention contributing to her overall comfort and her ability to cope with going home. These choices, aimed at optimizing the care of this patient, were not made.

If Linda and Janet's practice is not organized by or oriented to professional codes and nursing standards, what is its organizing principle or focus? The analysis in this chapter is motivated not to criticize, but to understand how Linda and other nurses working in contemporary hospital settings find themselves unintentionally subverting the standards of their profession. Using the approach of institutional ethnography (IE), our inquiry begins in examining the activities of Nurse Linda, Ms Shoulder, and Ms Leg Wound. That is, we investigate what we see happening and look for clues that we can follow to explicate the social relations of how it happens as it does. We notice in the story the way the needs of Ms Shoulder and Ms Leg Wound conflict and recognize that they both are urgent. The urgency that we see relates to several nursing priorities. One is the routine feature of nurses' work – that it is organized to articulate patients to ongoing hospital schedules, such as those of the operating rooms (ORs), or to a scheduled discharge. Nurses are trained to finely attune their attention to such schedules and to the associated standard requirements. (Where a patient is not ready for her or his turn in the operating room, there are ensuing consequences for everybody else – all the surgeries for the day will be late, the surgeons will be held up, irritated, and so on; or if Ms Leg Wound goes to the OR without the proper documentation, completed accurately, her surgery may be put off, again creating complications for her and others.) The routine features of the discharge that Janet was instructed to handle as she prepared Ms Shoulder for discharge are also evident. This chapter will have more to say about the consequences of a delay in discharge. But we need to mention here another feature of the urgency of the demands on Nurse Linda's time – both she and Janet are concerned about and trying to be responsive to patient comfort and safety. We see how Nurse Linda is caught up in addressing these demands, choosing to interrupt her pressing work with the OR-bound patient.

There appears in Janet's account to be more pressure on Nurse Linda than would be expected in the routine balancing act that is a nurse's everyday work experience. What accounts for this? Is it that she has had an extra patient dropped into her workload? To all outward appearances, Ms Leg Wound is not one of Nurse Linda's assigned patients. But it is not a coincidence that Ms Leg Wound appears now and can demand Nurse Linda's urgent attention. She has been organized to be there. Nurse Linda is not surprised and indeed Janet, too, can now understand why Linda's workload was expressed not as a definite number of patients, but as "all the patients in eight beds." We will discover a whole system of organizational texts and people's activity lying behind the arrival of Ms Leg Wound on Linda's medical and surgical ward that tie this admission to the predicted discharge of Ms Shoulder. Here we have an instance of the organization of admissions and discharges that appears to be placing more than one patient "in a bed."

The ADT system is instrumental in making the connection between a discharge and a new arrival and for bringing Ms Leg Wound into the Same-Day Admission Room (and into Nurse Linda's hands). The use of this computerized software program produces an apparently orderly and timely movement of patients into or out of pre-admission suites, the emergency room, the admitting department, surgical operating rooms, and beds throughout hospital wards and nursing specialty units. Its use generates the knowledge by which this hospital efficiently manages its "fixed investments"; but as we shall see, that is not all that happens. Also, as part of the tightened-up utilization of fixed assets (namely, hospital space), nursing knowledge is downgraded as a basis for nursing action to the point that we claim that the operation of ADT accomplishes a partial restructuring of nursing practice.

The ADT System: Knowledge for Restructuring

We might describe the ADT system as a patient-tracking system run from a computer on the top floor of the hospital where it is physically removed from the busily peopled settings of the hospital units. But ADT must also be seen as a technology that contributes to the textual (numerically based) monitoring and transformation of the cost-relevant use of hospital beds and other clinical resources. This particular system is a proprietary software program contracted from a company known as Meditech. A team of clerical staff, "patient placement clerks," work with the system, which requires them to enter demographic patient data into various fields on computer-generated forms. Through other entries in various fields on their computer screens, patient placement clerks keep an up-to-the-minute record of all ongoing hospital admission and discharge activity. The system creates a hospital "bed map," which is a bulky document that is printed twice a day. The bed map is organized by hospital units and provides a means of tracking the patients occupying beds throughout the hospital. Bed maps can be printed from computer terminals throughout the hospital and are used by unit clerks and nurses on the wards to keep track of where patients are located. The ADT system also has the capability to produce other documents that are not widely distributed throughout the hospital: for example, the Occupancy Summary by Location form, which lacks any specific patient information, is much less bulky than the bed map, and provides at a quick glance the total number of admitted patients per unit. Other forms generated by the ADT, such as monthly "inpatient location statistics" and "total occupancy rates," are available to departmental administrators and their clerical staff as they gather and monitor data about patient activity in their departments. At the hospital at which these observations were made, the ADT system and all the data it generates are the responsibility of the director of performance improvement and health information. The ADT system's "account" of beds occupied, spare capacity, booked and prospective patients, planned and actual discharges, and so on enters into and becomes part of a textual reality around which managerial action is coordinated.

The ADT system tracks and locates patients as they are admitted into, transferred among, and discharged from beds. A textual representation of the space availability, and who is assigned to what space, is made and kept updated by the software program. Actually, a patient placement clerk using ADT information, in concert with clerks in the hospital admitting department and the OR booking office and operating under the authorization of patient services managers, organizes patient arrivals into ward beds. The clerk's work with the ADT system determined Ms Leg Wound's timely arrival on Nurse Linda's nursing unit. It organized which bed she would be assigned to and who might be transferred in order to accommodate her (should Nurse Linda not accomplish Ms Shoulder's discharge on time, for instance).

Assigning patients to beds is no simple undertaking. Beds are chronically in short supply in relation to the number of patients waiting for them. As well, patients cannot be randomly placed into any available bed in the hospital. Patients are assigned to beds based on established protocols related to the nature of their illness, their sex (until recently, about which more is said shortly), and whether they have requested a private room and can be considered "revenue generating." The patient placement clerk uses computer-generated bed maps to locate patients and beds and, on occasion, to finesse bed allocation within the virtual reality of the ADT system's bed maps. A patient placement clerk explained this strategy: "We admit people but we [may] have no beds for them. They come in before the bed is ready for them. So, in the system we create this place called SDAs [Same-Day Admits]. They are fictional rooms."

Efficient bed utilization is constituted through a textual construction in which "fictitious" beds apparently expand the hospital's capacity. For instance, Ms Leg Wound was admitted to the hospital, and indeed underwent her surgery, before there was any confirmation that a bed (or a nurse) would be available for her recovery. In the ADT system, the problem of keeping the queued patients in view is solved by the creation of a textual space in which to house them. This capacity to expand fictitiously the number of available beds explains Nurse Linda's comment during an interview when she wryly said, "You should have been here last week when I had three patients for one bed." A hospital executive also recognized this phenomenon, calling it "110 per cent utilization."

The constant overlap of patients shapes the "speeded up" work processes of nurses who are always, nevertheless, irremediably grounded in the embodied actualities of their daily/nightly work. Patients have bodies and they need real beds. When new patients arrive, they require nursing attention, even if they do not appear in a nurse's assignment. And, besides their taking care of the extra bodies, the overlap that the use of fictitious beds creates is consequential for nurses in another way. It is up to nurses to see that the virtual bed into which the new patient is assigned is actually available when the patient needs it. This accounts for Nurse Linda taking "short cuts" when caring for Ms Shoulder. It explains why she would have given her discharge instructions when Ms Shoulder was in pain, and it explains why she put aside Ms Shoulder's nausea and discomfort and hurried her out of the hospital. Nurse Linda and her colleagues have learned to adapt their nursing care to the dictates of the hospital's overriding concern about excessive spare bed capacity. This is how the ADT system organizes and even restructures nurses' work.

Placing patients in beds is only one of the uses of the ADT system. Its capacity to represent textually this aspect of the operation of the hospital is important in many other ways. As the patient placement clerk enters information about patients into the computerized ADT program to create bed maps and assign beds, she contributes to the generation of a great deal of statistical information. The number of patients "in" and "out" of each inpatient area in the hospital is counted and categorized. Monthly reports generated through the ADT system are circulated to all the patient services managers at the hospital. The monthly reports, known as "inpatient location statistics," are organized under the system's headings – "bed days," "patient days," "average length of stay," "average daily and monthly census," and "percentage of occupancy." Other data generated through the ADT system, and known as "service statistics," are collected by the director of performance improvement and health information for reporting to the Ministry of Health. Accumulated "patient days" are broken down into various categories and subcategories. There are (1) "service" categories (e.g., medicine/general practice; surgery/ear, nose, and throat; medicine/neurology); (2) "payment" categories (e.g., billable categories such as long-term care and acute care); and (3) categories of "appropriateness" (e.g., acute care or alternate level of care).[4]

Information generated through the ADT system is also made available to the Canadian Institute of Health Information (CIHI), and it is this sort of information that the CIHI relies upon when developing case mix groups (CMGs). The product of an administrative classification system used in Canada, CMGs group and describe in commensurable form the patients admitted to acute-care hospitals. Modelled after the American diagnosis-related groups (DRGs), CMG systems use data that are routinely generated by hospitals to group together patients who are clinically similar in terms of diagnosis and treatment and, importantly, similar in their consumption of hospital resources. CMGs are then employed to make comparisons of resource use across hospitals with varying mixes of patients. The development of CMGs is thought to produce a sound, up-to-date method for assessing the relative efficiency of hospitals. In the early 1990s, the usefulness of case mix groups for determining hospital funding levels was emerging in Manitoba: "Thus far, Hospital Case Mix Costing is proving to be a highly effective means of assessing hospital efficiency. Ultimately, if analyses in subsequent years continue to support these initial assessments, such data could provide important information with which to adjust global funding" (Shanahan, Brownell, Lloyd, & Roos 1993: JS101).

ADT data collection and the various kinds of aggregations made of it render one hospital's costs and use of resources comparable with those of other hospitals. These comparisons (as they affect bed utilization) offer new means of influence over nurses' and physicians' practice. In this regard, a nursing team leader reported how an "older" surgeon tended to "hang onto his patients too long" and how this became a problem for her to resolve. She explained how ADT-generated data were useful to her to broach this topic with the offending doctor. She was able to show him how his patients stayed in the hospital longer, on average, than those of his orthopaedic colleagues, and how his practices reflected a wasteful use of the valuable bed resources.[5]

It is the virtual reality of the ADT system that makes it useful for managing beds efficiently. For instance, it is only in a system that creates fictitious beds that the sleight of hand by which people with no beds are counted as inpatients makes 110 per cent bed utilization possible. This careful tracking and overbooking reduces the possibility that any hospital bed is left vacant. However, the fictitious beds of the ADT system create challenges for nurses (such as Janet and Linda) to overcome in that their work is "on the ground," with actual beds and actual patients. It is important to recognize that nurses' work in the transformed everyday/everynight world of nursing brings together what actually happens with the virtually generated accounts. In doing so, nurses accomplish in actuality the efficiencies of the rapid turnover.

The ADT system is very much implicated not only in Nurse Linda's work with Ms Shoulder, but also in the work of nurse managers. Interwoven into Nurse Linda's practice are policies and procedures monitored by nurse managers to ensure program efficiencies. New policies must be generated to make the best use of the system's potential. The textual or virtual reality of the ADT system prompts managers to review and revise specific clinical practices. For instance, the decision to designate shoulder surgeries as same-day procedures, reducing the time these patients spend in the hospital, did not arise spontaneously. It was a knowledge-based decision of the sort we refer to as constituting a textual or virtual reality. A patient services director who reflected on how the "same day" designation was made remembered "a provincial trend to treat shoulder surgeries as day care." Knowledge of this trend came to the patient services director in the form of statistics, amassed through the ADT systems of several peer hospitals across British Columbia and reported to the Ministry of Health in the form of monthly statistics. There, relevant comparisons were made across peer hospital groups, and the information was distributed back to the hospitals, thus producing a knowledge base about bed utilization across the province. Prompted by this knowledge about the provincial trend, the patient services director and her management colleagues initiated an examination of their own hospital's practices.

In matters like this, it becomes apparent how the different authority accorded to statistical knowledge overrides a professional's experiential knowledge. One of the patient services managers identified some of the challenges she faced when reassigning shoulder repairs into the ambulatory care program. She explained that "when shoulders were first being considered for ambulatory care the nurses who were currently caring for these patients on the orthopaedic ward expressed many worries about patient's pain management during that first night at home." She then added, "However we knew it could be done, that it was working in other centres; patients at home do well." What this nursing manager knew was what her statistical information told her.

Her confidence that a patient will "do well" is based on data collection oriented to statistical outcomes, a major undertaking of health services research.[6] Researchers examine quantifiable measurements such as the number of clinic visits made post-operatively, the time it takes for patients to regain range of movement, and readmission rates of patients who are discharged to their homes on the day of their surgery. Length of stay (LOS) data is then compared with these sorts of (cost-relevant) outcomes. All these become indicators of a hospital's performance. ADT systems are relied upon to generate a great deal of the data upon which health services research is based. Mykhalovskiy identifies how this sort of research "is highly applied. It does not simply present research findings, but articulates them in terms that seek to organize evidential relations of hospital restructuring and management" (2001: 275). These sorts of evidential claims are different from those of the orthopaedic nurses who were worried about "how well" patients would do at home following shoulder surgery. For nurses, the patients' experiences of pain and suffering count. While they may be empathetic about patients' pain, another nursing issue is even more important. Before a patient leaves the hospital after surgery, the instructions that the patient is given at the pre-admission appointment must be reviewed. Post-operatively, patients must get explicit directions for their own care. Nurses recognize that patients have limitations in what they can hear when they are ill, stressed, or in pain, and that it is nurses' responsibility to ensure that patients (and most often a member of the patient's family) understand their recovery regimens. They know that patients need nurses' time and attention and also that different people need different amounts of instruction. However, none of these nursing concerns gets included in the official data gathered to make a decision about how shoulder surgeries are to be accommodated.

One patient services manager identified these differences in ways of knowing when commenting on an initiative she was involved in to make laparoscopic gallbladder surgery an ambulatory procedure. She said, "I personally am a little reluctant because I think it's a major surgery and I think they can benefit from an overnight stay. However, if I take on that role, that is the nurse coming out in me." This patient services manager understood that "the nurse in her" was not properly acquiescent to the authoritative statistical knowledge, and, in contrast, her job required her to override these sorts of "nursing" concerns. She continued, "We find that nurses do advocate strongly for patients. First of all, we have our doctors not wanting to send the patients home, then we have our nurses who can often find reasons why the patients need to stay, frankly some reasonable and some unreasonable, but that they do tend to be protective."

Such tendencies among doctors and nurses are something to be managed. Authoritative statistical knowledge provides the means through which standards can be developed to compare (virtually) and act on variations among patients themselves (for instance, the levels of pain and nausea such as that experienced by Ms Shoulder) and among professionals ("some reasonable and some unreasonable"). This (nurse) manager concluded by saying,

I have many years of practice. I am astounded at the changes. It is surprising to me. I have been here for a lot of changes and have been involved in the implementation of change – the pre-admit, and same-day admit procedures where people may have stayed for a month, and now they are going home the day of [surgery]. I am constantly amazed at people's ability, on the whole, to take that on.

The manager's knowledge about how well patients fare following day-care surgery seems at odds with Janet's experience of discharging a decidedly unwell woman with an emesis basin the morning after a rotator-cuff repair. The statistically generated information also seems at odds with other nurses' experiences of nursing post-surgery patients through the night, before shoulder-repair procedures became part of the ambulatory care program. These nurses explained how, in their experience, the anaesthetic block used to perform the surgery works better in some patients than in others. They noted how some patients experience a great deal of pain and require substantial nursing support, while others do not. Suppressing her own doubts, the manager quoted above remains positive about fulfilling her management responsibility to ensure that patients are not held in the hospital just because nurses or doctors have "found reasons" to extend their stay. Her role demands that she will monitor and use her information resources to override the "reasonableness" of the professional judgments being expressed. The new standard for length of stay for shoulder surgery is a case in point. Statistical comparisons such as those being used to justify the change in shoulder surgeries are used to validate that, in fact, patients at home "do well." A standard being imposed on all patients makes it difficult to express the sorts of variation among patients that nurses worry about.

Nurse Linda's ad hoc activities that produced Ms Shoulder's 11 o'clock discharge (the antacid, the advice about over-the-counter anti-nausea drugs, the vomit container to take in the car), examined along-side an administrative decision to categorize the needs and care of patients undergoing shoulder repair as same-day surgeries, provide a particularly compelling illustration of how administrative use of objective health information is employed to make efficiency-oriented decisions and how that reorganizes nursing care. The issue here is how a technology that, in the hands of patient placement clerks and management nurses appears merely to be a useful administrative tool, effectively organizes what nurses can do for patients. The patients, the subjects of nurses' attention, are objectified and become merely "discharges." Despite the nurses' qualms, the administrative review of the ADT data from other hospitals did result in an initiative to assign shoulder-surgery patients to the ambulatory care program. This kind of administrative knowledge "trumps" the local judgment of competent professional caregivers.

The ADT system appears to be a remarkably helpful way of keeping track of where patients are in the hospital in order to reduce excessive spare capacity. We see it as a technology that produces knowledge for managing bed utilization, a feature of the management of efficiency. As the system helps the hospital establish a speedier throughput of patients, the involvement of nurses encourages and even necessitates a restructuring of nurses' work and patient care. The management's version "of how well we are doing" enters into and displaces nurses' ideas about a patient and how well any individual patient is doing. Nurses' concerns about how well a patient is doing address patients as embodied individuals, the subject of nurses' professional assessment and judgment. The authoritative version reflects objectives related to efficient utilization of resources (reducing spare capacity). Displaced in the latter version are the options about care that nurses would choose and that would better stand up to professional tests of adequacy. Laid over the nursing setting, the objectified knowledge supports processes and procedures that rule the setting. What is known statistically dictates the way that patients will be cared for, subordinating nurses' experience-based worries about patients' variable recovery patterns and different levels of pain and suffering. This theme is repeated, again and again, in analyses that show virtual accounts working better for the managerial agenda than for the agenda of caregiving.

Knowledge Infrastructures Built for Managing Costs

The ADT system builds factual accounts about patients' movements through the hospital – information that stands as a representation of what actually happens as it mediates (or instructs) transformative action. In this section, we suggest how its character as a textual reality is important to its usefulness within the managerial agenda. We have already argued that a textual reality, "how well we are doing," should not be mistaken for what actually happens. The ADT information is a built infrastructure. It attends to the placement of patients in beds in a manner that foregrounds efficient bed utilization (costs and accountability) and not, for example, patient preferences. It does this through organizing what will be known in categories that make visible the cost relevance of space so as to support decisions that reduce the possibility that any bed is "inappropriately" staffed or occupied. With the exception of the actual bed maps, all the documents generated by the ADT system build utilization statistics through translating the work of nurses and clerks into data that reflect time utilization (such as length-of-stay data and cumulative transfers) or space utilization (percentage occupancy of beds). Constructing this visibility means that other knowledge related to the use of hospital space drops away. Other ways of knowing what is important are displaced by the more authoritative version carried in the ADT system. For instance, lost are the aspects of patient placement to which nurses might give priority, such as using space flexibly to enhance the comfort of patients. Nurses whom Rankin interviewed described how difficult it was for them to arrange to have dying patients moved into private rooms or to have patients who were having trouble sleeping moved out of rooms where a roommate snored loudly. They were critical of the amount of authority that the patient placement clerk held in relation to decisions to move patients throughout the hospital. They felt it constrained their own ability to accommodate patient care.

The ADT-inspired transformation of the hospital will have variable outcomes for differently located groups of people. ADT information fits with and advances actions framed in relation to efficiency. It does not have the same internal relation to nursing goals and actions. Managers are "instructed" in various ways by the ADT system's statistical information. In one case, a new policy about "same sex" rooms was generated to capitalize on the faster through-put of surgical patients. Speeding up the treatment of surgical patients through pre-admission and same-day admission procedures creates bottlenecks, with many more patients present than available beds. This combines with the inherent unpredictability of patients requiring emergency admissions, who also end up "lining up" in the emergency department waiting for available beds. Almost always, there is backlog of patients waiting to be accommodated. Customary rules about same-sex accommodations became a drag on the most efficient use of bed capacity, which ADT-based placement otherwise made possible. The placement clerks would have to handle the problem through complicated "transfers." A patient placement clerk described the challenges she encountered daily at 4 p.m. This was the "cut-off time" when further discharges were unlikely, and she could reasonably predict that all the patients in the hospital would be staying the night. She had to find everybody a bed, and eventually she would run out of appropriately sexed beds. Creating fictitious beds was no longer a solution because patients would be physically waiting in various holding areas of the hospital. Transferring patients among rooms would become the only way to "find beds." The clerk gave an example of the "just awful" work this entailed:

> I mean some of our moves are just awful ... [Say that] we have two four-bed male rooms, and each one has an empty bed in it. But we need three female beds. So you have two empty male beds but no empty female beds. So then you empty a semiprivate room, move two of the guys from the four-bed rooms into the semi, then you move the third guy from the four-bed room into the fourth bed in the other male room, and now you have four empty beds you can put ladies in. I mean they can even get more complicated than that ... Sometimes you're moving people all over the place just to get the right combination of same-sex beds.

She was describing the complexity involved in transferring patients virtually from one space to another, as she used her bed map to "juggle" and "squeeze" patients in, to maximize the bed resources within sex-segregated restrictions. For the patient placement clerk the work of transferring patients to find beds is a complex computer puzzle. Through manoeuvring patients on her bed maps, she is able to make highly pressured decisions about where patients can be placed in the hospital. But her account of "awful moves" is nothing compared with the embodied work of nurses who actually move beds, patients, and their belongings. When the instruction comes from the ADT clerk, nurses begin pushing the beds, gathering belongings from bedside lockers, informing the receiving nurses about the condition and needs of the patients being moved, and gathering and moving the appropriate records, medications, equipment, and so forth.

Using the cumulative ADT-generated statistics of "awful moves," managers, too, can "see" the labour involved in transferring patients. For them, costs and efficiencies are paramount. Transferring patients from room to room is yet another cost to try to reduce. When patients are moved from one bed to another it involves not only the patient placement clerks and nurses, but also ward clerks, housekeeping staff, medical records personnel, dietary clerks, and so forth. Records must be adjusted and extra work done to accommodate patient transfers. For this reason, the patient placement clerk explained, patients who are in four-bed wards or semiprivate rooms are seldom moved to accommodate mere preferences (for instance, a preference to be placed by the window or nearer the bathroom). Rather, transferring a patient from one bed to another is most often reserved as a tactic to "find beds" (or to accommodate a "revenue generating" patient who has requested a private room and can be categorized as a "paying private"). Transfers are carefully monitored. According to the patient placement clerk, when the ADT system showed a continual increase in the number of patient transfers – the "awful moves" – managerial attention was brought to bear on this issue. The resulting change in policy was unisex accommodations. Unisex realizes significant organizational efficiency by ensuring that no bed remains empty owing to it being treated as inappropriate by virtue of the patient's sex. One manager interviewed about the new policy viewed unisex accommodations as a way of "letting go of outmoded rules and moving into the new millennium."

It seems clear that ADT information helps hospital managers consider how to facilitate the efficient use of resources. In that light, the new unisex policy is successful in alleviating an apparently wasteful use of hospital space and of hospital workers' labour. What remains invisible within the picture created through the ADT system is the impact on patients. When the textual representation is substituted for knowledge of the local experiences, managers miss patients' responses. It is likely that the new work that is undertaken in order to function within the new systems is also overlooked. We learned about the discomfort of mixed-sex accommodations from Mary, a single woman of sixty-seven who was experiencing unstable angina and spent sixteen days on a heart monitor awaiting a coronary angiogram. Mary was accommodated in a room with three men, with whom she shared a bathroom. She found this upsetting. She felt it to be an assault to her "modesty." She said that she kept the curtains pulled (and pinned) around her bed all the time. Trying to maintain her privacy increased her isolation and her sense of vulnerability, as she adjusted to sharing sleeping, toilet, and bathing space with men. Such issues become a mere "preference" that hospitals cannot accommodate.

Even if managers were sympathetic to patient responses, individual managers do not have the privilege of using their discretion about such things. The ADT information is part of detailed information about hospital activities that is made available to managers with the expectation that it will be used to improve hospital performance. Performance here means adequate care with minimized expenditures (Shanahan, Brownell, & Roos 1999). ADT-generated statistical data, aggregated and fed back to the hospital managers, have already been used by government funders to establish "provincial averages" and "benchmarks" that hospitals have to live up to. Subsequent reports will compare them with like hospitals and like regions, and hospital administrators live in an ever-tightening loop of performance of efficiency in relation to other hospitals.[7]

Hospital managers are harnessed to improving hospital performance, not only through their job descriptions and upper management expectations, but also through the version of reality that the information provides. For instance, the patient services director's knowledge about how "well" patients do at home following shoulder surgery is factual. It is based on statistics. Standard statistical measurements offer the kind of description of hospital performance and health care delivery that produces unassailable accounts. Another director interviewed explained how having only just returned from holidays he had decided to take the "period statistics" home to review them. Embedded in his talk about his use of statistics is the reliance he places upon them for his decisions: "At any given time we can pull the statistics. Actually, we're not doing very well right now. We've started to vary a little bit with our hips and knees, probably by a day or two here and there. We have to get better at that." When he says, while looking at the statistics, "we have to get better at that," he is referring to his managerial responsibilities, organized through the facts generated by the computerized systems of counting, including ADT. The information-based work of these directors, and the accounts their work generates, produce the hospital efficiencies that are the imperative of cost containment demanded in health care reform. This is specialized work and it constructs a particular perspective. Pulling sheaves of paper from his briefcase the patient services director explained how he works in this textual medium, and how he is accountable to the ADT-generated data:

> We need these statistics for a couple of reasons. We [report] those ones that the ministry insists on and I need some purely to do my work. I use them as backup for proposals. I guess every second day you get involved with discussions with other hospitals in comparative talks. You get at the table in budget discussions or whatever, and you can talk statistics at people. We can say, "Okay yes, well we do 280 joint replacements a year, so we do need more money in our Joint Program." Utilization and length of stay

are big issues with the region. They say, "Look here, what's happening here? You're not utilizing well" ... and certainly, in our discussions with the ministry, in order to receive any extra funding, for the Joint Program for instance, they talk about length of stay and utilization a lot.

He uses his statistically generated knowledge when interacting and negotiating with people from the Ministry of Health, for whom "utilization and length of stay are big issues." As a manager it is his job to initiate strategies to address the problem of patients and practitioners who "vary a little bit," with the result that patients stay in the hospital "a day or two longer" than their allocated five days. It is his responsibility to organize professional practitioners and hospital employees to direct their work towards standardized length of stay for patients. For him, the ADT data provide the facts of efficiency, towards which his everyday work is directed. In our analysis, efficiency is shown to be a virtual reality, a construct of particular categories chosen for how they can make commensurable patients, treatments, beds, length of stay, utilization, and so on.

Information about the movement of patients through cost-relevant spaces is used to maximize the efficient use of resources not only in the day-to-day admission and discharge or sex-segregation practices being managed locally, but it also informs decisions being made by bureaucrats and public administrators far removed from the actual sites of patient care. In British Columbia, certain funding decisions are made based on a hospital's performance, calculated on the basis of the ADT data. In health care reform and hospital restructuring, hospital administrators, regional health authority administrators, and bureaucrats at the Ministry of Health all make use of the ADT-generated data to make decisions concerning, for example, the closure of hospital beds, the closure of hospital wards, or the closure of entire hospitals. Major redesign plans are generated by regional authorities. For example, one BC health authority cut nine beds from a local community's hospital, and when a great outcry ensued, relied upon calculations gathered through the ADT data to explain the proposed changes. Although it was true that service demands were high in that community (higher than in some comparable hospitals), length of stay was also "significantly higher [at 7.8 days] than the 4.8 average days per case for similar conditions in comparable hospitals." Better utilization management was expected to make the nine-bed closure able to be absorbed "without compromising patient care" (Petrie 2003: 3–4).

When patient placement clerks use ADT to distribute patients, the patients enter (and later, the system requires them to leave) a nurses' work purview. In drawing attention to how statistical information collected in this system informs policy decisions that are meant to improve hospital performance, especially the hospital's efficiency, we have shown how useful it is to have this kind of cost-relevant information. We want to put that together with our ethnographic analysis and reflect on the different standpoints represented. Our analysis draws attention to what is not known, at least not authoritatively, about the impact on individuals of policies that put efficiency in the forefront. At the level of managerial decision making, clinical relevancies about how patients are to be accommodated, or which patients require overnight care, fall out of sight. We showed Nurse Linda scurrying about making room for incoming patients, her nursing care being aligned with and constructing, in actuality, the hospital that is modelled in the ADT system's virtual reality. In these same activities, Nurse Linda's work is also being aligned with policy – the reform and restructuring agenda. She and her nursing colleagues work to the demands made on them.

We end this chapter on a troubling note. The accounting logic being appealed to in the restructure and redesign of health care systems propels continuous "improvement" in efficiency. The whole health care enterprise is being thought of as a virtual reality whose efficiency and productivity can be endlessly enhanced. A hospital president described an instance, in 1997, when the regional hospital he administered received funding for "673 acute inpatient days [i.e., funded beds] per 1,000 population." He explained how, statistically, this translated into two overnight beds per thousand people in the region. Then his hospital's same-day admission program and improved ambulatory care procedures generated improvements in utilization, which the data sent to ministry officials via the ADT system reflected. That year, the ministry readjusted the "benchmark targets" for "acute inpatient days," reducing the funding that would be made available from two to one-and-one-half beds per thousand of the population. A continuous ratcheting up of productivity expectations occurs. This accelerates the demands that are fed into nursing.[8] Nurse Linda's increased pace of work, her ad hoc nursing, and her suppression of nursing values are what it takes to coordinate the work on the ground with the virtual reality of the information-based technologies. Together they accomplish the goal of a restructured hospital and, at least for the immediate present, demonstrate "efficiency."

NOTES

1 Based on chapter 2 of Janet M. Rankin and Marie L. Campbell, *Managing to Nurse: Inside Canada's Health Care Reform* (Toronto: University of Toronto Press, 2006) , 45–64.

2 Called "chaotic" by the Steering Committee of the Western Canada Waiting List Project (Arnett, Hadorn, & the Steering Committee of the Western Canada Waiting List Project 2003), who have reported their early efforts to develop priority criteria for surgeons to help make assessments of prospective patients more objective and rational and thus fair. Physicians play the dominant role in managing waiting lists, and reliance on their judgment in this as in other clinical matters complicates rational management efforts.

3 Length of stay is planned before admission. Patients are informed about how long they will stay in the hospital and are expected to make arrangements for going home at the allocated standardized discharge time. (At this research hospital, patients are asked to sign a pre-admission agreement that commits them to make whatever arrangements required at home so that they can be discharged on time. Patients are advised that their surgery may be cancelled if they fail to comply. The standard discharge time is developed based on analysis of data from peer hospitals for similar surgeries.)

4 Alternate Level of Care (ALC) provides a means for screening patients related to whether the care provided *could* have been provided in an "alternative" as opposed to a "hospital" setting. ALC is discussed in more detail in chapter 3 of the book from which this chapter is taken.

5 See Mykhalovskiy (2001) for a more detail discussion about how physicians' and surgeons' resistance to reforming their approaches to care were being managed through discursive practices of health services research.

6 Health services research is a highly applied multidisciplinary field of research that addresses the structure, process, delivery, and organization of health services (Mykhalovskiy 2001). It relies on quantitative and positivist research methods using complex statistical analysis to establish relationships between health services rendered and health outcomes for a broad selection of populations and services.

7 In the spring of 1997, Management Information Guidelines (MIS) were developed by the CIHI that established "national standards that provide an integrated approach to managing financial and statistical data related to the operations of Canadian health services organizations" (Kerr, Glass, McCallion, & McKillop 1999: 255). The national standards are expected to inform decisions for "planning and budgeting purposes, especially when projecting the impact of expanding or downsizing health service operations

(1999: 259). Key categories in the MIS statistical system include "functional centre" (a category that monitors and calculates the accumulated costs of each hospital department such as health records, pharmacy, laboratory work, and nursing) and "service recipient" (a category that relates costs of "patient visits" to each hospital department). It is this system that contributes to the "case costing" predictions – aggregate calculations that report "typical" costs for various procedures. For example, an Ontario case-costing initiative compared the average cost of coronary artery bypass graft (CABG) across four medical centres: University Health Network, London Health Sciences Centre, St Michael's Hospital, and Trillium Health Centre (Couch and Sutherland, 2004). The ADT system produces a great deal of the data entered into the categories of the MIS system.

8 See also Willis (2004) for the analysis of similar effects in Australian health care.

PART 3

Experiential Ethnography

7 Doing Child Protection Work[1]

GERALD DE MONTIGNY

This chapter by Gerald de Montigny is distinctive in its execution of the phenomenological aspect of an institutional ethnography and its progression into description of conscious, active practice in dialogue with a professional discourse. He posed the problem this way:

> As a social work student and later as a social worker for several government ministries, departments, agencies, and hospitals, I constantly bridged the conflict between two apparently distinct worlds. I bridged the gap between the world of my experience and the world that denied my experience, a world of my thoughts and beliefs and a world that demanded that I perform other people's thoughts and beliefs – spoken through operational directives, policies and legislation. As a social worker, I bridged a flesh-and-blood world of embodied or immediate being and a textually cold world of disembodied or institutional being. (1995: 6)

Describing his experience on entering an apartment in response to a call to Child Protection Services, de Montigny provides a moment-to-moment account of the professional work sequence he is engaged in. He shows how the categories and concepts of the professional discourse learned in his training take over from the sensory responses (sights, smells, etc.) of his immediate experience. He shows how the categories organize a selective focus to bring the actualities he registers in his bodily being into a coordinated relation with the institutional text-work sequence enabling removal of a child from its home.

De Montigny then describes his own practices of producing and compiling the texts that will eventually go before a judge in court: he writes up his observations, selecting from what he noticed in the apartment where he found the child; he connects with the group home where the child will be cared for on a temporary basis; he prepares his report for his supervisor; he fills in a legal affidavit that will authorize him to make the account; and so on. He shows how this textual work builds exclusively on what the categories and concepts of social work discourse have drawn selectively from his experience in the home visit. His experiential description brings into view two segments of a sequence of action: (1) the situated practices of "apprehending" a child and writing up the experience-based report; and (2) the presentation in court of the "case" based on the report. The textual work links these two, the first in its vivid narrative and the second in its spare account of the institutional moment, a "court review." Together, these provide a detailed and experiential exploration of what George Smith calls "a mandated course of action."

Making Sense

As the intake social worker responsible for handling all child enquiries for my small community, on a Thursday afternoon, I received a phone call from the caretaker of an apartment building, who complained,

> Donna Trout is drunk again. She smashed her fist through the god-damned kitchen window. Last I saw her she went staggering off, swearing, saying she was going to go the hospital. She's left one hell of a mess. She's left her kid alone in the apartment, and sure as hell I'm not going to take care of it. You guys had better do something about that woman. I've come down here several times, after neighbours complained, to tell her to be quiet. She'll party all night if you don't stop her. I've had my belly full of her BS, and I want her out of my building.

When I asked, "How do you know what happened?" he responded: "I was upstairs cleaning the hall when I heard glass breaking, a commotion going on – a hell of a lot of hollering and screaming. I went down to the ground floor and found Donna staggering about the hallway. She was drunk out of her mind and bleeding like hell all over my floor. She'd slashed her arm, putting it through the window."

The Sea View apartment building was a familiar stop for me. I had other clients in the same building. It was slum, substandard, and low-cost housing. Its exterior had gone years without paint. The windows over the entrance doors were shattered. Graffiti was scrawled on the hall walls. The building stank of urine and filth. The floor tiles in the apartments were cracked and broken. The wooden front steps were rotting. The grounds were unkempt and littered.

As soon as I arrived at the apartment building, about fifteen minutes after the call, I tried to find a focus for building a case. I sorted through myriad sensual details trying to recover a professional standpoint. I noticed that the caretaker was outside at the side of the building boarding up a blood-streaked window. As I entered the building and walked down the hall I saw two older people were clutching each other outside an open apartment door. They looked very upset. They were Donna's parents. When I introduced myself, they told me, "We just got here." They said, "We came because Donna called us from the hospital." This last bit of information seemed important. It suggested that Donna had taken reasonable steps, following an obvious injury, to ensure supervision for her child in her absence. However, the grandfather continued, "We won't take care of Edith [the child]. This sort of thing has happened too damn many times before." The possible strength of Donna's efforts to ensure "continuity of care" weakened as a factor in her favour.

Although what usually mattered was quite simply whether or not a responsible adult was available to care for the child, I saw that in this case there were other factors that needed to be considered. It looked like there might have been a pattern of drinking, drunkenness, and grandparents being called out to pick up the pieces.

Donna's father groaned, "She has been drinking a lot since Christmas. We warned her that she had better stop." He added, "She wouldn't listen. I wish you still had the old 'interdict' list. I used to be on it, and I couldn't get any booze. Donna should be on it too!" The grandmother demanded, "The welfare should take Edith, teach her a lesson, she's got to stop drinking." Again, to cover myself, and to ensure that the grandparents were making a decision that they would not regret, I repeated my request, "Are you prepared to take the child?" Again they both refused. Donna's father burst out, "We've bailed her out of trouble too many times. She never learns, that girl."

From this exchange I learned several vital pieces of information for building a case of neglect and for legitimizing a decision to apprehend Donna's child. First, Donna was not present to care for her child. Second, I could see that her absence was most likely due to self injury brought about by drunken action. Third, I heard and had noted both her father's and mother's stories about her continual drinking. Fourth, I heard the grandfather admit to his own drinking problem, which suggested a pattern of alcohol abuse in the family. Finally, and perhaps most important, the grandparents had refused to take the child into their care, meaning that at that moment it seemed as if the child was without a caregiver, which then required that I act to protect her.

Producing Evidence

I entered the apartment and moved from room to room to observe and to record mentally those particulars which as a child protection worker I, and others, would recognize as worthy of documenting. I noted the pools of blood by the shattered window, the bloody trail of chaotic hand prints smeared on the walls (signs of stumbling, halting, and confused movement), empty beer bottles strewn across the floor, the stench of booze, urine, and unwashed bodies, and the filthy and disordered state of the apartment, and – with greater surprise as the grandparents had not mentioned him – the dark hair of a man apparently "passed out" on the couch. As I walked into the back bedroom I found an infant, apparently Edith, perhaps 10 or 12 months old, lying asleep on top of filthy sheets turned brown by dirt. I saw that she lay on a bed, not in a crib. I knew that a child that age should not have been left unattended on a bed. I anticipated a series of potential dangers against which the mother failed to protect her child. The child could have accidentally rolled off the bed and could have been injured in a fall. I looked at the child's body to note that she was wearing only a faeces-soiled and urine-soaked diaper. Faeces had dried, and caked her torso and face. I could see that she had been left unattended for several hours without attention to her needs.

Even more disturbing to me was that when I picked her up I saw that the back of her skull was flattened. I assumed that the flattened skull was not natural. I guessed that it signified the parent's failure to attend to her, and rotating her while sleeping or to pick her up when awake. The flattened skull could be an invaluable piece of evidence before the court. It would serve as a powerful and graphic sign of abnormality resulting from serious neglect. It showed that the child had been left alone lying on her back hour after hour and day after day.

I looked under the diaper and saw that the child had a red rash and had a small patch of two or three open sores. Her face had several infected scratches about her nose and eyes, probably from her fingernails, which were jagged and unkempt. I made a mental note to myself, "Remember to have the group home parent take photographs of the flattened head, the sores, and the scratches!" As I stood in a dimly lit room and breathed in putrid air, I held a groggy child who was beginning to emit frightened cries, yet, my mind was focused on an institutionally defined problem of making a case. I had to establish that this was a child in need of protection. I had to compile sufficient evidence of neglect to make a case, that is, to justify my apprehension, and to be granted custody before the judge in court. Although I wanted and had decided to apprehend the child, I needed to proceed cautiously and to assemble my observations as facts and particulars that would stand as compelling evidence of child neglect. Even as I stood in that apartment, breathing in the stale air, holding a distressed child, I anticipated a future course of action in which I would need to display, through the presentation of observed "facts," the warrant of my actions. I anticipated the possibility of a battle in court between myself and the child's mother and lawyer. To win the battle, I needed to identify those facts which could be assembled to tell a convincing story of neglect. I could tell a story of alcohol abuse by referencing the empty beer bottles strewn about the living room, the half empty bottle of rye whisky by the couch, the empty wine bottle on the kitchen table, and the sickly sweet smell of alcohol from body pores that permeated the apartment. "Neglect" could be signified by the putrid smells of faeces, urine, and filth, and most importantly by the observed condition of the child. That the child was in need of protection was evident by the absence of her mother and the refusal of the grandparents to assume custody. From experience doing child protection work I believed there were enough indicators to sustain an apprehension before the court.

I asked the grandmother to find a clean diaper while I took the child to the washroom, where I placed her under warm running water in the bathtub. I washed off the faeces and was able to do a quick check for bruises, scars, and other injuries. I assessed the severity of her sores, and tried to determine if there were other more serious injuries, which would have required taking her to the hospital instead of the receiving home for observation or treatment.

I made a final surveillance of the apartment. I noted the piles of dirty and smelly clothing littered about the bedroom floors. I moved to the kitchen, opened the refrigerator, gasped at the stench, and noted that it was empty except for a few wilted carrots and two open bottles which contained mouldy food remnants. The cupboards were almost bare except for an abundance of small black droppings. It seemed that the apartment was infested with mice. The kitchen sink was filled with dark water and grimy dishes. The counter and stove were littered with unwashed pots, plates, bottles, and cutlery.

As I sat on a chair in the kitchen, I passed the child to the grand-mother, and pulled out my black notebook (my daily log) from the satchel I had deposited on the kitchen table earlier. Log in hand, I began to ask a series of routine questions. I wanted to establish the particulars of the case. I asked the grandmother: "What is your daughter's full name? What is her birth date? What is the name and birth date of the child? Who is the father? Where does he live?" (I had already gathered that the father was not the drunk the grandfather had roused and or-dered to leave.) "What do you know about what happened here today? How do you know Donna was drunk? What is your name, address, and phone number? How long has Donna been drinking? How many times before have you had to take the child? Are you willing to testify in court?"

Producing Parental Failure

As I moved about the apartment I was building a case to justify an apprehension, while trying to anticipate arguments against my assess-ment. I wondered, could Donna have accidentally put her arm through the window? Could Donna have been locked out of the apartment? Had she called or banged on the door to try to waken her drunken friend inside? Did she smash the window to regain entry to protect her child? First, the location of the shattered kitchen window revealed that Donna could not have accidentally fallen into it. Second, even if Donna had been locked out, she could have contacted the caretaker who could have let her back into the apartment. Third, even if she could not find the caretaker she could have picked up a board or a rock, rather than used her fist, to smash the window. It seemed evident that Donna had not acted rationally. She had not taken proper care of herself. If she could not care for herself, how could she care for her child?

I appreciated that the apparently simple facts at hand could rather easily be assembled to produce a case of immediate parental failure. However, I also recognized some troublesome details that threatened this account and that needed to be contained by my story. First, Don-na's self-mutilation required immediate absence from her child. She had taken the precaution of phoning her parents to ensure continuity of care. Perhaps she had relied on the fact that the man on the couch was home with her child. Had she thought that leaving him with her child was adequate? However, she did not wait until her parents ar-rived before leaving for the hospital. Could anyone expect that Donna could have waited? Would Donna have bled to death if she had waited? The large pools of blood on the floor indicated that Donna probably could not have waited for her parents. What would a physical examination of Donna's wounds reveal? Had Donna taken reasonable steps to ensure continuity of care in her absence? Could Donna be faulted for leaving her child without adequate adult care? Partially. Could an apprehension be sustained on this point alone? Unlikely. It seemed most important that Donna's wounds were self-inflicted. The severity of the injury signified Donna's disregard for her own care. Furthermore, her parents, although at the apartment, had refused to assume responsibility for the child. Their verbal complaint that "this type of thing has happened before" was important. It suggested a pattern of drunkenness and parental neglect. Finally, these elements could be combined with the sensory evidence of prolonged alcohol abuse and resulting neglect, for example, the filth, disorder, stench, and, most important, the physical condition of the child.

Implicit in my construction of Donna's parental failure was the normative model of a rational actor. If I showed that Donna's actions were irrational, this would be sufficient grounds for claiming that she had failed to exercise her duties as a parent. If I could sustain an account in the court that Donna's actions were irrational, then my intervention in her life and that of her child would be justified.

Seeing the Tear

This work, which described Donna's action as irrational, was not innocent. Its good sense articulated a domain governed by the dual imperatives of rational action and mastery of self and others. Smith understands that the normative model of the rational actor is problematic, as it is grounded in the social relations of a ruling apparatus:

> The rational actor choosing and calculating is the abstracted model of organizational or bureaucratic man, whose motives, methods, and ego structure are organized by the formal rationality structuring his work role. At work his feelings have no place. Rationality is a normative practice organizing and prescribing determinate modes of action within the bureaucratic or professional form. Responses that do not conform to these modes of action, by virtue of how they are excluded from these domains, are constituted residually as a distinct mode of response and being. (1987: 65)

Smith argues that the lives of women, and I add Donna's life and the lives of clients in general, do not conform to this voluntaristic model of rational action.

As a social worker, I focused my attention on creating a professional account of Donna's actions as not rational. In my social work accounts Donna was drunk, irrational, and out of control. I developed a tentative history which suggested links between the moment of my arrival at the apartment and other moments in Donna's life, as accessible through her parents' stories at the door. I was attuned to see a pattern of parental failure. I worked to see a pattern through the connection of case details to professional understandings about normal family life, child development, and personal care. I identified patterns by weaving together the caretaker's and the grandparents' statements, the evidence of disorder about the apartment, and, most important, the fact that I found the child on a bed, not in a crib, the faeces dried on her body, her flattened skull, diaper rash, uncut fingernails, and scratches.

At the moment of raising her fist, hurling her hand through the window, and ripping it back through shattered glass, Donna expressed her experience of being in a lived world. Just as there are realities of fantasy and of dreams (Schutz 1973), so too is there a reality of alcohol intoxication. Beyond the reality of alcohol intoxication there is a social organization of "being" drunk. These are forms of being in which others who are not "drunk" assess. The reality of a person who is drunk, although outside the logic and rationality of organizational work, mandates, and records, is nevertheless subject to the surveillance, powers, and judgments of those inside such organizational work processes. As a social worker I had the mandated authority to enact institutionalized courses of action which appropriated and defined the nature of Donna's reality on that day. Surely, Donna's act gave voice to her place in a world. This may have been a world whose boundary was a locked door, a window, a shabby apartment, a cry from her child inside, the sound of her own voice yelling and her banging the door, the lack of response from the man inside her apartment, a mounting sense of anger, desperation, frustration, and rage, and ultimately the panic of hurling her fist through the glass window.

When Donna slammed her fist into the window, she gave voice to something that was real for her. She meant to do it. Her voice was not necessarily expressed in words – perhaps other than through a scream or a profanity – but in a form of action that flowed from her history and her lived world. When the tip of her knuckles first touched the glass, her voice lacerated the tranquillity of still glass. Her voice shattered a silent second. When her hand withdrew, jagged and ripped, her voice was pain and rage. Her voice reverberated through the echoes of experience over her lifetime.

In my report to the court what disappeared – as not worth reporting – were the conditions of Donna's life and her lived experienced as expressed from her standpoint in the world. The report to the court did not address her situation nor her understanding of what it meant to be a First Nations person, a young woman (nineteen years old), a single mother, a woman who had dropped out of school in grade 8, and who had struggled with a physical disability throughout her life. Certainly as a social worker I could guess that Donna's life had not been pleasant. Her father had already told me enough for me to know that he had had a serious drinking problem. Later, Donna told me that she, her brothers, sisters, and mother had all been victims of his rage, beatings, and abuse. But this information was peripheral to the work at hand of determining whether or not there was a child in need of protection.

Professional Entries and Exits

As a social worker, my entry and my work upon entering was structured by my location inside an organizational work process. I entered as a professional, not as a friend. As a social worker, I entered Donna's home to do child protection work. I did not tisk tisk, shake my head, or cry over her injuries. I did not mop and sweep up the floor, rouse the drunk, and wait for Donna to return home. I did not put on a pot of coffee, try to sober Donna up, have a "heart to heart" talk about what was wrong in her life, or agree to take the child for a few days until she sorted things out. I acted as an agent of the state with the legislated authority to enter her home, to investigate, and to apprehend her child.

I had neither the time nor the authority to wait at the apartment. Indeed, while I was at the apartment I was consuming precious organizational time. Back at the office I knew that I had people scheduled to meet me for appointments, there were piles of paper work to be completed that included court applications, case recordings, applications for service, and case progress reports. Fortunately for me, the decision to apprehend the child was easily made. I left the grandparents my business card and instructed them to have Donna call me first thing in the morning. At this point the organization had assumed custody of the child through my action as agent.

Placement

I left the apartment, taking the child to go to a receiving home. The receiving home was an approved "group living home" as defined by the British Columbia Family and Child Services Act (1980). A legal contract specified the organization of the receiving home, the number of spaces (beds) available for children, the types of services provided in the home, the group home parents' responsibilities, and a budget for salaries and services. The receiving home had become available for placement of children only after it was approved by the child protection agency where I worked. The building was inspected by the fire department and by city health officials. The home's parents were interviewed, investigated, and approved as caregivers by social workers. A contract was signed between them and the district supervisor and the regional manager. Only after these procedures were in place could the home's parents receive children.

When I entered the receiving home I left behind the worlds of Donna and her parents' daily lives. I left behind their pain, chaos, and disorder. I was entering a familiar institutional setting. This was an institutional world occupied by co-workers employed in child protection work. I had moved from the disorder of clients' daily lives into an administered and mandated order. In the receiving home, I could begin to relax. I knew the group home parents and the childcare workers, so they invited me to sit down at the kitchen table for a cup of coffee. As I sat at the table, I calmed down and organized my thoughts. As I talked about what I had seen and what I had done, I began to assemble a coherent version of my intervention work. Again, just as it was after every apprehension, in telling the story I searched for and received support and encouragement. On that Thursday, the group home parents affirmed that my actions were necessary and that the child would benefit from placement in their home. We talked, and they shared their understandings of what this particular child would need. I appreciated their practical knowledge about children and their support for my actions.

My knowledge that the receiving home parents would assess and monitor this child allowed me to justify my actions, as I knew that I had removed a child from a place of "risk" to a place of "safety." I knew that I could rely on the work of the receiving home parents in the coming days, and that they would report to me further information about the child which I could then present to the court. I expected that they would assess the child's intellectual and emotional development and look for behavioural or emotional problems. I also expected that if the child's mother requested and was granted supervised visits with her child, they would report whether or not she showed up, and that they would provide an assessment of the nature of her interactions with her child during those visits. Simply, I expected that their daily work would provide additional information for building a case of child neglect.

In the modern kitchen chair and sitting before a clean table, I had returned to friendly and supportive institutional relations. Inside the receiving home, I found like-minded people who understood my work and the language I employed. Together our talk affirmed the correctness of our enterprise. This comfort was in contrast to the world from which I had come. There I had entered as an intruder, a stranger, as someone unfamiliar with people's histories and daily lives. Despite such ignorance, I was empowered to intervene dramatically in their lives.

I hunched over the cup of fresh coffee and breathed in the aroma. It erased the lingering cloying stench of urine in my nostrils. The sparkling cleanness of the kitchen washed away my memories of patches of blood on a floor. In the calm of this kitchen, I continued my search for order in the disorder that had become a memory. I returned to memories and impressions to search again for patterns. Once away from the chaos of the front line, I worked to recover a frame of mind and a centre of being essential for getting on with the next challenges of the work. Inside the safe space of this kitchen, I could reconstruct a professional persona, detached, objective, observing, emotionally controlled, evaluating, and acting in accordance with regulated policies and protocols. I was out of danger.

Despite the obvious sensibility of my professional self, there remained an inner unmediated fragment. Behind the social worker who calmly sipped his coffee, there remained an insecure man. I sensed that what I had done and what I could do as a social worker failed to adequately address Donna and her parents' pain and problems. As a child protection worker, the time I had to spend with Donna and her family was work time, paid for by my employer. The form of my action was mandated, regulated, and accountable to my organization, and ultimately the courts. As a social worker, I could not act informally to take the child for a few hours and return her later once Donna had sobered up. I was unable to work with Donna to help her resolve the practical conditions of her life.

Although my actions of investigation and apprehension were properly executed as defined by legislation and policy, I felt that I had failed

Donna, her parents, and her child. I felt that I had not done enough and that what I had done was wrong. My doubts remained silent. My words briefed the receiving home parents. I pointed out my concerns. I gave them a list of instructions: "Observe the child to assess her mental development. Pick up the child's permanent medical record form at the office tomorrow. Take the child to the doctor for a full medical examination. Ask the doctor to make a report concerning the flattened occiput. Ask her to look for other signs of neglect. Make sure she submits the bill and report to my office."

I interrupted my coffee to take a final trip to the washroom, where the childcare worker was giving the child a proper bath. Again, I observed and checked the child's buttocks, back, chest, and legs for signs of old bruising and deformity. I looked for any additional signs of neglect that I might have missed during my first hasty examination. However, no additional signs were visible. I had been away from the office for almost two hours. I had to return to the work waiting for me.

The Report and Power

After I apprehended Edith Trout, I not only had to complete the standard documents required to open the family-service and child-in-care files, I had to prepare a report to the court. The report to the court entered my activities on the doorstep and inside the apartment that Thursday afternoon into a formal document. The documentary entry:

1 provided my activities with the sanction of a legal apparatus and provided for a legal determination that the apprehension of Edith Trout was properly executed, warranted, legitimate, and legal; and
2 provided for a formal organizational appropriation of my practice as a sanctioned moment of work or task performed for the child protection agency.

I want to turn now to explore the activity of documenting a report to the court. The objective will be to highlight how I and other social workers practically inscribe the everyday worlds of our work and clients' lives into institutionally manageable forms.

To complete a report to the court, I was guided, as were other social workers in our office, by the instructions and directions set out in the Forms Manual. The Forms Manual provided facsimile reproductions of all forms, including the report to the court, and detailed instructions about how to complete or fill them in. Instructions insisted that no deviation or modification of standardized forms was allowed. For the report to the court to be sustained, it had to be recognizably complete, accurate, neat, legible, and professional. It had to demonstrably conform to a predetermined format.

The report to the court was a four-page document that included a one-page affidavit or sworn statement of fact. It interlocked my activities as a social worker engaged in child protection with a legal apparatus. The report to the court enveloped my actions into a properly legalized, and legalizable, form, where my actions as reported in documents, and perhaps supplemented by sworn testimony, could be presented, questioned, and subjected to scrutiny, evaluation, and eventual legal sanction by the court.

The mundane truthfulness of the report to the court depended on an institutional and historical matrix that includes child protection legislation, prescribed agency forms for case work, policies and protocols, and past judgments and legal precedents. The report to the court and the court work that follow articulated highly ritualistic language, grammar, rules, and codes. Even for most social workers, I suspect that the rituals of the law and court, on first encounter, seem strange. However, I, like most other social workers, quickly learned how to manage my work in court. Although many of us might be unfamiliar with the specific nature of the law and court, we do know how organizations operate. We do know how to generate proper documentary accounts and organizational records of our clients' daily lives. We know how to inscribe the everyday into the organizational. As we will see in greater detail below, for most clients, however, the law and court remain a strange and foreign realm. Court work confused most of those who were my clients, as its order and codes and the orientations of its functionaries are far removed from their own everyday experience. Although many clients may have been confused by court, they clearly recognized the power over their lives of the people who run the courts, and the courts themselves.

The Cover Page

The report began by identifying the legal jurisdiction of a provincial court over a particular matter as defined in legislation. A typical first page of a report to the court read:

In the provincial court of (province)

in the matter of the act

x.x. xx – chapter xx

and

The matter of the child

Trout.

To the court

1. Section X(x) I, Gerald Alexander Joseph de Montigny am duly authorized, pursuant to Section X(x) of the Act, by the Child Protection Agency of the (Province name), to present this written Report to the Court.
2. Interpretation
   Section X The Child listed below is under the age of 18 years and is hereinafter referred to as "the child."
   The Child Birth date
   Edith Trout 1 April (year)
3. Section XX(1) The child was apprehended on the 1st day of January, (year) in (town and province name) by Gerald Alexander Joseph de Montigny.
4. Interpretation
   Section X. The child was apprehended as being in need of protection by reason of being (a) abused or neglected so that her safety or well being is endangered.
   This is "Exhibit A" referred to in the Affidavit of 2 January 19XX, sworn before me at (town and province name), this 2nd day of January (year).

The cover page provides a warrantable account in a prescribed documentary form of practical social work activities as informed, guided by, and acted out as legally mandated courses of action. The account in the report to the court is organized by the relevances of statutory provision and authority, by authorized organizational policies governing the enactment of provisions, and by the requirement to document and to cite the sanctions for the local application of legal powers. The specific site, time, and people involved in the exercise of legislatively mandated authority are documented. The legislative provisions that warranted my actions are cited as the basis for those actions, that is, determining that Edith was "a child in need of protection by reason of being abused or neglected." Finally, the document references the ritualized legal practices of taking an oath and the swearing that that which is said is true.

The second page of the report is designed to allow the social worker to provide a narrative – albeit still formal – account of the particular circumstances that led to the apprehension. It is intended to set out in more detail the observed conditions and circumstances that led the worker to take action, and by extension to sustain a case of abuse or neglect. Social workers account for their activities on page two of the form inside the four inches of blank space provided under the heading, "Circumstances of Apprehension." The section begins, "The circumstances that resulted in the apprehension of the child were as follows." The accounts provided, although varying in details from case to case and from worker to worker, have to be recognizable for supervisors, legal counsel, and the judge in court as properly constructed and warrantable. The account addresses the time and place of apprehension, the people encountered when apprehending, their involvement and conduct (if relevant), and the condition of the child(ren). The account generates a base for seeing that there are legislatively defined grounds for apprehension. For example, a child is apprehended by reason of being found to be in a situation or condition provided for by legislation, that is, that she is "(a) abused or neglected so that his or her safety or well being is endangered; (b) abandoned; (c) deprived of necessary care through the death, absence, or disability of his or her parent; (d) deprived of necessary medical attention; or (e) absent from his home in circumstances that endanger his or her safety or well being." In the case of Edith Trout the "Circumstances" might read:

> Attended at apartment 102304 Zenith Drive, at 1:30 p.m. after receiving a report from the caretaker, Frank Valley, that a child Edith Trout was unattended in the apartment. Met the grandparents of the child at the doorway. They refused to assume custody. The child was found unattended on a filthy bed. She was covered in dried faeces, had diaper rash, and appeared to have been unattended for several hours. The back of her skull appeared flattened, indicating inattention. The apartment was filthy, empty liquor bottles were evident. Donna Trout the mother was not present, as apparently she was drunk and was at the hospital receiving care for self-inflicted wounds. The child was apprehended and placed in the receiving home.

The above would stand as a fairly detailed version of the circumstances. Shorter versions were also possible, such as, "Attended at

102304 Zenith Drive to find the parent absent and no responsible adult present willing to assume custody. Apprehended the child, placed her in the receiving home."

Regardless of how I or another social worker might present the circumstances, we would focus on one issue alone, namely, whether or not we had reasonable grounds for believing and acting as though this was a child in need of protection. All other information that did not directly address the issue of child neglect and inadequate parental or other adult supervision falls outside the legal definition of a "child in need of protection."

After I provided the circumstances in the report to the court, I supplied the names, addresses, and marital status of the parent(s). This information is often not available in veridical documentary form, for example, a certificate or licence of marriage. Indeed, on rare occasions, particularly in cases of abandoned children, the name of the child and her date of birth are not available. However, the process of naming identifies, for this moment in the process, the people who are considered the subjects of the case, and who might, following the report to the court, be served with notice of hearing. Finally, the second page requires that the social worker address the present whereabouts of the child. In the Trout case, I indicated that the child "remains in the custody of the child protection agency ... pending further investigation and assessment." In other cases I might have indicated that the child "has been returned to the parent(s) apparently entitled to custody pending further direction of the court."

Finally, the report of the court requires that a short-term plan for the child be created by the social worker. Is the child to be retained or returned? Can the parent(s) care for the child? Should temporary wardship be requested? If so, what amount of time would be necessary to correct the situation in the family? Three months, six months, a year? Should crown wardship – a permanent order – be requested? Should the social worker merely request a supervision order?

The third page of the report to the court addresses the interim order requested. Proper completion of this page requires that the social worker check off the particular order requested from the possibilities provided for by the act. For Edith Trout the interim order requested was:

XX(2)(c)

The child protection agency requests that the Court order that the child protection agency retain custody of the child until an order is made under Section YY of the Act.

Although this addresses the legal provision for maintaining custody, in the majority of cases I was involved with the child was returned to the parents without proceeding to a court hearing. In the small town where I worked, children who have become lost or who have wandered away from home were routinely reported to the police, who in turn called us. For example, one afternoon I was called to the police station to pick up a three-year-old child. Apparently, he had wandered into the local taxi stand to ask for candy. He could only tell people his name and did not know his address or how to get back home. I picked the child up and took him to the receiving home. When I got back to my office, the boy's mother was there to meet me. She was frantic with worry. She told me, "I lay down with him for his afternoon nap. I must have dozed off. I guess he got up, undid the safety latch on the apartment door, and wandered off." The woman explained that she did a search of the apartment, the building, the grounds, and then the neighbourhood. Finally, in tears she phoned the police. By the time she had phoned, I had already picked the child up and taken him to the receiving home. This set of events, although happily resolved, was nevertheless an apprehension, which requires a report to the court. In this circumstance I requested the following order:

> Section XX(2)(a) The child protection agency requests that the Court make an order approving the child protection agency's action in returning the child to Madeline Trouve at 93 Perdue Boulevard, Viking, who appears to be the parent apparently entitled to custody pursuant to Section XX(2)(a) of the Act.

Producing the Form

After I had written out a longhand version of the report to the court regarding Edith Trout, I submitted it for typing. I placed it in an "Urgent" box, with a short note attached requesting that the clerk also type an affidavit (all the information she needed was contained in the report). The clerk usually gave the request top priority, generally typed it within an hour or two, and returned it to me by placing it in my intake box. This mundane office organization of employee In and Out boxes, as well as boxes marked Urgent, were important tools for organizing the practical flow of work through the office.

Specific rules existed for workers using such an office system. It is assumed that social workers will not place work in the "Urgent" basket unless it genuinely was urgent. All court documents and overdue work were considered urgent. The routinized systems for regulating work flows allowed social workers to take for granted an orderly productive background of clerical practices to produce documents in the warranted forms. The day-to-day and routine character of office organization allowed clerical staff, social workers, and others to take documentary work for granted. The remarkable quality of workers' everyday documentary productions and the workplace divisions of labour for their production came to be taken for granted through the sedimentation of experience and familiarity with routines.

The Affidavit of Service

After the report was typed, I proceeded to another social worker's office to swear an affidavit. After the affidavit was sworn, it was attached (stapled) to the report to the court. The affidavit read:

In the provincial court of (province)
In the matter of the act
x.x.x. 19xx – chapter xx

Edith Trout

1. I, Gerald Alexander Joseph de Montigny of Viking make oath and as:
2. That I am the person whose Signature appears on the report dated the 2nd day of January 19XX, and attached as Exhibit "A' to this my Affidavit.
3. That the information contained in the said report is true to the best of my knowledge, information, and belief.
   Sworn before me in Viking, (Province) this 2nd day of January, 19XX.

My affidavit, like all other affidavits, was produced through an iterative, repeated, and routinized procedure for taking affidavits. To produce an affidavit, social workers enter themselves into a ceremonial, iterative, and routine set of activities. The iterative ceremony and routine for producing such activities provides for workers' post-facto claim, if questioned, to rely on an invariant process for producing oath-taking occasions, such as an affidavit of service. After I signed my name in the designated blank on the affidavit, the social worker who acted as the commissioner would ask:

COMMISSIONER: Are you Gerald de Montigny?
GERALD: Yes.
COMMISSIONER: Is this your proper name and signature?
GERALD: Yes.
COMMISSIONER: Do you swear that the information you have provided is
    true to the best of your knowledge, information, and belief?
GERALD: Yes.

As social workers, we had been instructed by supervisors and
trained to adopt an invariable procedure for swearing affidavits. We
were warned that we might be compelled to testify before the court
regarding the subject of an affidavit (i.e., details of a report) which we
had either sworn or witnessed. If this were to occur, we needed to sustain our claim to properly swear an affidavit by referencing as a certain
and unequivocal matter our personal use of an invariant procedure. If
challenged to demonstrate how we could know that the affidavit was
properly sworn, we could in turn swear under oath, "I always swear
an affidavit in this way. It is my habit. I never swear an affidavit differently." This process of swearing and witnessing implied a possibility of
conflict, variation in lived memories, and the indeterminacy of situated
forms of being itself. The institutionally controlled acts of swearing and
witnessing are designed to transcend the equivocalities of the everyday, which even permeate our office work.

When we made a sworn oath, this ceremonial act constituted a relation between a particular document and ourselves as social workers.
Our oath-taking absorbed our particular actions as candidate members
of universal courses of action and legal sanction. Swearing an oath created a bridge between the social worker and the law such that the sequence of events we pursued, the investigation, entering an apartment,
apprehending a child, and so forth, could be properly identified for the
court as being our actions performed on behalf of the child protection
agency. Swearing the oath established that the social workers (I was
one) appearing in court were in fact those who had observed what was
reported and had acted as described in the report.

The Court Order

Once the actual form was completed, I took photocopies of the report
to the court, placed those in the file, and, with the original in hand,

walked to the courthouse and gave it to the clerk in the Court Registry. The court clerk assigned my report to the court a file number, date-stamped it as "Received," placed it in a court file, and assigned it a date to be heard before the court (the next Wednesday, as was usual). At the same time, I deposited a copy of the report to the court in a file folder for our lawyer, who also had a box at the Court Registry. By duly registering the report to the court, I enacted my compliance with the legislation and policy demands for a legal review by the court of my activities as a social worker. Once my work at the registry was completed and a date had been set for the report to be presented, I attempted to deliver and recorded all efforts to deliver a copy of the report to the parent(s) "apparently entitled to custody."

When the following Wednesday arrived, I appeared in court at the scheduled time to present my report to the court. In the case of Edith Trout, I requested an interim order for custody until the hearing. The interim order was produced from the work of the social worker, the lawyers, the court clerks, the court stenographers, and the judge. The interim order affirmed that my activities on this occasion were properly conducted on behalf of the child protection agency.

The Interim Order

The deliberations of the judge who considered the matter brought before his court resulted in a court order. The act required that the court would do one of the following: "(a) make an order approving the child protection agency's action in returning the child under section XX(5) where he has done so; (b) order the child protection agency to return the child to the parent apparently entitled to custody; (c) order that custody of the child be retaken or retained by the child protection agency until a further order is made under section XX; (d) make an order under section XX(1)." The legislation provided sanction of the social worker's activities as properly those conducted on behalf of the child protection agency. Only after a court order was issued could I as the social worker proceed to the next stages of child protection work, that is, either to make an application for a hearing to seek state custody of the child or to seek approval to return the child.

When a judge hears evidence in court, he or she poses a series of questions both explicit and implicit based upon knowledge of the law and as demonstrably being oriented to and inside legal procedures and principles. Were the social worker's actions justified by the law? Did the social worker have reasonable grounds to make an apprehension? Did the social worker take all reasonable steps to avoid an apprehension? Has the child been returned to the parents since the apprehension? Was this a reasonable and proper decision? If the child was not returned, should the child remain in care? Should the matter proceed to a hearing? Once such questions are answered to the judge's satisfaction, a ruling is made on the case which is documented as an interim court order.

From the moment I answered the call regarding Edith Trout, began doing an investigation, made a decision to apprehend her, and in fact did so, my practices anticipated and intended that moment of presenting my work before the court. That moment in court, in turn, served to retroactively subsume my situated and particular work activities into general and universalized policies and law. As a social worker does child protection work, he or she collects evidence that is intended to be sufficient for presenting and making a case in court. In turn, the court, in the person of the judge, considers the evidence brought before him or her, and determines whether or not the social worker's activities can legally and warrantably be appropriated as proper instances of child protection work. If the judge determines that this is proper work, then he or she will produce an interim court order that affirms and validates the social worker's practice.

The twofold dance between situated practice and court review produces a hermeneutic circle that establishes the hegemony of the institutional sphere over the spheres of daily life. Institutional hegemony is constructed through day-to-day practices that come to be articulated in textual form. The texts can then be circulated to weave together various moments as properly sanctioned, legal, and warranted. The production of texts anticipates further legal review, the presentation of documents in court, the textually-mediated assessments and reviews of those documents in court, and the interim court order that frames particular activities as instances of generalized institutional practice. D.E. Smith has observed:

> The articulation of different segments of these social relations are [sic] not obvious, yet they create the actual linkages between a lived actuality and the event as it becomes known in the documentary forms in which it circulates for further work. Whatever else may be going on in this interchange between the professional discourse and the institutional structures of state

control, it is a process which continually integrates, circulates, feeds back and coordinates the continually changing relations of the bureaucratic apparatus to the actuality of everyday life. (1990b: 147)

What emerged as the situation of this child, Edith Trout, her life, her history, her relationship with her mother, her mother's history, their situation as First Nations people living in poverty, being unemployed, marginalized, and struggling to survive a life of abuse and addictions dropped out of sight as irrelevant for the immediate court work at hand.

NOTE

1 This chapter is based on parts of G.A.J. de Montigny (1995), *Social Working* (Toronto: University of Toronto Press). All the names of places and persons are pseudonyms; descriptions of places observed and situations experienced are artificial assemblies based on the experience of many.

PART 4

Text–Reader Conversations

8 Reading Practices in Decision Processes[1]

SUSAN MARIE TURNER

Susan Marie Turner's ethnography examines a sequence of naturally occurring talk in which a visual text is central to a city council "making a decision." Her chapter illustrates how individual reading practices take shape within an ongoing organizational process. It looks closely at how the text coordinates individuals' consciousnesses and how text-reader conversations bring institutional objects of knowledge in the text into active dialogue with what's happening in the setting. Turner proposes that reading practices deserve further ethnographic attention as organizational forms of activating texts that make specialized forms of knowledge present and enable local action. Such inquiry can tell us a lot about what happens in institutional settings and decision processes where what's in the texts is considered, contested, or negotiated.

Her methods comprise observation of a sequence of talk in a setting in which multiple "text–reader conversations" are integral to "discussion" and "decision making," recording, transcribing, and examining text-reader practices applying institutional ethnography's (IE) conceptual framework for inquiry into language–text interaction in action in the setting. She shows how IE orients to what conventionally are seen as individual internal practices, and makes visible the conceptual and language resources of different realms of experience as actual spheres of activity – the "interindividual territories" that reader-speakers' practices and utterances rely on. She illustrates how to take up V.N. Vološinov's analysis of historically concrete and living language to attend to the way speakers formulate in everyday speech an interpretive frame for reconceptualizing everyday realities. Her analysis shows the practices as they are coordinating diverse readings and utterance, "cling-wrapping" them to the fixed and stable forms of representation provided in the text being read and discussed. She uses multiple "exhibits" of sequential readings to show the institutional procedure of reaching a municipal decision as it is being organized in ongoing text–reader–speaker interaction *that takes up objects constituted in the text.*

Turner's practical goal is to open up ways to explore reading practices in workplaces where such specialized forms of action are taken for granted yet central to how organizational work gets done and accomplishes institutional outcomes. Laying out to view procedural forms for accomplishing organizational tasks provides a critical analytic description. Turner shows us how reading practices can be explored as procedures integral to organization and how an organizational concept like "decision making" can be ethnographically discovered as text–reader–speaker interaction among participants in an institutional process. Her description and analysis has thereby the potential of opening up such institutional processes to intervention and change.

This chapter analyses data from an earlier study in order to treat afresh how different "readings" of a site-plan diagram of a development project operated in a decision-making sequence of action. The readings examined are integral to what took place in a public municipal council meeting. In addition, the chapter also tries out ways of analysing and describing the distinctive procedural forms in which institutional texts – words and images in a definite and replicable material form – organize and regulate diverse local reading practices, talk–text interactions, and sequences of action. Decision processes have been a focus for my work on development planning (Turner 2003).[2] Taking up the decision-making process as the institutional context, the chapter explores how different readings engage with the technical details and surface features of a diagram – a text in action. Also, it contrasts the distinctive reading practices that produce a text as institutionally actionable in the setting with others that do not. The segments of conversation are taken from my 2003 ethnography. I observed, recorded, and transcribed the council decision sequence, which was also broadcast on the local cable television station. Reading practices are setting-specific, text-based work. They bring texts into the course of action that is being put together as participants speak. Reading practices themselves are organizational courses of action to be explored.

Reading also plays a central part in the apparently specialized intertextual work people do in the setting that goes on in standardized and mundane forms of talk. Specialized "work knowledge" (Smith 2005) in this setting can be seen to involve knowing just which of a text's features to "activate" and knowing how and when to do so as well as the particular textual formats, who reads them, and what kinds of utterances can produce the next institutional action to move the work sequence along. Activating – a socially organized form of drawing the text into action in the setting (McCoy 1995) – involves distinctive procedures. Readers must find in the text objects beyond it that can be recognized as the object or objects to which the text refers. Practices of referring require distinctive kinds of looking and recognizing.

In the following segments of talk, readers visibly employ a strategy of looking and finding in the text what can be recognized as objects known in common that can be spoken about, or they employ a quite different strategy that goes from the text to the particulars of a local actuality known outside and beyond the text. Some employ both strategies, going back and forth, in a course of reading. Individuals' reading practices take shape in the context of a particular organizational process. Complex, varied, and emergent in actual settings and courses of action, reading practices are "situated" practices deserving further ethnographic attention and descriptive language. In a preliminary way the chapter demonstrates the importance of developing a range of research and analytic strategies that attend to people's practices of reading texts as integral to what happens in institutional settings.

Reading Practices as Social Courses of Action

The problem of how individual reading practices function in coordinating sequences of action is of central concern for institutional ethnographers. The ethnographic investigation of reading practices is also a productive line of inquiry for people working where organizational decision processes are of practical concern to them. Institutional ethnography takes its standpoint within institutional relations and local settings wherein people are actively aligning their actions and accomplishing what happens in a course of action. Institutional ethnographers have broached reading practices with analytic strategies that rely mainly on interviewing or experiential ethnography. Smith (1990b: 177–96) examines her own reading of Quentin Bell's account of Virginia Woolf's last days, showing how Bell's text organizes a reading that transforms Woolf's primary narrative into an ideological frame and an account of her as "mentally ill." Smith (1999, 2005, and chapter 9 here) takes up George Herbert Mead's conception of "the social act" and M.M. Bakhtin's of an "utterance" to examine speech and writing for how they coordinate individual consciousnesses. She develops further the experiential ethnographic strategy to explore her own "text–reader conversation" and to explicate the dialogic relation in which theory regulates local reading practices. Smith draws further analytic attention to institutional text–reader conversations (2006), demonstrating two research approaches. The first is interviewing the producer(s) and reader(s) of a text, locating their text work in an act-text-act sequence. The second approach is close examination of the text itself, uncovering traces of its production and what it projects as the organization of what comes next.

In an experiential ethnography of his own "front-line" social work practices, de Montigny (chapter 7) shows how, in the extended course of action producing an institutional text, a "sworn" report to the court, what he sees, says, and does is organized by the text's features that project its future reading by a judge, in a court setting, in the next institutional step in a sequence. McCoy (chapter 4) interviews a manager, accountant, and department chair in an institution in the midst of being restructured to explore how a newly introduced text is read by and plays a part in reshaping their work and diverse work knowledges.

What I am doing here is somewhat different. I am analysing reading practices as they happen in a sequence of "naturally occurring" talk. The sequence is elected officials' discussion of a developer's proposal. The transcript of the discussion provides evidence of how participants take up the features of texts as the discussion goes forward in talk. I was a participant observer in the meeting. I've extracted sections of the transcript and present those extracts as "exhibits" that open windows onto social organization and make available evidence of the speaker's reading of the diagram. Also, I am drawing on Bakhtin's (1986b) dialogic approach to language and social organization to examine reading practices as local courses of action that link reader–speakers, via their language practices, in a "chain of speech communication." Describing "speech genres," Bakhtin (ibid., elaborated by Smith 1999, 2006) gives us the distinction, however, between speech genres that are based on direct experience and those that are based in texts. Smith pursues the distinction for ethnographic practice, for exploring how language coordinates what people are doing, built on different "territories." Vološinov (1973) distinguished language that coordinates people's actions and sequences of action, relying on what people are doing in an interindividual territory of shared sense-based experience and language that coordinates what people do, think, and say in an interindividual territory mediated by texts (academic and professional discourses in journals, email, Internet media, and so on). In text, the stable form of the utterance is visible to all, carrying the objects, relations, actors, and resources upon which reader-speakers can draw upon in the course of action. At the same time as the reader reads, s/he responds to the text, bringing to the present setting its terms and order. Individuals take up differently a particular text as "utterance," reconstituting it in producing their own unique "utterance" in speech or in text. It is an active dialogic relation.

Smith's (2006) "institutional forms of text-reader practices" find the text's logic *within it*. These forms require reading practices that draw on resources of a specialized discourse within which the text was produced. Reading imposes a sequence out of time and place and categories empty of historical particulars. Conceptual "shells" operate to give a particular coherence and cling-wrap the reading to a discourse narrative that displaces both the reader's primary and other narratives she tries out. The reader occupies a distinct interindividual territory that is text-mediated. The "required" reading practices link the text via the reading into specific forms of organization – "into specific forms of social relations constituting the ruling apparatus of the specific social form" (Smith 1990b: 178) and authorizing the text as a factual account. Other forms of reading practices draw on different territories. Here's Smith on other forms:

> The *text of a map* never stands alone; it is always waiting for its connection with the local actualities it intends; the sense that it can make is incomplete without the local practice of referring, yet that reference is not contained within it ... It *relies on the actual terrain it can reference in the hands of the map-reader* ... Fictional maps mime the operation of a map that enables the complete sequence of reading and taking the map's instructions to look beyond it and recognize in that beyond-the-map the features it instructs the reader to find. They *instigate the motion of referring to a somewhere sometime, but it does not exist*; the map has no indexical complement ... [In fiction the] grammar projects the map's complement into the imaginary. (1999: 129, emphasis mine)

Reading the Text as a Map and Reading the Text as a Plan

Local practices of finding and identifying are required of readers of the diagram titled "proposed site plan." In the following extracts we see how some readers look *outside the diagram* to find and recognize the ravine's actual slopes – reading the diagram as a map. Others activate its surface features and draw on a discursive realm of already constituted constructs of land use planning they find *in the text* – reading the diagram in the institutional form of text–reader practices in this planning decision setting – as a plan. The peculiar finding, identifying and recognizing work of those in the setting is part of the task required of councillors in a public meeting where they engage in "general discussion." At this point, a developer or his planner has presented a proposal to develop a particular piece of land within the municipal boundaries, and residents or other "delegations" have spoken. During general discussion, the mayor and councillors speak about what they've heard, seen, and read, and may call on the planning director and lawyer for clarifications or other information.[3] Discussion focuses on the diagram (figure 8.1). It is a visual text that stands in for the actual land on which a developer proposes to build and for the proposed development. The diagram is read in multiple planning settings and is central to work that goes on in diverse processes. It is designed for intended multiple readings in the multiple institutional settings of a legislated and standardized process. In this setting, the diagram is part of a larger document municipal officials have in hand – the staff report. Compiled by the municipal planner, it incorporates information regarding the proposal from staff in various departments. Its organization carries concepts, categories, and visual markings as facts laid out for councillors' reading in this setting; the information in it is required by legislation to be made visible so that multiple particular participants – lawyers, planners, engineers, councillors – can look at the diagram, talk about what is in it, and do something.

Understanding how the text can be operated seems to require a technical expertise not equally available to everyone in public decision making. However, the production of the technical aspects of "site plans" is accomplished by readers' practices and talk interaction in planning settings. Technical information is not just transmitted by the text. The diagram provides evidence of a plan and a site and its features that people have to take up, look at and discuss, and make a decision about. The diagram adds theoretical information not available in a walk around the property. It integrates and assembles the operating conceptual procedures of diverse professional processes including surveying and mapping, law, real estate development, engineering, and construction. Produced in and for the administrative and governing processes of planning, it makes present specific types of information in its visual representations and not others. Taking it up and "reading" it as a plan is central to councillors' decision-making task.

The Reading–Text–Talk Relation in the Setting

The diagram is the authoritative text in the discussion. The site is already created, already constituted. At this point in the process, people who have not been involved in its technical preparation talk about the diagram and are making a decision about whether the developer's plan is "suitable for the site." They make their decision on the basis of the diagram's textual features that stand in for the actual physical land, and they rely on what they see in the diagram and the verbal statements of the developer's lawyer, planners, and citizens as a resource for "knowing" what they are seeing and making a decision about the "plan." The "facts" of the case are textually represented and are thus made present to everyone in the setting. The texts are already authorized accounts of the plan, but council must approve the accounts and pass a resolution approving in public a bylaw that will change what can be built on the land. As the people in this setting take up the diagram and attend to what is in it, they bring about a relation between the actual physical land worked up as "the site" in the texts, their own and other individual action, other texts and prescriptive legal texts, and the production of the routine, formalized features of planning. In order to do what counts as planning in this public setting, participants must engage with the technical details in the texts and what is said, and do something with them.

In this particular process, a developer wants council to approve a zone change in order to build several luxury homes in a small wooded ravine. A group of residents has come together to oppose the development and protect the ravine, which they experience and value in their everyday lives as a natural area and a tree buffer for the neighbourhood. They are asking that the plan be amended, that council add a condition to prevent development into the ravine. They suggest that houses be built on the high, flat area surrounding the ravine and the ravine itself left untouched. In order to enter this request textually into the proceedings, to make it something that can appear as a measurable and enforceable restriction, the residents refer to the diagram. It contains graphic features meant to represent topological features of the site. These take the form of wavy lines that are known as contour lines. Contour lines are to be read as showing changes in height or depth

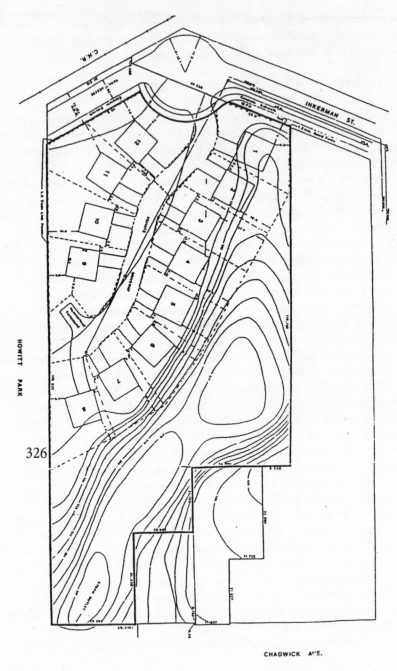

Figure 8.1 Proposed site plan: "326" marks contour line being discussed.

relative to other areas on the two-dimensional image. This is a way of representing three-dimensional features on a two-dimensional surface, a representation that can be reproduced and entered into multiple sites for discussion.

On their copy, the residents have indicated a contour line that they understand represents the "top" of the ravine. It is labelled "326" on the diagram. They have submitted a copy of the site plan with this 326 contour line highlighted in yellow marker. Their act of marking up the text brings into the setting evidence of their reading of the diagram and their response to it, presented in text as an alternative to the developer's representation of a proposed future state of affairs on the land.

The Diagram and Its Situated Readings

What happens at the city council meeting is an experience that will be familiar to people who have participated in decision processes in which they are excluded from the discussion that is part of actual decision making. Councillors appear to read the diagram "wrong." The planning director's reading instructs them in reading its surface features. Residents watch councillors unable to read the contour lines on the diagram as relevant to their decision. They see and hear speakers go from the local historical, sensually known world that is within someone's experience to an out-of-body, in-text world. While residents read the diagram as referencing the actual physical ravine to argue about what should not be developed there, councillors, the developer's lawyer, and the planning director operate the diagram at a purely textual level – as a plan. All have before them the same text. It can be treated by any one of them as present to the others in the same way it is to her or him. Speakers can refer to features of it, point them out to one another, ask questions about them. The text "regulates" in this way: its features are what is there in common for participants to refer to as present for everyone in the same way. The text carries in it and into the reader-speakers' consciousnesses and utterances the terms of a development and planning discourse in the form of lines and shapes in the diagram's visual representation of a plan.

The disjuncture between reading practices in the council meeting reflects and expresses the intersection in this setting of social relations – or interindividual territories of knowing and activity of fundamentally different kinds – in which "the site" and its features are known and figure differently. How individuals operate the diagram's features, and thus read *it* differently, enters into and shapes what they come to say, concerting the discussion and revealing their location in these different relations. And we can see just how the distinctive reading practices are integral to the talk as courses of action in which the speakers are engaged.

The Residents' Reading

In the council meeting, councillors have in front of them the texts, compiled in the staff report, required for development approval under the Planning Act – a description by planning staff of the rezoning proposal, the diagram labelled "Proposed Site Plan," and a list of legal clauses called "conditions of approval." The diagram shows the ravine by contour lines. This council also has a submission from the residents – a set of four recommendations and a duplicate of the diagram with the 326 foot contour line highlighted with yellow marker. The line marked in yellow on the residents' submission intends to foreground the actual physical features of the particular ravine. The residents are trying to express through the diagram their local perspective and experience of the ravine. Their reading assumes that the physicality of the ravine represented in the contour lines could be seen and treated as a basis for council to possibly alter the plan. They rely on the contour lines in the diagram as representing the actualities of what they know of the ravine in its wild wooded state, assigning a kind of temporally prior status to the wavy lines, a status prior to the text's other graphic features laid over them on the texts' surface. These are reading practices that look outside the text to find actual particulars to which the text's conventions can be connected (Smith 1999). Their reading locates the ravine's existence in present time and space. Mapping, however, is a procedure for moving from local historical settings of living to the in-text construction of an Archimedean, position-less space. That planners and councillors can speak competently about plans in the planning setting relies on the ability of the map-reader to read and reproduce the site plan from a subject position outside the local and particular and in an Archimedean point.[4]

Councillors' Readings

The following extracts of council's discussion (exhibits 8.1–8.6) make it clear that the diagram's features as a plan are powerful in coordinating "political" decisions. Councillors work back and forth between the textual realities presented in the text and the legal course of action they are putting together. They look at and take up the diagram's surface features and orient to an in-common in-text world. They read its features as presenting evidence of "the site" and "the plan," which participants then can operate to warrant their discussion, consideration, and decision.

The diagram presents standard planning-relevant features that can be treated as there for everyone in the same way. Participants' readings of those features coordinate how the discussion goes forward. How standard features of the diagram are operated in the talk is how the text regulates and is powerful in this and multiple other settings. How the text coordinates the talk in a setting as authoritative, impenetrable, is part of how it operates to produce participants' readings and talk – and here also council's evaluative work – regarding it as a plan.

Vološinov (1973) suggests that we can identify particular authoritative forms of reporting (oral and written) which express the active dialogic of the social relations in which they are situated constituents. They are well worked out forms for assimilating various aspects of reality in words (1973: 320–1). In the analysis of historically concrete and living language, we must, he says, attend to the way speakers formulate in everyday speech an interpretive frame for reconceptualizing everyday realities. We must orient to the ways the assimilation of another's utterance does not simply provide "information," "directions," "rules," or "models." Rather, we must attend to the ways it determines the basis of our ideological interrelations with the world it represents as it performs authoritative discourse. A feature of authoritative regulating and organizational discourse is that it is impenetrable. It cannot be shifted or changed. What I am showing here is just how this impenetrability is visibly accomplished in local and mundane active utterances including procedures of reading.

Councillor Y's Reading

Councillor Y is addressing the developer's lawyer, who has presented the proposal. When Councillor Y is talking, he is looking at the diagram. He reads the surface features of the diagram as a fully external object and display that is accessible in the same way to anyone. He wants to establish the different graphic features of the text in hand as properties *of a plan* and reads contour and dotted lines as equally available to surface manipulation as the "dividing line" between "properties" and "parkland."

Exhibit 8.1 Councillor Y's reading

Councillor Y: Mr H [developer's lawyer], I don't know if you're familiar with what is termed the proposed site plan? ... that Mr M [resident] [presented, with the highlighted line on it] ... are you ... [Mr H replies "Yes" as Councillor Y continues] ... The 326 foot contour line that runs through two of the homes as I see this, possibly three, touches on a third one ... this yellow line on the single sheet ... what I don't understand, Mr H, is if the neighbours are in general agreement, uh I don't see how they can be, and I'm confused with this because they're saying they're in general agreement but they want the development to leave the land below the 326 foot line free, and yet it's not just the 326 foot line that I see here, you've got a dotted line on this diagram that seems to come alongside the ends of the properties as I look at it. I may be incorrect in looking at it but that's what I see. In other words, the park area that is shown here is quite a bit less than what is below the 326 foot line? (ll. 58–72)

Councillor Y picks out features in the text. Not confounding diagram with actuality, he operates it as a kind of virtual reality itself constituting the site and its features as shared objects of reference. He draws on the resources of zoning and land use categories to "see" homes, properties, park land, and lines dividing private and public properties. Lines *do things* in the present-for-everyone pure text moment: "the 326 foot contour line ... *runs through* two of the homes" (he can read the rectangles as substantial objects); the "dotted line *come[s] alongside* the ends of the properties." This talk differs from talk that addresses the textuality of the residents' diagram – "this yellow line on the single sheet." The yellow line is not a feature of a plan, as are the contour and dotted lines. It is a line that is not officially drawn. Nor does the residents' "single sheet" have in his reading the status of the "proposed site plan" that is part of the staff report. On the other hand, Councillor Y's "You've got a dotted line on this diagram ... I may be incorrect in looking at it but that's what I see" displays the ambiguous status of the dotted line on the diagram in terms of its being a plan, but also its availability as a feature of a plan and a product of the city staff's work. Councillor Y talks about what is "shown here," and he can "see here" using the deictic "here" to reference features appearing in-text that are equally available to him and others.

Here is the significance of multiple identical copies of the diagram/ site plan in constituting a common reference among speakers. Speakers can evaluate what proponents and opponents of the developer's plan have to say in the terms of the lines on the diagram. The lines provide the properly constituted properties of the site and the plan for development. Roweis (1988) views the technologies of planning and design professions as extended processes that "manipulate messy ground surfaces to fit to human projects." I am making the distinction between the local historical process that is necessarily always from within someone's experiencing in an ongoing course of living and the abstracted, textually-inscribed relations that position the subject outside the local and particular and in an Archimedean point. The lines on the diagram provide the ground for, and coordinate, practices of reading that require taking that position. Councillor Y's reading demonstrates the confounding effect that the contour lines and the ambiguous dotted lines present to reading the diagram as a plan. We can see Councillor Y's attempt to find its coherence as a plan and to produce a standard reading course falter and veer off.

The Lawyer's Reading

In his response to Councillor Y's quasi-question regarding the dotted lines, the developer's lawyer orients himself to the peculiarity of the diagram as a plan, but one that temporarily establishes a present onto which a future state is projected. His hesitations ("if … if," "a … a,""all, all, all," and "yes … the …") display a practice of reading different possibilities into plans. What is represented as already there is given. But representation of what will happen on the actual land is open to negotiation. The lawyer is negotiating the plan's properties throughout. Negotiation will enable his client to go ahead with the development in some form or another and make a profit on his investment. The lawyer's talk evidences a reading of the plan as flexible. Its features are not fixed, but the plan must be considered and dealt with in this setting.[5] He has an intimate working knowledge of what is going on where its representation is being read and discussed in other settings. His reading references this other routine course of action and negotiation that is going on outside the public setting in which his client is "quite willing to settle on a line."

The lawyer's reading practices and talk orient to the character of council deliberations in which planning texts are meant to be interpreted in the terms of a predetermined schema focusing on a development

---

Exhibit 8.2 The lawyer's reading

DEVELOPER'S LAWYER: Oh quite so. Quite so. The dotted lines, if … if this
is to proceed under … [the plan of subdivision, the lots would be] 50
by 100 feet. If we can work out a method without putting it under the
Condominium Act, then the, those would all be parts 1 through 3 – 4
through 12 on a reference plan and each of those parts would then be
conveyed to separate people. Instead of the condominium corporation owning that, individual people would own that. Now, my client
is quite happy, or quite willing to settle on a line below which no construction will go, but it may be not necessarily always the 326 line. At
some points it could be the 326, but when you get up to number 1 it
may have to switch to the 324, 323, that house may be farther down
the hill. That's all. But to arbitrarily pick out of the air 326 and put a
yellow line on it and say "We don't want anything below that" is a …
a bit difficult to deal with, because you can't necessarily site all, all,
all your houses.
COUNCILLOR Y: Right, I understand that. In effect are you saying that
the dividing line between the parkland and the development is the
dotted line?
DEVELOPER'S LAWYER: Yes … the bottom … (ll. 73–93)

---

outcome; that some future favourable to his client should be a product
of these deliberations. He does not orient to the features of the diagram as fixed, as either referencing a current or a future actuality, but
to its relating of a present to a projected future in which the phrase
"a line below which no construction will go" may be fixed but will
not be "arbitrarily picked out." Reading the text in its present state,
and with the council's decision-making task in mind, the lawyer puts
forward the possibility of a modified future that also attends to features of the present diagram, but "not always the 326 line." He orients
momentarily to the diagram and the residents' yellow line as referencing the actual ravine. However, in doing so he is introducing into the
discussion what is beyond and not represented in the diagram, namely,
the developer's (his client's) practical problems with developing the
real physical land of a ravine in all its local historical messiness. The
developer's lawyer orients to his client's job to "site all … your
houses" somewhere on "the hill," and to the neighbours' interference

in that business, not to site features to be read in the diagram. But here is the coordinative effect of the lines on the diagram highlighted in Councillor Y's reading. Councillor Y can be seen to still be trying to establish the representational status of the dotted line for his reading, hence to establish its character as a feature of a plan that can be read by everyone as against an unofficial or unstable line. The lawyer takes up this possible reading practice for the moment and capitulates to Councillor Y's insistence on establishing the dotted line as a feature of the plan.[6]

The problem of "siting" all the houses can be resolved on the diagram for this particular moment. Whether to use the dotted lines, which would indicate parts on a subdivision "reference plan," would be part of the negotiative work being done – and to be done by the lawyer and developer – with the city's planners and other professionals outside the council setting. The lawyer relies on his working knowledge of this sphere of activities to align his reading practice for the present setting and task.

The Planning Director's Reading

The planning director is looking at the diagram with the yellow line on it, but when he speaks of its features he uses legitimate zoning categories and descriptive terms – "units," "exclusive use areas," "open space" – to read features of the diagram that have already been assigned a determinate representational value as part of a plan. "Ravine" is not a standard discursive category or diagrammatic feature of plans. Councillor Y's phrase "ravine or passive parkland" in his question to the planning director marks the lack of diagrammatic conventions in planning for "showing" the ravine as a proper category that would provide for its reference as an object and a feature of a plan. Councillor Y is still trying to establish the status of the dotted line as a graphic feature integral to a plan.

Exhibit 8.3 The planning director's reading

COUNCILLOR Y: I'd like to pursue the question with Mr. V [the director of planning] about this dotted line and if what is below that does provide about 1.1 acres of ravine or passive parkland, or is it a lot less than that and in which case how much less?

PLANNING DIRECTOR: [inaudible] … drops down, so that's the beginning of the ravine. The 326 contour line, uh, represents that. If you look at the plan and you look at the units that have been designed on the plan as exclusive use areas, those areas extend further south or further down from the yellow line and those exclusive use areas would be exclusively used for the units, for the occupants, so therefore the backs of those dotted line areas would not form part and parcel of the open space. So and I if … just by taking a look at what's left over, and just eyeballing it, it looks like it'd probably be an acre even if that, that would be open space. (ll. 128–43)

The planning director finds and recognizes the 326-foot contour line as representing "the beginning of the ravine." He recognizes the diagrammatic convention of representing by contour lines, but he is almost exclusively oriented to the diagram as a plan. Discursive objects, "exclusive use areas," extend "south or further *down from the yellow line.*" The planning director is operating the diagram almost exclusively in a textual mode, at the surface of the text.

The planning director produces for those present a procedure for reading the textual surface features of the diagram as a plan. He takes the text and tells how to see its features and how they are intended to be seen: "If you look at the plan and you look at the units that have been designed on the plan as exclusive use areas, those areas extend further south or further down from the yellow line." His phrase "designed on the plan" relies on and refers back to the extensive work processes that have put this plan together before it arrived in this setting. He is not talking about the actual physical land, but past and future together in the present *as* the plan. The categories of "exclusive use area" and "open space" are standard devices for categorizing land and for distributing private and public rights to land use. With regard to their mandate to mediate the social use of land, councillors must rely on the technical and professional competence of the municipality's staff to produce planning texts for their decisions. That competence and professional expertise is also embodied in the texts. In this way, the issue of individuals' competent readings and work with texts in doing planning may arise, but not the text-concerted organization of the process itself.

The lines the planning director reads as representing "exclusive use areas" carry in them the economic construct "future occupants." It is an important construct his reading finds in the text, one that the de-velopment industry relies on. In the public discourses of development, various participants describe people as having needs that the indus-try is meeting. Future homebuyers, owners, and occupants and their lifestyles are a textual feature of plans, active constituents of develop-ment discourse as well as the organization of research, marketing, real estate promotion and sales, and planning. These other work processes produce resources (statistics, etc.) that, in planning settings and in the news media, development industry representatives can routinely draw on to speak *for* "future homebuyers" and "future homeowners and oc-cupants." Here, the director pulls them and their needs out of the text, introducing them into the deliberations as constituents of the plan. The planning director's practices can thus also read the dotted lines in the same way the developer's lawyer does, referencing the sphere of nego-tiating they both are in outside the setting which could result in those lines representing fixed, surveyed individual lots for homes constitut-ing "a subdivision" plan.

With their consciousnesses aligned by the planning director's instruc-tive reading, all but one of the councillors then read and operate the diagram's features as those of a plan, read in this purely textual mode. The diagram supplies the graphic features required under the Plan-ning Act. Local reading practices establish in it the known-in-common evidence they can find and recognize as sufficient for council's task of "considering" it as a plan and evaluating whether "the site" is "suitable for the proposed use."

Councillor L's Reading

Councillor L takes for granted the diagram's property of bringing together the site's "given" features and a future proposed state, mak-ing them present for her so that she can formulate the decision-making problem facing council as "we have development below the 326 foot line" (l. 255). She reads the contour lines as representing a physical actuality in the present, as a map. But choosing the 326 line, as the resi-dents suggest, would undermine the diagram's character as a "good" plan, one that council can deal with: "We have development below the 326 foot line." Choosing it would mean that "our site plan is no good." Council should change the plan; it is simply a matter of picking a line "a little bit further down" … "We have to pick another number" (ll. 254–7).

Exhibit 8.4 Councillor L's reading

COUNCILLOR L: There's only one problem with that. If we say no development below the 326 foot contour line, our site plan is no good because
we have development below the 326 foot line. So we have to change
that number. We have to pick another number. 320 or something a little
bit further down. Maybe (inaudible) can comment on that.

MR V: Your worship, through you Councillor L has raised a very good
point. If we take the plan as presented, and uh, we're assuming fairly
large units here in this development, and we're also assuming a fairly
large exclusive use area. These are not your standard townhouses or
your standard townhouse lots, these are single-family condominium
developments and they will equal a fairly large single-family house on
a fairly large single-family lot. I don't see how we can accommodate
a plan of twelve units picking the 326 contour line because that line
goes into three units and also the recommendation was that no patios
or anything else be constructed within that and if you look at unit
number 3 and 4 and 5 and 6 and that would preclude them having any
patio or anything else in that area and that would make it very difficult
for this plan to proceed. (ll. 253–72)

Councillor L slides between reading the diagram through to a ravine
and reading it as a text whose features as a plan can be altered as
part of council's decision-making task. She recognizes the interchange
between reading it as a map and reading it as a plan. As a plan, the
diagram exists for her as a reality itself – simply changing the number
to manipulate its problematic surface features is the way to go to get
on with the task at hand. The pure in-text possibility of her orientation – "pick another number" – at the same time references the actual
physicality of the ravine. She also reads the diagram as a map, referencing the physicality of the ravine through the contour lines. However, she sets aside the fact that the 326 line marks the "top" of the
ravine, which residents want to preserve whole, pointing to the haz-
ard of picking the 326 and proposing that councillors pick a different
line, a lower number, that would "accommodate the developer's plan
of twelve units" – the text as a plan with recognizable development
objects designed on it.

The planning director operates the diagram again at the purely textual level to take up Councillor L's reading and her "very good point": "that line [that the residents want recognized as a feature of the plan] goes into three units ... That would make it very difficult for this plan to proceed." Here we can see the power of the lines on the diagram to shape its reading as a plan, designed for this sequence of action. It is a property of specialized or technically produced texts in decision settings that professionals and elected officials can routinely find in them resources for their defence, and advocate for them, in this pure in-text mode.[7]

The Mayor's Reading

In this exhibit, reader-speakers operate both specialized visual and written texts in intertextual work in the organizational setting. The mayor reads the text as a properly produced plan, in which contour lines are not constituent features. When Councillor Y is trying to get the planning director to suggest how to operate the surface features of the diagram by writing something into the legal clauses in the staff report called "the conditions," to "safeguard the ravine which remains," the mayor intervenes.[8] Councillor Y wants to operate the dotted line as a constituent feature of the plan through a condition to "allow the development ... [and] safeguard the ravine which remains" – literally whatever land is left over below and after "whatever line there has to be" is picked. The mayor reads the diagram's features as those of a pure text plan, a reading that sidelines other readings.

Exhibit 8.5 The mayor's reading

COUNCILLOR Y: Well, your worship, I was going to ask [the planning director] a question somewhat along the same lines but somewhat different. Mr V, what could we write into the conditions ... what could we write into the conditions to safeguard the ravine, below whatever line there has to be ... in order to allow the condominium development [?] and the line that has to be is this dotted line that I asked [the developer's lawyer] about. What can we write into the conditions to safeguard the ravine which remains? [3-second pause]

MR V: The only thing we could do would be, uh, to pick a contour line and put it in as a condition – an agreed-to contour line ... um and I'm having difficulty trying to pick one, because the contours "are not uh that straight, they do curve over as you get further over to Inkerman Street and they really drop off there. So it's ...

MAYOR: The trouble is, we're trying to redraw the thing tonight in the council meeting.

MR V: That's correct. (ll. 274–92)

Councillor Y treats the text of condition clauses as if they reference the diagram and have a direct intertextual relation with it. He reads the diagram as if it holds in it actual physical features and a future reality which legal clauses in the text could act upon to "safeguard" them. The planning director's hesitation to "pick a line" (ll. 305–9, 313) marks the disjuncture between two orders of relations in which the physical site is linked to the text.

Where the residents try to express their concerns through the contour lines, the text-mediated relations of planning are organized through and reference other surface features of the "proposed site plan." In these relations, graphic marks on the diagram are not treated equally as constituent features of a plan. Different reading procedures take up different graphic features, using these to link the text to the site and thereby producing differing, conflicting, outcomes. One procedure references a world in which the "natural" contours of a ravine hold its features and are prefigured in a future state: the other procedure references and prefigures properties, units, exclusive-use areas, parkland, and so on.

The councillors' textual mode of reading emerges in the course of action which "implements" the city's land use policies and manages the relations between private land owners, the development industry, the province, and a general "public interest." It is an institutional and organizational mode. The readings I have examined here rely on the individual's ability to recognize the planning-relevant marks on the page as a plan's features properly presenting a future state of affairs and also on an understanding of how the diagram "works" in the decision processes regulating and distributing rights regarding uses of land. We see the organization of the council, its meeting, and its consideration and decision through the site-plan diagram which is embedded in different discourses. The visual text is the interactional object in a series of procedures that produce the land–text link in numerous settings. It is these reading procedures in the public council meeting that produce the site–text link authorizing and standing in for various activities connected to the visual text. The mayor's "The trouble is, we're trying to redraw the thing" refers to and makes present for others in the setting a proper separation and coordination of activities regarding the production and readings of the diagram in an ideal and legally defined planning process. In that ideal process, the division of labour is the production of texts by experts and their reading by councils. The text's features are given and read in the textual mode. However, also in this particular institutional mode, the physical land of the ravine that the residents and Councillor P reference is unavailable.

Councillor P's Reading

Councillor P's reading is the exception. He orients to looking and language practices. He sees the differences in how people are operating the text. He seems to be trying to operate the diagram to express the features of the real ravine, and literally does not have the words. Councillor P is saying something along the lines of "We should not be talking about the diagram here in front of us as a site plan. Site plans should only exist as objects for our attention in sequences of action that occur later on in the process. If we treat the dotted line as a feature of a site plan, we are then going into development." Councillor P is pointing out that councillors are reading the lines on the diagram standing in for houses as real things, and yet these lines are not. His reading of the text is opposite that of Councillor L, who calls it "our site plan." His reading practice draws on the sense-based interindividual territory of experience where the wooded ravine exists; he can read by referencing that experiential realm, so that in this setting the contour lines figure and the text is not a plan as such. This reading allows him to say, "We should be talking about altitude or the sea level."

Exhibit 8.6 Councillor P's reading

COUNCILLOR P: I was happy with the wording when it was the 326 contour line, but now we've gone into the dotted line. I'm not happy with the wording "below" because we are dealing with a site plan, and when we look at the plan and when we're talking about the word "below"

> the dotted line, we are then going into development. We should be talking about the altitude or the sea level or … it should be reworded. We're directly into development if we're talking about a site plan.
>
> MAYOR: Alderman L?
>
> COUNCILLOR L: Just a comment further on Councillor W's point …
> (ll. 411–21)

While the diagram is the same for all participants in the setting, Councillor P can read the text as a map *or* a plan. He is also displaying an ability to see how participants shift between reading practices that operate the diagram as a map and reading it as a plan. He can also locate and envisage those distinct forms of representation in different courses of action or different moments in the same course of action. He's able to identify the kind of language that you use to work those representations and he is showing what happens if you mix them up. This is what he is trying to make visible when he says: "I was happy with the wording when it was the 326 contour line." It's as if there are for him two different texts: Text 1 is a kind of geographical map which is directly referential to an experienced physicality, in which the relevant markings to-be-operated are contour lines, sea levels etc.; "but now we've gone into the dotted line," this is a different kind of text. Text 2, in which dotted lines show and display the features of buildings and structures, facilities and works, is an institutional text designed for site plan readings and development outcomes. Councillor P is trying to show how language operates and how the text is organizing the council's discussion; how people are talking about the lines on the diagram in a way that their discussion is "directly into development." Councillor P does not know how to talk about the problem of language and texts in the council meeting. He does know he is "not happy" about it. No one takes up his utterance. The mayor directs discussion back to Councillor L, who, by referring back to a prior speaker, clinches Councillor P's intervention as irrelevant in the ongoing discussion.

In attending to how texts in front of councillors produce an orientation to a future state which is "development," Councillor P can be seen to want to change councillors' reading practices and, as a consequence, to change how the discussion goes forward. He makes visible, but not hearable by other councillors in the flow of their talk, the temporal disjuncture between relational sequences and their objects that collide in this setting.

Conclusion

We've seen reading practices that take up the diagram in planning terms, as a plan, and those that read it like a map. I've examined reading practices as courses of action. We can see two different kinds of reading procedures as readers go back and forth to draw on resources in the text and in other's utterances in a setting, on the discursive constructs of a course of action and a particular task, and on readers' experiential work knowledge of worlds or spheres of activities in which they can reference past and future acts. Here, the specific reading practices are articulated to a course of ongoing, face-to-face talk that shapes and is shaped by them. The institutional forms of reading can be seen to proceed to:

1 shift the referencing of the contour lines on the diagram away from a reality of physical particulars (land);
2 assign them status as alterable;
3 confine them to the text's two-dimensional surface;
4 substitute the (empty) terms and categories of discourse ("properties," "exclusive use areas," "units," "park land," "open space") that are the legitimate properties of a site plan, and move into aligning with others to speak about recognizable features in the text;
5 recognize, identify, and point to surface features as familiar and sufficiently present for a setting-specific task (decision); and
6 locate what is being accomplished in an organizational sequence of work.

Reading practices can be seen to translate the terms of the discourse for the specific task in this setting. Readers also align their individual readings for their co-consideration and decision. They fill the "shells" of the professional and institutional lexicon, picking out the graphical markings in the text as they bring the terms of the discourse into their utterances to accomplish a council's "consideration and decision" task. They establish the lines as providing evidence of the text as a text that is suitable for the decision-making task and, in doing so, for the particular institutional function and work in the setting. This procedural form of reading that goes forward exhibits a more general form, one that aligns reader-speakers' courses of action to:

1 assign definite status or meaning within an interpretive frame given by discourse to graphical marks on the text;

2 set aside other readings;
3 locate the text in a temporal sequence of organizational work; and
4 treat what has been established as in the text as sufficient for the
   task in this present setting.

Alternative reading practices whose procedural form is, first, to assign
prior status to [wavy] lines that conflict with the categories of the development planning discourse ("units" etc.) and, second, to locate a temporal sequence that runs counter to and out of sync with the ongoing
organization do not work. Here the procedure is rendered useless by
the mayor's "The trouble is, we're trying to redraw the thing tonight in
the council meeting."

Here is Dorothy Smith on different ways of referring: "Referring to
an object is a social act, performed in actual settings of people's activities, and producing for those present what is first named, or pointed to,
or referred to in some other way, as what is to be dialogically achieved
in its 'recognition' by another, whether the actual other of the local setting or the virtual others of text-mediated discourse" (1999: 128). We've
seen how to make visible reading practices in the context of ongoing
courses of organizational action such as a "discussion" period of a
meeting. We see how, as reader-speakers go back and forth, they use the
text, employing these different types of reading practices that operate
the text's surface differently. Institutional procedures come into view
as referencing established concepts, categories, and frames of planning
discourse, bringing them in ordinary ways into the organizational task
in the setting and the work process being put together. The alternative
or non-institutional procedures – those that do not fit a local historical experience to the governing framework and categories – work from
surface features to an actuality of particulars the reader draws on, a
resource of experience, knowing, and cognitive awareness outside of
language, texts, and resources of institutional discourse or diagrammatic representations.

I have aimed to explore ways to analytically describe reading practices as courses of action integral to people's work in organizational
processes and institutional action. A goal was also to make visible distinctive procedural forms for reading in actual situated practices in
action. The practical consideration has been to open up ways to explore
reading practices in workplaces where they are taken for granted
yet central to how organizational and institutional work gets done
and to how specialized forms of reading integral to talk accomplish

setting-specific tasks and institutional outcomes. Laying out to view the procedural forms for assembling and organizing the particulars of experience into "factual accounts" for accomplishing organizational tasks provides a critical analytic description. As a practical matter, reading practices can be explored as procedures intrinsic to organization and decision making, opening them to intervention and change.

Further, I want to offer more general ways to explore institutional action and organization as it is *going on* and being put together in people's actual activities and work in organizational decision settings and processes. Investigating how work processes are governable and governed by standardized textual practices, including reading practices, can show us the essential power of texts in decision processes and explicate the operations of their textual technologies and procedures. Here we can see in individually unique reading practices the diagram's power to orient and shape readers' consciousnesses, organize readings and talk, and coordinate the knowledge and actions of even diversely located co-readers of the same text. That power is extended when texts are replicated for use in multiple settings of work.

When notions like "decisions" and "decision making" are attributed to organizations or institutions to describe what goes on and how they operate, people and their actual practices disappear. This close-up look at different ways of reading a text brings into view the vivid detail of how development decisions are actually made as individuals align their activities in these very ordinary and observable ways in going about accomplishing their work. Over two decades ago, Sally Hacker (1988) pointed out the problems that researchers doing critical ethnographies of organizations and institutions have when trying to get into an organization's inner workings and finding out how professional discourses of science and engineering shape organizational "acts." The way of looking at institutional practices offered here presents possibilities for investigation of decision-making processes that environmentalists and other critics of contemporary institutions could use. In policy studies or in studies of organizations and decision making, these acts are usually treated as acts of individuals or of the organizations as bodies or entities in themselves. The ethnographic strategy used in this research focuses on reading practices. Such an approach shows that accurate accounts of textual practices and their function in decision processes and organizational action can be accomplished by situating them back into the settings of their use and by observing the relevant reading practices in action.

Bringing to the analytic project the conception of different interindividual spheres of activity that people can draw on as resources for producing their spoken and written "utterances" is useful to exploring and describing reading practices in contemporary situations in which readings seem to confront one another on fundamentally ontological grounds. The concept of distinct territories of experience, knowing, and working in language can be put to work examining different readings of the same text that often divide people and groups in organizations. Doing this ethnography of situated reading practices can bring into view different organizationally relevant procedural forms of reading and working with texts that are operating in an institution. It can also bring into view how each relies on distinctive yet connected forms of work organization within the same organization (staff versus managerial forms of knowing organizational work is a common division that emerges; faculty versus administration in universities is another example). Exploring such distinctions within work organizations might give us interesting and useful insights into just how specialized yet mundane forms of reading–text–talk interaction function in institutional and organizational action.

NOTES

1 This chapter is based on a section of my "Rendering the Site Developable:
   Texts and Local Government Decision Making in Land Use Planning,"
   in Campbell & Manicom (1995), and on a paper prepared for the annual
   meetings of the Canadian Sociology and Anthropology Association
   (Ottawa, 2009), for the session "Producing Textual Realities." I thank
   Dorothy Smith for encouraging me to revisit this work and for
   comments that assisted me in revising it for this collection.
2 I am interested in the application of what I am learning to community
   organization action. My experience working with community organizations
   in a five-year community-based research program funded by the Social Sciences and Humanities Research Council under its Community-University
   Research Alliances (CURA) program and work with groups on organizational change suggests the usefulness of looking closely at reading practices
   in organizational decision processes. The CURA took up various partner
   organization managers and staff researchers' concerns about how to access
   and influence policy – and decision-making processes. In a project with
   collaborating organizations working on rural women's employment and
   poverty, we interviewed our individual partners, managers in their "sister" organizations, councillors, mayors, and social service managers about

their work. We made maps of government decision making for a guide for community organizations on government services and mapped how local governments work and how to make presentations to them. We did not explore ethnographically the texts and reading practices that are so powerful in organizing and accomplishing governing decisions.

3 A subsequent sequence of councillors' work in this setting constitutes "the decision": the mayor will call for a "motion," a councillor will "make a motion" to approve, refuse, or defer the application, and a vote is taken and recorded.

4 There are other texts that participants orient to in the discussion, including a set of four "condition clauses" that the residents are recommending. In the meeting, the developer's lawyer disagrees with two recommendations the residents make, and proposes a new clause, "or such other binding arrangement satisfactory to the City Solicitor," which is accepted. The future that would be represented on a revised diagram could be very different from that represented in the present diagram.

5 The lawyer orients to the deadlines within which the future projected on the plan or some other future to be determined at that meeting must be dealt with within 30 days. Should they not be accepted, both non-decision and refusal can be appealed. The developer can appeal to the Ontario Municipal Board (OMB) for a hearing *de nova* in which the documents are brought in and reviewed by the board chairman, and the board's decision is final. The lawyer relies on this resource of a sphere of work external to this public setting – activities that are a resource for his "quite willing to settle" statement.

6 In conversation the city's planner told me the dotted line "doesn't mean anything. It just shows what it would look like, what the lot lines would be," if the plan was for standard homes on lots in a subdivision rather than a condominium, which it is at present. Technically, the dotted line has no legal status on this diagram that accompanies an application for a zone change to allow a condominium development. But notice that the developer is looking to "work out a method without putting it under the Condominium Act" (ll. 75–6). Unhooking the plan from the condominium process and instead hooking it up with the subdivision approval process would have currently unknown and different outcomes in the ravine. The subdivision process is prefigured in the dotted lines. Subdivision is attractive in terms of its investment value to the developer; it has fewer restrictions, does not require public participation, involves fewer "up front" finances for the developer, and, notably, it produces a "reference plan" through which individual lots can be sold and the burden of financing is borne gradually by future home builders and buyers.

7 In other accounts of what goes on in the business of land-use planning and decision making, this has generally been seen in terms of the "dilemma"

of the planner's "role" that individual planners experience or the political "alliances" bureaucrats form with business interests in the "informal process" – or "systematic corruption." This coordinative and concerting business of planning has also been a subject of activists' theories.

8 Legally, councils can amend the conditions as part of their decision-making mandate, as it is "the city" or "the municipality" that imposes conditions on a development via legal clauses. This is what the residents wanted council to do using the 326 contour line. The diagram, the product of many hired professional experts doing the developer's technical work with "the city," stands in for his "plan." The legal "condition" clauses, the work of city staff, stand in for the planning administrative work of "the city."

9 Discourse as Social Relations: Sociological Theory and the Dialogic of Sociology[1]

DOROTHY E. SMITH

Drawing on the thinking of George Herbert Mead, V.N. Vološinov and Mikhail Bakhtin, Dorothy Smith has conceptualized language as coordinating individuals' consciousnesses (Smith 2005). In moving that concept to explore how texts coordinate, she has introduced the notion of a text–reader *conversation. In this new version of the chapter originally published by the University of Toronto Press in 1999 in* Writing the Social, *Smith explicates practices of reading in dialogue with texts of sociological theory. One of these is an experiential ethnography of her own reading of a text by Anthony Giddens. She draws on Mikhail Bakhtin's emphasis on dialogue and dialogic, how utterances are always actively in dialogue with the pre-established discourse that frames them. Smith's concept of* text–reader conversation *extends this line of thinking to understand reading a text as a dialogue in which the reader plays both parts, taking on the given words of the text in organizing her consciousness and at the same time bringing the text into dialogue with where she, the reader, is and what she is connecting it up with.*

Here Smith brings concepts, knowledge, and theoretical discourse into the same world as people's activities, laying them open to ethnographic attention, exploration, and explication as actual practices. She shows language as "an actually happening, actually performed local organization of consciousness." This fundamental insight – that language coordinates consciousnesses in ongoing courses of action – catapults discourse out of "textual security" so it can be seen as a sphere of activity.

Smith builds a conceptual scaffolding – around Bakhtin's active utterance and speech genres in particular – allowing us to see how discourse regulates in and through local practices in which texts are central. *She shows how a reader must activate and respond to what is in a theory text and how its discourse reduces what can be heard, read, seen, and so on – how it reduces and "manages" the "heteroglossia of society." The chapter gives two demon-strations, each showing how experiential ethnography of reading practices can proceed. Both examine how the text goes to work in the reader as they are activated in text–reader conversations. One draws on her own experience of how reading a sociological text managed the heteroglossic world of other texts she'd read, subduing their voices, bringing this text's theory, as utterance, into dialogue (or resistance or confrontation) with other texts she was reading at the time. This intertextuality is activated in the moments of text-reader activities: practices of remembering, noticing, looking out for, passages that bear upon it, that it bears upon. She shows how text's theory as organizer of her attention and reflection structures the intertextual dialogue.*

If as sociologists we begin as ourselves, active in the local settings of our living, we know sociology as we live it, as its readers, writers, speakers, and hearers. We are in the middle of it, in our reading in a library, in an office, at home. Our reading is active, responsive, attentive to possible uses, reactive to what we identify as error, anger sometimes, pleasure sometimes. Though we rarely if ever attend to sociological discourse in this way, it is always in practice being discovered as an actual course of action projecting into what comes next – teaching, writing, speaking at a conference. The process of writing sociology at particular times and in particular places engages actively with the discourse; it references and is in dialogue with our reading. Explicit references are only a small part of it; it is deeply embedded in and draws on language uses as they come to hand already determined historically by their uses in multiple disciplinary sites – and from beyond the discipline. For, of course, sociological language is not clean. It is contaminated in multiple ways by sociology's dialogue with the heteroglossia of contemporary society. Sociology pulls other forms of language in to do its discursive work, language that trails with it a debris of meaning from its original site. Reciprocally, the language of sociological discourse goes out into the world and is taken over to do other and others' work.

This paper draws on Mikhail M. Bakhtin's theory of the novel, of language, and of speech genres to investigate discourse as social organization. It takes up this project as an investigation into sociology as a discourse because I know it as an "insider"; I am a participant; I know it as a local practice in my own life; my experiences provide the main resource for this study. In this I move away from Foucault's (1972) conception of discourse. Brilliant as it is, it accredits the stasis of the text. In so doing, he displaces the materiality of the text as in print, on screen, or other mode in which it enters local settings of reading, watching, etc. I have no thought of returning to the older history of ideas that Foucault sets aside. But here the materiality of the text, its replicability and hence iterability, is key to addressing discourse as actual social relations between reading, writing, speaking, hearing subjects – actual people, you and me. Just as in Marx's *Capital* the commodity mediates the concrete and particularized labour of the producers and the abstract and universalized relations of exchange, the printed or electronic and hence many-times-reproducible text mediates between the actual people engaged in their particular local activities as participants in a discourse and the intertextual organization of the discourse.

Bakhtin differentiates between two kinds of speech genres: utterances in and of direct encounters between people and those mediated by texts which he calls "secondary speech genres" (Bakhtin 1986b). Though all areas of human activity involve language, speech genres "originate" in distinct "spheres of activity" and secondary speech genres/discourses are just as much spheres of activity as the specialized speech genre of pickpockets (Maurer 1981). Discourse, as the term will be used here, is recognized as relations coordinated by texts, a secondary speech genre in Bakhtin's terms, but discourse is also itself a sphere of activity, of the doings of actual people who are actively engaged in utterances, their own and others. Hence, in this paper, discourse is explored as what we are part of and active in, including our local practices of thinking, writing, and listening to what other participants have to say and reading texts, our own and others. I want to lift the discourse off the page and give it presence in the everyday. I want to step outside the artifice of the text's stasis and rediscover discourse as an actually happening, actually performed, local organization of consciousness.

David Maurer's (1981) account of pickpockets' "talk" shows us a speech genre viewed in relation to a sphere of activity:

> When a professional criminal learns his occupation, as, for instance, thievery, with specialization as a pickpocket, he starts with the very specialized techniques of pocket picking in terms of a specific language. More than that, he constantly thinks of his occupation in terms of that language and discusses his work with other pickpockets in terms of their common language. In other words, his entire occupational frame of reference is both technical and linguistic, and the language is fundamental not only to the perpetuation of the craft of thievery but to its practice. (261)

Maurer's account shows the intimacy of learning an occupation and learning a language. He emphasizes here and in his study of the practices and social organization of pickpockets, *Whiz Mob* (Maurer 1964), how the "language" of thievery (surely what Bakhtin would call a speech genre) organizes a thief's activities and his (or her) working relations with others. In the study from which the above quotation is taken, Maurer has worked up his materials as a lexicon of pickpockets' language. Scanning the lexicon, we can see how the terms locate categories of person in the organization of a division of the "labour" of thievery: there is the "mark" – focus of the pickpocket attempt; the respectable-appearing "front" who unbuttons the mark's coat so that the "tool" can get into the mark's inside pockets; a "cannon broad" is a skilled and experienced woman pickpocket; the "local" will not work outside the area with which he or she is familiar. Hazards are named, including, of course, police and detectives; settings and areas are constituted in relation to the relevances of thievery – a locality that is "burned up" is one that has been hit so often that it is "hot" (Maurer 1981: 234–56).

These are more than items in a lexicon; they are terms that operate as the carriers of an interindividual organization of consciousnesses among pickpockets, constituting a shared universe of actors, practices, environment, objects, and their relations on which practitioners can draw in coordinating their work. The terms transport the sedimented experiences of previous usages into the current situations of utterance among the thieves. Language does not appear as if it were detached from the settings, objects, persons, and activities that it names. It coordinates the focus of the speakers' and listeners' consciousnesses in ongoing courses of action, marshalling news, passing on tips, sharing achievements and failures, telling jokes, locating known-in-common points of reference and filling out future projects with local detail.

Precipitated out of its textual security, sociology is a sphere of activity. Sociologists are reading, writing, teaching, learning sociology; going to conferences and listening to other sociologists; worrying about their sociological competitors; getting together in departments to defend the sociological enterprise against administrative marauders and upstart theoretical factions; participating in networks, orienting to leaders, deciding who's in and who's out. All this is not apart from its texts, for its texts are "activated" in these activities as local events coordinating the local practices of this sociologist here with those of others who appear to her at the moment of reading only as virtual participants of discourse.

Language, "Speech Genres," and Social Organization

Language comes to be thought as distinct from local practices of speaking, writing, hearing, reading when technologies of print have created the conditions under which it can appear as replicable independently of particular contexts of reading or writing (Smith 1999: chap. 5). That language and meaning can be abstracted via the text from local settings is foundational to semiotics or semantics. Texts are artifices that, in separating and preserving utterances independently of local settings, also make possible the regulation of language through the development of technologies of meaning, as in dictionaries and thesauruses. Such models of meaning are grounded in an experience of language as meaningful independently of its local practice among people. The artifice of the text is presupposed in lexical models that locate meaning in the coupling of word and meaning or reference, signifier and signified, even when meaning is held to arise as a function of differentiations within a system. Within this approach, words/signs carry meanings around, can be carried from mouth to ear and transmitted unblemished from one mind to another.

The view of language on which the investigation that follows relies differs significantly from the lexical semiotic approach. The theories of Bakhtin, Vološinov, and George Herbert Mead offer a radical contrast to the approach summarized above. Vološinov's conception is of language as essentially social, and signs as both within and external to the individual. It is not "communication" from one consciousness to another but "interindividual" (Vološinov 1973: 12); further:

> A word is a two-sided act. It is determined equally by whose word it is and for whom it is meant. As word, it is precisely *the product of the reciprocal relationship between speaker and listener, addresser and addressee*. Each and every word expresses the "one" in relation to the "other." I give myself verbal shape from another's point of view. (86, emphasis in the original)

Similarly for Bakhtin, the meaning of an utterance always arises "two-sidedly" in particular local settings, and for George Herbert Mead the spoken word appears between people, heard by both, and generating the same responses in speaker and hearer, its meaning organizing the consciousness of both in the ongoing social act. For these thinkers, meaning is always relational, processual, and two-sided. In moving away from lexical models of meaning, speech/writing (or "utterances" –

Bakhtin's term includes both) is conceived as projecting organization into ongoing sequences of people's activities and bringing them into an active coordination with the activities of others. Such a formulation is readily expanded in terms of my interests in the social as the concerting of people's activities (Smith 1999, 2005), enabling language or, rather, speech and writing to be explored for how they coordinate or align individual consciousnesses – hence as organization.

The organizing work language does, its selecting, ordering, assembling, operations, is transferred from setting to setting. A word exists already "in other people's mouths, in other people's contexts, serving other people's intentions" (Bakhtin 1981: 294), such that

> Each separate utterance is individual, of course, but each sphere in which language is used develops its own relatively stable types of these utterances. These we may call speech genres ... Each sphere of activity contains an entire repertoire of speech genres that differentiate and grow as the particular sphere develops and becomes more complex. (Bakhtin 1986a: 60)

The speech genres that are the dialogic ground of the novel are themselves grounded in "spheres of activity" – scientific, literary, political, bureaucratic, criminal, occupational, regional, and so on.[2] The "social organization" of what Bakhtin calls "spheres of activity" is carried by the ordinary and taken-for-granted terminologies and syntactic conventions enabling the utterances of its participants. Here is the familiar feeling that you have when you are new to a socially organized setting, of not knowing quite how to speak. It is not a problem strictly of knowing the language, but rather of how to insert properly made sentences into local sequences of action (including, of course, talk and writing).

Since Bakhtin is concerned with a literary form, his focus is on language. Though he sees speech genres as arising in the spheres of activity of groups of people, he is interested in the forms of language and not in its relation to the people who use it or the activity it arises in and organizes. Because he is working exclusively with textual materials (and almost exclusively with novels), he can lift out the speech genre and forget about spheres of activity. The operation then is entirely within language. The fictional form does not claim to represent a reality beyond itself as sociology does. Whether or not these forms are actually sociology's topic in any particular case, sociology is always and necessarily grounded in the actual "spheres of activity" that bring its phenomenal universe into effective being. Hence, it is also implicitly and for the most part unknowingly grounded in the speech genres that express, arise in, and organize spheres of activity. Speech genres are distinctive language uses – terminology, syntactic conventions, stylistics, and so on – that carry and regenerate the social organization of groups, large-scale organizations, discourse, indeed all forms of social life in which people together are concerting their activities.

We could say that talk, as with pickpockets' cant, "expresses" a social organization. That would direct us to an analysis of such speech genres for what *underlies* them. We would be instructed to look for structure or organization that is expressed in the form of words the utterance, whether text or speech, contains. We could also confine our interest, as ethnomethodology's conversational analysis does, to the ordering of the talk itself. But carrying Bakhtin's line of thinking into the analysis of spheres of activity attends to how utterances generated by the relevant speech genre organize consciousnesses among people in action. Utterances regenerate or activate forms of coordination that have been laid down in the past and are carried in the terminology, the characteristic syntactic forms, the styles, and so on. Social organization is continually reanalysed, explicated, and elaborated in talk and writing/reading that concerts particular activities ongoingly across particular local encounters, occasions, and so on. In coordinating particular local sequences of activity among participants, utterances reaffirm, regenerate, and modify social organization as it is projected towards the next occasion of action together.

No less, then, the social organization of those spheres of activity we call a discourse (an instance of what Bakhtin refers to as a secondary speech genre). The peculiarity of a discourse is the standardization of ways of producing utterances from many sources and over time that can claim membership in it. Indeed, membership is claimed in part by explicit conformity to such standardization. In sociological discourse, theories, however various, provide standardized strategies for reducing the multiple voices and speech genres of the society to monologism. Sustaining the dominance of a particular standpoint as universal means excluding alternative practices of sociology's dialogue with the world full of other voices – the contemporary heteroglossia to use Bakhtin's term – which it must bring to discursive order. A variety of theoretical enclaves have formed in sociology around competing monologisms. No one procedure for producing monologism will suffice; each one is exposed to the possibility of being unseated by what it cannot subdue.

The "work" of sociological theory in regulating the potentially de-
stabilizing dialogues of sociological discourse with people is a local
practice of sociologists. It is at work as sociologists plan and carry out
research, devising interview schedules and coding systems, and interpreting the product as they write it up for presentation or publication.
It is at work also as sociologists read sociology and hence in sociology's dialogic relationship to the unregulated intertextuality and heteroglossia of the contemporary world. Reading sociology is no less a
local practice than doing research. Reading is not entirely in the text,
for at the point of reading, the reader both activates the text and is
responding to it. Here is another dimension of the regulatory work of
theory. While practices that rework, reduce, or mush the heteroglossia
of our time are organized or instructed by the text, it is the reader who
performs these practices. The following two sections examine how sociological theory controls the potential discursive disorder threatened
by the multiple voices of societies in which we, as sociologists, are
both present and active in our bodily beings while at the same time being involved in and contributing to a discourse which reflects on and
represents them. In both sections, the regulatory work of sociological
theory is explored, using my own experiences of reading. The first of
these explores sociology's dialogic and how it manages its necessary
engagement in and with a contemporary heteroglossic world; the second is an experiential ethnography of my own local practices of reading a passage of sociological theory in a particular local setting and at a
particular time of my life and discovering theory's regulatory capacity
as it organized the dialogic of my encounters with voices from other
sources – the heteroglossia of the textual world I was active in at the
time of its reading.

Sociology's Dialogic

I have written of texts as "active" (Smith 1990b). I mean to see them as
like a speaker in a conversation; one who is deprived of the possibility
of hearing and responding to us, but nonetheless as present and active
in "speaking" to us as our reading activates it. Our reading operates
the text; in our reading it becomes active; we become the text's proxy
in the text–reader conversation. The artifice of the text detaches it from
the local historicity of living and activity of the reader's or writer's
bodily site – or seems to do so. But its making was work done in actual settings by one or more people and as part of a course of action,

whether of an individual, a group, or an organization of some kind or of an extended social relation concerting the activities of many. And its reading also is in time and in an actual place and enters again into someone's course of action and has, in that course of action, a speaking part; it becomes active in that course of action (Smith 2006; Turner 2006). The texts of social scientific discourse are active in just this way.

Such a conversation does not take place in isolation. Bakhtin (1981) in theorizing language and the novel insists that the meanings of words have already been given determination as they have been used in multiple local settings; they enter local utterances trailing debris of meaning from the past, "tasting," to use Bakhtin's term, of the settings and intentions of their use elsewhere and else when (294). To speak or write is thus always essentially dialogic. A given utterance (acts of speech or writing) is intrinsically dialogic in its reworking of terms that have already been given determinate, if essentially pliable, meaning elsewhere and else when in the utterances of others. And it contributes prospectively to what others may be able to say down the line.

Bakhtin's theory of the novel builds on this notion of dialogue. Our everyday use of language appropriates, for what we want to get done, meanings determined by a multiplicity of contexted utterances. Of course these are not unique to individuals. Bakhtin stresses language as a property of groups and relations. As we have seen in the instance of Maurer's study of the language uses of pickpockets, styles of usage are integral to established groups or forms of organization, professions, bureaucracy, trades, in social circles, social movements, generations, regions, and so on. In Bakhtin's analysis, the novel's distinctive project draws such speech genres into a dialogue within the text. Its themes orchestrate diverse speech genres, bringing them into dialogic relations with one another. Dialogue is present not only in the overall thematic organization of the novel. The dialogic thematic organization is worked out in and worked into specific passages and even sentences. The diversity of voices in dialogue is not only in the representation of different voices as speakers in the text and in reported speech, but also in hybrid sentences in which the author's voice draws in and subdues another's speech – in irony where the author's voice reflects on others and in movements between one voice and another in narrative sequences so that one reflects on (is in dialogue with) another.

Sociology too is embedded in the heteroglossia of a diverse society. Sociology too relies on and writes into its texts and hence draws into its discourse (as the text-mediated conversation among sociologists) a diversity of voices. It relies on the same resources as the novel does; indeed, sociologists have recognized this kinship though not knowing quite what to do with it. Perhaps we should be writing novels rather than sociology; some sociologists have written novels (Harvey Swados, for example); some have said novels are a better form of sociology than sociology itself. Sociology draws into the discourse, covertly or explicitly, the social organization carried by the "speech genres" of the people who have been its object or resource. It brings into the text, though not necessarily explicitly, not just a language but a linkage back into the "sphere of activity" in which the language originated.

Think of sociologists reading newspapers, magazines, novels, poetry, biographies, history, and watching television and going to see films, as well as doing our proper sociological reading. We participate in the multi-discoursed and text-mediated relations that coordinate people's everyday doings beyond and across particular local settings and we are competent practitioners of the speech genre bearing the social organization of our place of work. There is constant leakage from the multi-voiced society in which we do our work into our sociological work. More than that, however, is the discourse's necessary dialogue with its subject matter. It is full of voices, though often they are unrecognizable as such because before they even arrive at the threshold of sociology, they have already been transformed into textual products, for example, in the demographic data produced by the state census procedures or the legally mandated procedures for registering births, deaths, and marriages and so forth. The dialogic of the interchange between state and people who are the originals of the data enters sidling into the sociological text. Sociologists listen to conversations, record them, and analyse them after converting them into texts as recorded voices or visual images and then as written transcripts; we talk to people out there in what we call the "real world" in contradistinction to the world we generate in our texts which is not real; we ask them questions and bring their answers home with us to build representations of those with whom we spoke. Some script the dialogue between sociology and respondent so that the latter's voice is heard only as a refraction of the sociological discourse; other methods, such as oral history or ethnography, expose the sociologist to the native speaking of society, leaving it for her later work, after she's brought her notes, recordings, and recollections back to home or office, to subdue the original genres abstracted from their sphere of activity to the magisterial language of the discipline. Within sociological texts themselves we find traces and presences of diverse voices: passages quoted from interviews, passages from field notes giving accounts of what was said and done on a particular occasion, texts of a variety of kinds used for what the sociologist thinks they might be able to tell her about what was on the other side of the text in the "real world."[3] Recommendations and prescriptions for how to regulate these dialogues appear in the endless publications on methods of "qualitative" research.

Sociology's dialogic has the potential for eroding from within the discursive coherence on which sociology's existence as a discipline depends. The speech genres drawn into its texts carry their own intentions, perspectives, experience. and social organization:

> There are no "neutral" words and forms – words and forms that can belong to "no one"; language has been completely taken over, shot through with intentions and accents. For any individual consciousness living in it, language is not an abstract system of normative forms but rather a concrete heteroglot conception of the world. All words have the "taste" of a profession, a genre, a tendency, a party, a particular work, a particular person, a generation, an age group, the day and hour. Each word tastes of the context and contexts in which it has lived its socially charged life; all words and forms are populated by intentions. Contextual overtones (generic, tendentious, individualistic) are inevitable in the word. (Bakhtin 1981: 293)

In a sense, sociology is exposed to capture by ways of seeing and representing the world that are those of speech genres other than its own. In such ways, sociological discourse is everywhere fractured with traces and presences of a diversity of voices that are methodologically regulated through formalized accounts of interviewing procedures, protocols provided for interviewers specifying the sociological script for their part in dialogue with respondents, procedures for coding that impose the disciplinary interpretation on the original and above all by the interpretive dominance of sociological theory.

Unlike the natural sciences, sociology does not have material technologies producing specialized representations that differentiate its objects from the local actualities of the world it explores. The tenuous separation of sociology from actualities is achieved as participants conform to its discursive order. In contrast to the novel, as Bakhtin theorizes it, sociology's stylistics, rather than preserving the "inserted genres" and the "speech of characters" as with the novel form, are regulated theoretically so that the diverse speech genres or voices that appear directly in the text are provided with standardized discursive frames. Dialogue is subdued to the monologic or unitary language that Bakhtin contrasted with dialogized interplay of voices in the novel.

Monologism, for Bakhtin, describes a condition wherein the matrix of ideological values, signifying practices, and creative impulses which constitute the living reality of language are subordinated to the hegemony of a single, unified consciousness or perspective. Whatever cannot be subsumed under this transcendent consciousness is regarded as extraneous or superfluous (Gardiner 1992: 26). Constitutional rules of one kind or another – for example, Emile Durkheim's *The Rules of Sociological Method* (1964) – objectify sociology's phenomena, producing a discursive universe in which the people's utterances and other actions can appear as if there were no actors or in which uttering, acting agents are subordinated to discursively authorized concepts or theories. In the context of the genre of the novel, Bakhtin (1981) has described such practices as "hybrid utterances." In hybrid utterances, there is one authorized speaker (the novelist) who introduces the utterances of others speaking other speech genres to contrast, sometimes to mock. Sociology's monologic practices, which insert but subordinate others' utterances, are analogous. The voices of those who in various ways came within the sociologist's research scope are not framed by the author's voice as in the novel but are instead framed by a monologic that is discursively standardized and adopted by individual participants in the sociological discourse as a "single, unified consciousness or perspective" (Gardiner 1992: 26) that all know how to practise as their sociological competence. This is, I suggest, how sociological theory regulates the order of sociological discourse.

Sociological Theory as Regulator

The textual substance of sociological discourse originates in the actualities of people as they are and act, including their utterances (oral or writing). Sociology's relation to the diverse speech genres of contemporary society is analogous to Bakhtin's account of the novel as embedded in heteroglossia. Sociology works with multiple and diverging voices; its dialogue with and in their diversity is regulated theoretically. As a regulator, sociological theory subordinates the intentions and perspectives of the original speakers engaged with sociological researchers to the "order of discourse" (Foucault 1981), an order managing sociology's intratextual dialogues and supplanting the original intentions of those who were the sociologist's research "subjects" with an authorized system of discursive intentions. Theory standardizes the local interpretive practices of its sociological participants and sets up a unitary organization of subject positions organizing how the reader enters into the dialogic relations of the text.

The regulatory work of sociology's theoretical vocabulary can be seen in the following two examples. The first is from a paper by Hilary Graham and Ann Oakley (1981) called "Competing Ideologies of Reproduction: Medical and Maternal Perspectives on Pregnancy." Two different and conflicting "perspectives" on childbirth are described, that of obstetricians and that of women in childbirth. "Specifically, our data suggest that mothers and doctors disagree on whether pregnancy is a natural or a medical process and whether as a consequence, pregnancy should be abstracted from the woman's life-experiences and treated as an isolated medical event" (56). Obstetricians and patients are not observed arguing with one another. The conflicts are "between medical and maternal frames of reference" (ibid.: 56). These are the researchers' discursive construct. "Perspectives" or "frames of reference" are assembled in the text from rather different kinds of original activities and happenings among the people studied. "Perspectives" or "frames of reference" are attributed to the obstetricians on the basis of observations obtained during consultations with patients;[4] the mothers, on the other hand, were interviewed extensively using an open-ended format – the respondents speaking directly to the researchers. These two very different sources are synthesized first as perspectives or frames of reference which mediate their theoretical elevation to "competing ideologies of reproduction." The theoretical concept, ideology, that defines the paper's topic subsumes the lower-level array of categories, "perspective," and "frame of reference." The latter concepts have in their turn subsumed the actual observations and talk out of which the researchers produced their data. Hence, the original stuff of observations and interviews can become expressions of "conflicting ideologies." Utterances recorded from the original setting are cited as "manifestations" (ibid.: 56) of an underlying ideological reality. Theoretical management of the original dialogue which produces "data" can be recognized as operating as a circuit[5] – from the sociologists' original dialogue through talk or watching with their subjects to descriptions which reconstitute what was learned to fit a theoretical framework; what has been described can then be treated as an expression or manifestation of that theory. This is sociology's distinctive form of hybrid dialogue in which original voices may indeed be heard, but only as illustrations, examples, expressions – not of the individual author, as in Bakhtin's analysis of hybrid utterances in the novel, but of a theory coordinating sociological discourse.

The second is Eric Rothenbuhler's (1990) interpretation of the reporting of the 1912 strike of workers in the textile factories in Lawrence, Massachusetts, that built on concepts derived from Victor Turner's (1969) analysis of liminality and Emile Durkheim's *The Elementary Forms of Religious Life*. The strike was organized by the International Workers of the World (IWW), and it is this that is Rothenbuhler's focus of how it was represented in an editorial in a local newspaper. Rothenbuhler's analysis is essentially a theoretical reconstruction of the editorial – written during the strike. Here is part of it:

> Are we to expect that instead of playing the game respectfully, or else breaking out into lawless riot which we know well enough how to deal with, the laborers are to listen to a subtle anarchistic philosophy which challenges the fundamental idea of law and order, inculcating such strange doctrines as those of "direct action," "sabotage," "syndicalism," "the general strike," and "violence?" (Rothenbuhler 1990: 68)

The editorial has already organized its representation of what was going on in the strike at Lawrence. Something strange and new is going on; the laborers are listening to a new philosophy which undermines law and order. Rothenbuhler creates a theoretical gloss that re-presents the newspaper account to produce its objectified and generalized version as follows: "when ... some members of a society reside in a liminal zone that is not part of that society's legitimate ritual code, their behavior cannot be meaningfully explained by the governing myths" (ibid.: 67). Here, Rothenbuhler's theory transposes the standpoint of the newspaper editorial into the monologic of the sociological text, elaborating theoretical categories that build the editorial into a generalized and generalizing statement and, incidentally, depriving the striking workers of even the marginal voice to be heard in the original editorial's hybrid citing of the categories of the "strange doctrines." The subject–other relation projected in the newspaper editorial is preserved in and yet displaced by the higher-order monology. In these two instances, we see sociological theory being brought to bear in subduing what people have said or written or been doing in different actual settings to intentions projected at the level of sociological discourse. Theory is deployed to pick out and tailor extracts from the original events to appear conceptually reconstructed or as fragments of speech or writing sustaining the theoretically regulated discursive theme.[6] The hybrid text is riddled with the dialogics in which it originates, but theory represents their fragmentary appearance at the surface of the text as its instances or expressions, assimilated to the order of discourse (Foucault 1981) and appropriated by the latter's "transcendent consciousness" (Gardiner 1992) as its own.

Reading Theory: An Experiential Ethnography

In this section, I report observation and analysis of my experience of reading a passage from an essay on sociology by Anthony Giddens. My experience is explored and explicated as a text–reader conversation, that is, as an active engagement in a particular time and place of a reader engaging and activating a specific text. A footnote to Giddens's essay tells us that it was originally written for presentation to the assembled dons and fellows of Cambridge University. In this dialogue, Giddens plays a kind of ambassadorial role, acting as sociology's representative and champion. At the same time, it is written to be "overheard,"[7] reappearing in a collection of Giddens's writing entitled *Social Theory and Modern Sociology*; readers are thereby admitted to a text–reader conversation as official eavesdroppers on this earlier occasion.

If we think of an actual local setting of reading, we can see how it becomes a setting of sociological discourse as the reader picks up the book

---

Exhibit 9.1 Passage from Giddens

It is intrinsic to human action that, in any given situation, the agent, as philosophers sometimes say, could have acted otherwise. However oppressively the burden of particular circumstances may weigh upon us, we feel ourselves to be free in the sense that we decide upon an action in the light of what we know about ourselves, the context of our activities and their likely outcomes. This feeling is not spurious for it is arguable that it is analytical to the concept of agency that the actor in some sense "could have done otherwise" – or could have refrained from whatever course of action was followed. (Giddens 1987: 3) (she bought it recently at the university bookstore or got it out of the library or is reading it on her e-reader) and begins her conversation with it. She engages the discourse at this moment and in the particular local setting and time of doing reading. It comes into play as she, the reader "activates" or "operates" the text, deploying the methods of reading of the discursive genre in which the text is written. In this instance, the discursive setting is signalled by the title and related cues such as the name of a well-known sociological theorist, Anthony Giddens, as its author. But reading, like conversation, is also two-sided; the reader's consciousness is not wholly subdued to the text; she brings her own sociological projects and concerns to the reading, as well as resources of memory and attention. As is typical of sociology, the interchange between reader and text is not insulated from other, non-sociological speech genres/spheres of activity. Activated by a particular reader, the text provides a set of instructions organizing the reader's selections from other texts and even from the local relevances of her life.

For the reader, so long as she is reading, the text pursues its remorseless way unresponsive to the impassioned marginal notes, the exclamation points of question marks, the underlining, through which the reader tries to force dialogue on it. It is untouched by the reader's part in her conversation with it. It scripts her part in the conversation and, in the order of reading, she has no choice. Yet text and reader are in dialogue and not only at the time of actual engagement in reading the text. Dialogues may also appear as afterthoughts, supplements, additions, a return to particularly troubling passages, or connections between the dialogic of the text and other texts or talk that the reader is engaged in – or this analysis. This is the dialogue which I am exploring here as I was active in it when I was reading Giddens's book some while back in an apartment in Eugene, Oregon. When I became engaged in the text–reader conversation to be analysed, I was on leave from the Ontario Institute for Studies in Education and enjoying a dispersed and less focused range of reading than is usually practicable. I noticed, as I read Giddens, how a particular passage occasioned a kind of argument with other things I was reading or had been reading, and also how it regulated, *through me*, their admissibility to or implications for sociological discourse as Giddens interprets it – at least as exemplified in this passage. I found the latter observation troubling and decided to investigate it. Here is the passage:

The author has a dual role, or perhaps better, is present at different levels of the text. He is scripted, as any of us is, as participant in the "we" to whom all these scripted determinations of subjectivity apply; he is also Anthony Giddens, major sociological theorist, whose authority has already passed from the title page to the text we read. He speaks in the magisterial voice of one who can claim to speak for sociology, even legislate for it. The magisterial voice is more than just the voice of the sociologist. He is not alone; one sentence bears an internal dialogue – a hybrid utterance to use Bakhtin's term. A proposition is embarked upon – "It is intrinsic to human action ..." – and then interrupted to make explicit its appropriation of phraseology from philosophy for its concluding clause: the agent "could have acted otherwise." An intersection of discourses is signalled; a kind of collaboration in which the phraseology of another discourse is deployed to buttress the discourse in situ. The appeal is to a discourse that is in the business of formulating rules, principles and procedures for thinking and inquiry for other discourses. A supplementary authority is invoked.

Our participation in the text is directly scripted. The use of the pronoun "we" enters us as subjects into the text as a course of action. "We" are accorded properties of consciousness: "we feel ourselves to be free"; "we" "decide on a course of action in the light of what we know." As reading subject I come to stand as proxy for the text; in a sense I speak its sentences. It is I, as reader activating the text, who enunciates "we feel ourselves to be free ..." The statement that "we feel ourselves to be free" establishes the application of what philosophers sometimes say to she who reads. She is / I am among those who feel free. The subject thus positioned in the text participates in a scripted dialogue with the magisterial and positionless voice: "We feel ourselves to be free," we intone and, antiphonally, the magisterial voice assures us "this feeling is not spurious." Our feeling is authenticated theoretically: "It is analytical to the concept of agency that the actor could have done otherwise." Our textually scripted subjective states of consciousness are properly authorized. At the time of my reading, because I was on leave, I had time to read eclectically and for other than strictly sociological purposes. Under the text's mapping of my consciousness I began a dialogue between me, Dorothy Smith, as its local proxy and other texts that I had been reading. In the account that follows, intertextuality is transposed from its primarily literary force to explore a particular reader's local practice of dialogue among texts, escaping in this way from the stasis of the text into the lived actuality where discourse, like any other speech genre, is indeed a sphere of activity.

Here during the course of my reading, the concepts of "agent" and "agency," and of "freedom" to choose a course of action, select and collect beyond the terms of the text, hooking into other and subversive discourses. Memory, like a northern flicker hunting ants, skitters over a meadow of texts, plucking out items from various, earlier, ongoing, and later readings. In this intertextual activity, arguments against the constant and impervious text are engaged. Passages from newspapers, books, what people say emerge or are located. I recall Jessie Bernard's (1973) early feminist critique of the agentic assumptions of sociology, and my use of that in reflecting on my own experience as a woman who did not choose (Smith 1987) or, I suppose, had chosen a form of marriage that relinquished choice.

In Giddens's text, "we feel" locates us, readers/audience, as members of the class of human agents, summoning us to join the text's course. Yet rereading it in the course of analysis, I suspect the pronoun creates a rent in the text which a more impersonal form might have avoided. The formulation claims universality that the pronoun subverts. The "we" is for anyone, but not everyone feels free. My intertextual dialogue, thinking about Giddens and reading eclectically over several days as well as remembering earlier reading, engaged with more than one passage in which people wrote or were recorded as saying they do not feel free. In a study of women and depression (Jack 1991), I encounter women who lacked a sense of themselves as agents: one of the women says "that the traditional sort of role that I played in my marriage was almost like an automatic pilot" (73); another, "Most of my feelings about what a woman is are tied directly into a man. A woman isn't anything by herself" (116). I remember a woman speaking in a group of "psychiatrized" women (the self-naming by women who have been hospitalized for mental illness). She described herself as having been taught as a girl that she was not an agent, that she did not have the power to decide anything for herself, that she existed purely as an extension of, a means to, men's doings, men's actions, men's projects. How can their experience be "claimed" by this theory of human action and agency?

I had just read Marcia Dimen's (1989) experiential and analytic account of sexual domination. Giddens's text as regulator of my own, as reader's, consciousness singled out a passage that also registered as an exception. Dimen writes of "the loss of one's sense of and wish for autonomy, as a result of processes that play on one's doubts about the reality and validity of one's self, one's perceptions, and one's values" (37). Her experiential account is more powerful still. It begins with an incident where she is followed by a man on the street telling her he wants to fuck her; it recounts the responses of her mother who criticizes her manner of dress, her father who wants to beat the man up, her conscience echoing many voices. An uncle, not himself blameless in such matters, tells her to ignore the man. To the last of these she replies in the text: "*My mind doesn't work as rationally as yours. How can it? My brain hears, my desire is stirred, I lose control of my body. On the street my body is theirs. I am a body on the street. Two tits and no head and a big ass. I am a walking Rorschach. My body becomes a cunt and I am sore from this semiotic rape*" (ibid.: 73, italics in the original). I remembered also a passage in Zora Neale Hurston's novel *Their Eyes Were Watching God*. Nanny tells her granddaughters, "Ah was born back due in slavery, so it wasn't for me to fulfill my dreams of whut a woman oughta be and to do" (Hurston 1937: 31–2). Slavery deprived slaves of freedom. They did not cease to be human or indeed to act. What sense of agency or freedom to choose applies here? Reading an Iranian labour newsletter that I then subscribed to, I located another voice. An article in it told me that, under Iranian labour law, "the worker is considered a minor and the employers as the owner of the society." "Any worker who reads this law carefully will say to himself or herself: This law considers me part of the means of production, without a tongue or will of its own" (Saber and Hekmat 1992). The law is enforced by the police and courts. The employer's will is sustained with beatings, jail, and sometimes by death. Iranian workers do not have, they want, the freedom to decide.

In sum, as the text's proxy and at that time engaged also in an eclectic array of other texts, my practices of remembering, noticing, looking out for, passages that bear upon the theoretical text, that it bears upon, become organized by the theory. Though my input is argumentative, it is the text's theory as organizer of my attention and reflection that structures the intertextual dialogue. The text provides me/the reader with instructions on how to handle instances that "come to mind" of people who have not felt free. It is not the feeling that validates the generalization. Not any old feeling can be admitted as relevant. The parameters of admissible feelings are laid out. The theory validates feelings selectively. Some would be authorized and others discounted. As proxies acting for the text we know how to discard the relevance to the argument of the voices of those who declare that they are not, and do not feel, free. What is validation here? It is not simply the text's work, but an implicitly dialogic aspect of the reader's work as proxy of the text. The text lays out theory's command of relevance, but the reader must assent and activate to regulate what feelings of freedom may be entered into the feeling of freedom of those who can enter the "we" of the text. As the text's proxy, the reader is accountable to the text; she is its enforcer.

The text's trap is that in its conversation with the reader its part is reader-activated. In becoming the text's proxy, she takes on the text's organizing powers as her own. Just knowing how to read it enables the text to creep into her consciousness and take over (Smith 1990a; 2005). Not necessarily to agree with it, of course, but to adopt its organizing framework in selecting and interpreting other texts. This is the special competence of theory. Giddens's text in my consciousness singles out passages read or recalled; it also instructs me on how to subdue them to it. Can it not be said of any of the instances I have adduced that "the actors in some sense 'could have done otherwise' – or could have refrained from whatever course of action was followed" (Giddens 1987: 3)? An Iranian worker could choose to do otherwise and risk death. "However oppressively the burden of particular circumstances may weigh upon us, we feel ourselves to be free in the sense that we decide upon an action in the light of what we know about ourselves, the context of our activities and their likely outcomes" (ibid.). In Hurston's story, the grandmother could choose within "the context of [her] activities" as a slave. I have to contort the others, discounting the women with depression (they are "ill") and treating Dimen's text as metaphor. So long as I undertake to act as its proxy, the text remains impregnable.

The cunning of the theoretical formulation provides for the problem that in none of these accounts do those represented report themselves as feeling free. Here are people who state clearly that they do not feel free or are clearly described as not being free. How to exclude their testimony so that the text is not impugned? The text itself provides instructions for how to handle such difficulties right there in the passage I quoted. Feeling free in the text's sense cannot be equated with people's self-reporting of their feelings of freedom or unfreedom. A special sense of feeling free is put in place. It is this: "We decide upon an action in the light of what we know about ourselves, the context of our activities and their likely outcomes." If the likely outcome of what we choose to do is torture and death and deciding to avoid them is to accept slavery or forced labour, we have been free to make that choice. The order of the discourse imposes its interpretive authority against the authority of the voice I bring forward in contention.

Giddens has been careful to define what feeling free might mean. While we, who feel free, are validated – our feeling is not "spurious" – those who do not feel free drop outside the circle of shared subjectivity constituted in the text–reader dialogue. For within that circle it seems that "however oppressively the burden of particular circumstances may weigh upon them, they could have refrained from whatever course of action was followed." Here is demonstrated theory's capacity to control the bolt-holes through which the meaning of other texts or voices might escape its regime. And note that the printed published text has this powerful organizing effect of making the same "instructions" available not just to me, but to any other reader who can activate it. Any such reader becomes its proxy. Just as I became proxy of Giddens's text in my reading, others reading his text in his chapter may find themselves taking on the same role, saying, as a colleague of mine did when she read a draft, "but doesn't she [i.e., Dorothy] see that they [Dorothy's collection of other voices] don't apply?" Another might move to a larger scope of the hermeneutics of discourse to point out that I have misinterpreted the issue: Giddens surely is addressing the traditional problematic of the regional moral discourse of Western European philosophy since the Enlightenment, namely, that of free will versus determinism: "Smith has missed the point altogether." Here is theory at work in the social organization of discourse.

There is repression here. Whatever way I turned, my collection of stories from people who do not feel free cannot engage with the text or enter the circle of authorized subjectivity it constitutes. Trained readers of such texts know how to suspend their own or others experience when it challenges the theoretically regulated order of the text. They know how to take up instructions provided by the text to subdue the intrusive and potentially disruptive other voices. The dialogue with the text offers no purchase to challenges offered by counter-examples. They will not fit and cannot be spoken without a discursive shift that repositions the subject outside the scope established by the theory organizing and generated in Giddens's text.

Within the theory-regulated dialogic order of the text, the possibility of feeling otherwise, perhaps not free, perhaps not really feeling either one or the other, is not open. The reader who feels a disjuncture here has also been given instructions to bracket the sources of disjuncture emerging for her from the actualities of her own life, or from her participation in other discourses. No feeling other than that prescribed is admissible to the dialogue within the text and the reader as the text's proxy is enforcer of that rule.

It is here we find theory's part in organizing the discursive exclusions that are the local practices of monologism. I don't think Giddens would have felt comfortable telling an audience of Iranian workers that "we feel ourselves to be free," when "we" is intended to include them. They would be indifferent, perhaps enraged. I imagine Zora Neale Hurston's grandmother turning away in contempt and disgust too profound for rage. The cogency of Giddens's passage is at least in part sustained by the lack of disjuncture between the reader's/audience's feelings of freedom and the subjective state it assigns them. They/we do feel free, or at least don't feel strikingly unfree. "We" (is there an implicit class and racial referent here?) have no sharp history of recent slavery; we have not experienced being confined to a ghetto or to an aboriginal reserve; "we" who are men do not experience masculine sexualization of women's public life as a young woman might; we are not Iranian workers; and so on. Here's where an organization of class, race, and gender subtends but yet is written out of the text. Should *agency* itself be recognized as constructed in social relations much as *subject* is of discourse?

The override clause that specifies the sense in which we feel free relies for its operation on our being able to centre ourselves where the text centres us, setting up instructions for its exclusionary work in our consciousness. The heteroglossia of oppression into which my memories of eclectic reading had tossed me were controlled as I returned to functioning as the text's proxy. Excluding those other voices relies on the lack of specification of who this "we" is, and on our knowing how to participate in it and adopt the enclosures it calls on us to inscribe. There is no space, operating under the text's instruction, for an alternative "we" offering a contentious identity. The stylistics of theory universalize, and s/he can find no ground within the text enabling her/his speech. The participant as text's proxy adopts its instructions for her/his local practices of inclusion and exclusion. S/he is not alone. Others, also readers of the theoretical texts, are observing the same boundaries. Our local practices of interpretation are, in this fashion, coordinated across the multiple local settings in which sociological discourse is realized as such.

I notice retrospectively that this passage of sociological theory could subdue these divergent voices only because I treated its unitary standpoint as mine. In the text–reader conversation, the reader becomes the text's proxy as well as responding to it. Hence, the theoretical position embodied in the text was the effective authority in my local practice of reading. Sociological theory is one of a family of discursive devices which shares with other institutional processes the capacity "to operate on an account of experience in such a way that it can be seen as an expression of, or as documenting, that institutional process" (Smith 1990b: 154) or, in this case, that theory. Theory coordinates the local practices of discourse, aligning the practical exercise of consciousnesses of participants. Perspectives and voices presenting alternative standpoints are subdued to the status of expressions or examples of the theory (and as I read and argued, I was also doing the subduing). The stylistics of universality are preserved against the threat of fragmentation and disorder, a threat sociology cannot evade in its dialogue with and within a heteroglossic society, a society of many and diverging voices. All this, of course, is the work of participants in the discourse who know, as I did, how to take up the theory as regulator, making its monologic organization of dialogue their own.

I did not know when I started on this analysis that I was going to discover how a passage such as this might inscribe hidden subjects who are the not-female, not-African-American, not-Iranian worker, and other "nots" that my eclectic reading at that time in Eugene did not encounter. The subtextual subjects are constituted in the reader's theory-governed dialogue with the various voices threatening its claim to universality; there are those who would not enter or be entered as subjects into the universalized "we" of Giddens's text. Here, then, theory can be seen in action as regulator of sociology's dialogue with other voices, inhibiting their capacity to intrude and disrupt the consolidation of a unitary "we" among members of a discourse.

Discussion

In my introduction to the collection of papers that made up my book *Writing the Social* (Smith 1999), and later in my book *Institutional Ethnography: A Sociology for People* (2005), I wrote of the ontology of the social that I have come to work with and of how this breaks with the ontologies in which experience, activities, or practices appear on one side and beliefs, concepts, ideologies, knowledge, theory, and so on, on the other. Recognizing the latter also as activities or practices pulls them into the same space of investigation as, say, conversations or local work organization. In exploring my own experience of deploying a piece of theoretical text in argument with other texts, I have been exploring a discourse as that which Bakhtin calls a sphere of activity. It is explored not as statements, but as actual practices that are organized as and into a discourse across local settings. Sociology has as deep a dialogic ground as Bakhtin has argued for the novel. These are in its texts (as we have seen), in the making of its texts, and in their reading. My interest has been in exploring theory as it regulates the order of discourse. What I discovered had not been pre-visaged. Analysis of the kind I have done here discovers beyond what the researcher knows before she starts. I learned in the process just how the particular text I had chosen blocked any avenue I could discover to making it responsive to the various voices I used to interrogate it. In the course of my analyses and of my experiential ethnography of reading a theoretical text, I have been discovering just how theory organizes and defines the sociological project and how it comes into play in regulating the discourse, a force very clearly declared in Jeffrey Alexander's argument in support of the teaching of the "founding fathers" of sociology. A classic, he tells us, "establishes the fundamental criteria in the particular field" (Alexander 1995: 22), citing the Bible and the works of Shakespeare as instances. But I have also been interested in developing further the project of bringing the notion and investigation of discourse into the living space of readers' and writers' (and researchers') everyday living, since it is here, of course, that discourse happens.

I did not intend an irony in drawing on pickpocketing as an example of a sphere of activity and the speech genre that organizes it. I introduced it in part because I had admired David Maurer's study of pickpockets through their language (Maurer 1964). At the same time, as is so often the case, there is a kind of inner logic in the choice of metaphor. I see in the retrospect of writing this concluding section that I have displayed a sociology that has found ways of appropriating others' voices and that reduces the essential dialogic character of the society to the monologic of the order of its discourse (Foucault 1981).

In exploring my local practices of reading and reflecting on a piece of Giddens's text, I learned something of the power of a theoretical text to insulate the discourse against subversive voices. Though I could set up an argument with it, I could not make a place for them in it. At every turn, their experience had to be denied. You could choose the theoretical text or choose those voices, but there was no way in. Oddly enough, the very conception of agency that rescues the scholars of Cambridge from feeling that they are somehow pushed around by society, and allows them to claim for anyone some kind of autonomy as a subject vis-à-vis the determinations of structure, fails at a critical juncture, namely, in its capacity to recognize people as subjects speaking for themselves.

Earlier in this paper I described how Rothenbuhler's theoretical moves rewrite monologically a standpoint in the ruling class of the eastern United States in 1912, constituting the striking workers organized by the IWW as an Other beyond understanding. When I originally read Rothenbuhler's paper I was, as I've described, on sabbatical leave and had time to go to the library of the University of Oregon and read up on the extensive IWW literature from that period. The voices of people active in the struggle are strong and immediate. People are named and known. They argued and struggled with one another as well as fighting against a ruling class. They sang; they spoke on street corners; they went to jail; they lived in camps and travelled on the rails. Here was another dialogue I could have written, bringing their voices to bear on Rothenbuhler's theoretical gloss. But again, the order of discourse would have gone unmarred and unmarked by my argument on their behalf in terms of an actual course of reading. The uses of theory to circumscribe a standpoint and export it to the discourse as its order is obvious here, but no less present in the extract from Giddens with which I worked. I do not imagine you can have a sociology without standpoint or interests. Rather, the sociology making inquiry – that is, inquiry into the social as people bring it into being as its central project – is necessarily in explicit dialogue with them and is necessarily exposed to being changed by that dialogue. Here is the move that institutional ethnography has made by starting in the same world as that which it explores and with actual people and their doings viewed under the aspect of how they are coordinated. This is the approach that I have applied in this paper to my ethnographic account of reading a theoretical passage written by Anthony Giddens in a setting in which I had been actively engaged in text–reader conversations that generated challenges and resistance to Giddens's formulations. And yet, engaged as I was in a conversation with Giddens's text, the distinctive logic of the text–reader conversation ensured that in my reading I became his text's proxy. As proxy, I had had to give way to the power of a skilfully developed theoretical fabric which left no holes through which those voices – the voices of the IWW strikers of 1912, of African-American slaves, of women denied agency, of Iranian workers, and, of course, of the unheard Others – could intervene in and potentially disrupt the order of discourse. This paper exploring my text–reader conversation with Giddens's paragraph is also my escape from its theoretical enclosure.

NOTES

1 This chapter is based on a paper prepared for the annual meetings of the Canadian Sociology and Anthropology Association, Montreal, 1995, that was subsequently published as "Discourse as Social Relations: Sociological Theory and the Dialogic of Sociology," chapter 7 of my *Writing the Social: Critique, Theory and Investigations*. The chapter here is a substantial rewriting of the original paper.

2 Other theorists in other fields have made analogous formulations, suggesting that all are pointing to the same beast, like the six blindfolded Jains holding different parts of an elephant. G.H. Mead argues that the "significant symbol" always presupposes a "universe of discourse" as the field within which it has significance. His notion of a universe of discourse is not a notion concerning a purely conceptual object, but as "constituted by a group of individuals carrying on and participating in a common social process of experience and behavior" (Mead 1934: 89). Wittgenstein uses the term "a form of life" to emphasize how "meaning" is embedded in and arises as it comes to mean in the contexts of its use. Bologh (1979) has developed Wittgenstein's thinking as the basis of a phenomenological sociology. She writes that language must be understood actively as a form of life and not passively as a totality of names for things that exist independently of subjects. A form of life, or language-game, may be understood in terms of unspoken rules or presuppositions for knowing an object. These rules constitute a "game," a purposive activity, within which acts and words, like moves in a game, come to make sense. Only within the game are the moves or word intelligible as such (ibid.: 2).

3 There is another level of dialogic organization in the sociological text on which this paper does not focus: other sociologists appear as characters in the text; they are cited as authorities; attributed theoretical positions; attacked; quoted to support a position taken by the writer, or to illustrate the writer's interpretation. The sociological text is written such that it is positioned, during a course of reading that follows the text's instructions, intertextually within the discourse, locating and relying on formulations, theories, positions, methodological procedures, of the discourse; it may

draw similarly on related discourses such as those of cultural theory or philosophy.

4 "[S]ome of the ways in which the differences between them [the two frames of reference] are displayed in antenatal consultations and women's experience of having a baby" (Graham & Oakley (1981: 52).

5 See my analysis, based on Marx and Engels's *The German Ideology*, of the ideological circle and in particular of "the three tricks" (Smith 1990; Marx & Engels 1976).

6 Compare Giltrow's analysis of an ethnography that also inserts the notion of a ritual (Giltrow 1995).

7 A form of "hybrid" utterance, to use Bakhtin's term (Bakhtin 1981) – dialogue embedded in a covert secondary dialogue, the overhearing characteristic of Shakespeare's dramas.

PART 5

Extended Institutional Ethnography

10 Standardizing Child-Rearing through Housing[1]

PAUL C. LUKEN AND SUZANNE VAUGHAN

In this long chapter, Paul Luken and Suzanne Vaughan are doing something rather different from the ethnographies that, until this point in the book, have focused on specific institutional settings. They are investigating the emergence of a public discourse originating in the early twentieth century that has organized a moral relation between suburban style housing, single family dwelling and the well-being of children. They begin with oral histories of women's housing experience told them in the late 1990s by women over 60 living in Phoenix, Arizona and go on to trace the historical work of professionals, intellectuals, government agencies, and construction industry and real estate interests, in the invention and dissemination of a public discourse idealizing the suburban home.

Luken and Vaughan's exploration of the emerging complex of the public discourse standardizing child-rearing through housing began as they observed how the women they talked to reflected on it in various ways. The stories from interviews included in this chapter give us the women's practices, including their consciousnesses – "the things that they did, the materials they used, the people with whom they interacted, and their enjoyment or dislike of their activities and circumstances." Luken and Vaughan go on to locate how the women spoke of their housing experiences to the public discourse relating child-rearing to housing that was being invented early in the twentieth century. They open up a wealth of primary sources of texts circulating between 1890 and 1930, including from the US National Archives and Research Administration, the Library of Congress, historical societies and museums in cities where each of the women had lived as children and parents. The texts make present the work of departments in the federal government responsible for housing policy as well as the work of professional and business organizations promoting and facilitating the constructing and purchase of a type of housing. They bring into view the texts active in an overarching discourse establishing an "ideological code" they call the "Standard American Home" (SAH). And they show how, widely distributed through home, health and agriculture programs of the time, the texts created a dominant "discursive terrain" and a set of valued concepts which the women Luken and Vaughan interviewed drew on in their talk and to which they related their own and their mothers' practices of child-rearing and homemaking.

"Normal family life cannot exist apart from a normal home," the noted housing reformer Edith Elmer Wood proclaimed (1931: 7). Later she added,

> American authorities agree with the British and a majority of Continentals that a single-family detached house with a garden all around it forms the ideal setting for the life of growing children ... The only excuse for apartments is for celibates, childless couples, and elderly people whose children have grown up and scattered. Newly married couples, especially where the husband and wife are both working, will naturally turn to them. And herein lies the danger, if they stay on after children are born. (41)

At the time of her writing, these ideas were becoming commonplace and formed the basis for much criticism of housing in the United States. In this paper we demonstrate that the standard of the proper home environment for raising children, alluded to above, was articulated by the concerted efforts of three state-affiliated organizations: the Children's Bureau, the Own Your Own Home campaign, and the Better Homes in America movement. The work processes of these organizations – research projects, the production and distribution of pamphlets, articles, and newspaper advertisements, demonstration projects, and other discursive practices – connected anxious parents to the newly professionalized child welfare experts (Levine & Levine 1970), to an emerging market of consumer goods and services for the home (Bronner 1989), and to the depressed consumer market for housing (Luken & Vaughan 2005). In doing so they authorized these agents to be the holders of child welfare solutions.

A number of sociologists and historians have examined the "child saving campaigns" during the Progressive Era in the United States, particularly with regard to the discovery of child neglect and abuse (Nelson 1984; Pfohl 1977), the creation of juvenile justice systems (Platt 1969;

Rothman 2002), the establishment of the child welfare system (Gordon 1990; Skocpol 1992; Trattner 1984), the development of child labour laws (Trattner 1970), compulsory education for children (Chapman 1988; Cremin 1961), and the sacralization of children's lives (Zelizer 1985). Much of this research (see Frankel & Dye 1991; McDonagh 1999) suggests that the Progressive movement in the United States was a response to rapid industrialization, immigration, and consolidation of economic interests after the Civil War, and that embodied in the movement was a faith in the state's ability to overcome these problems. As Julia Lathrop, noted Progressive activist and chief of the Children's Bureau, proclaimed: "The success of our future civilization lies in government adding to their responsibility and taking on work which people have not hitherto been willing to entrust to them" (quoted in Rothman 2002: 6).

Our research extends these analyses to the activities involved in the early formation of child-rearing practices around a gendered and familial organized, single-family, detached, suburban dwelling, and it elaborates the ways in which the numerous institutional agents – local and state public health officials, home builders, academics, early child welfare activists, magazine publishers, medical doctors, government officials working in the US Department of Commerce and the Department of Labor and, of course, mothers and fathers – came to participate in the American Dream business. Although a number of institutional actors were involved in child-rearing and housing, our focus is on the coordinating efforts of the state and the ways in which people activate and use institutional discourses and the conceptual frames they circulate (DeVault & McCoy 2001).

In this paper we explore the processes by which an institutional discourse combining child-rearing and housing was formulated through the work practices of three state-affiliated organizations between 1900 and 1930 and how this discourse was used by parents. For us the discourse is a window into ruling relations organizing the local sites of parents in the everyday world. While we argue that this discourse was pervasive, we are not suggesting that parents always enacted it. Rather, the discourse's organizing character can also be seen in the ways parents use it as a standard to which their everyday practices are compared, evaluated, or even rejected, and to which parents feel accountable. In addition, the discourse provides courses of action through which the work parents do in child-rearing and housing are linked to the marketplace selling and leasing housing, household goods, and services.

Standpoint and Method

We use institutional ethnography (IE) (see Smith 1987, 2002, 2005) as a method of inquiry to examine the formation of a segment of ruling relations governing, coordinating, and standardizing child-rearing practices through housing in the early part of the twentieth century in the United States. With the emergence of large-scale organization and printed text, Smith argues, the social organization of direct relationships between people was displaced increasingly by "exogenous systems of rationally designed, textually-mediated forms of organization" (Smith 2002: 39). IE aims to uncover this organizing process from the standpoint of people differentially located within an institutional site by describing how people in the everyday world bring into being the social relations of ruling within their social practices and at the same time through their actual social practices.

Social reality is the ongoing coordination of what people do, say, and write (Smith 2002) and arises within people's everyday activities. Included in these activities are language, thoughts, concepts, beliefs, and ideologies. As people discuss their activities, the language of the everyday world is grounded in extra-local social relations and expresses relations not limited to the local, particular setting. Hence, the relationship between people's everyday world and generalized social relations is a property of social organization (Smith 1987).

Smith (1990) argues that discourse is important in that it mediates relations between active, creative subjects and the market and productive organization of capital. Although discourse appears as objectified forms, it can be examined as "actual social relations ongoingly organized in and by the activities of actual people" (160). Thus, for IE, because consciousness cannot be separated from the individual, discourse (or other social forms of consciousness) is never an agent, but is only accomplished through people's doing in the everyday world.

Following the extra-local textual production and distribution practices of organizations, people's activities are coordinated and made accountable to themselves and others in local settings as they discuss, make decisions, and work to organize their lives in relation to the discourse. While people do not necessarily enact discursive prescriptions, discourse provides an orientating framework to which people feel accountable. Thus, *the relationship between the discourse and local practices is not determinant in this process; yet, the relevancies of those authoring the texts transcend the local historical setting and often become points of reference for people in their everyday world.*

Although IE assumes that people experience and understand things differently, those forms of social organization that generalize and objectify – overriding individuals' perspectives – are of great interest. Texts are fundamental to these generalized forms of consciousness since the production of texts in standardized and replicable form organizes discourse. Even though discourse is not limited to texts, those translocally produced relations of objectification and generalization in texts enter actions and organize actions at multiple sites as the discourse is taken up in local settings either by reading, talking, or acting (Smith 1990b). In IE, discourse does not only include texts and intertextual conversations, but also incorporates people making texts active at any local moment of its use, including its use in their talk (DeVault & McCoy 2001).

Public text-mediated discourses emerged, particularly in the early part of the twentieth century, as a distinctive form of social organization. Smith notes that the development of these forms of ruling produce "an increasingly co-ordinated complex, forming a system or field of relations occupying no particular place, but organizing local sites articulated to it. Since the relations of this complex are based in and mediated by texts, important functions of coordination are performed by ideologies, concepts, theories that insert their ordering capacity into specialized sites otherwise operating independently" (1999: 157). Texts produced by researchers, government agencies, the mass media, and so on are often coordinated conceptually through ideological codes, that is, discursive schemata and concepts that generate procedures for selecting and interpreting syntax, categories, and vocabulary in other texts and in talk (ibid.). Ideological codes produce a unified understanding of the social world and a framework for engaging textually-mediated discourse across diverse organizational sites and in people's everyday lives. They also generate evaluative procedures for determining what is a deviant or defective case. In this way, these ideological practices are powerful forms of ruling as people take up the framework in talk and/ or action. The aim of IE is to uncover these discursive practices as they coordinate and implicate the work activities of people in local settings (ibid.).

Investigating ruling relations involves a two-step process, since the goal of IE is not to explain the behaviour of the subjects or to simply describe the local social organization of people's lives, but rather to examine a segment of the institutional regime that coordinates the activities of the subjects as well as others by tracing how people living in different circumstances are drawn into a common set of organizational processes (DeVault & McCoy 2001). Thus, research begins with locating the problematic from which to explore experience by collecting data about people's everyday activities. Second, the researcher traces the extra-local discursive relations, which may be textually-mediated.

Step 1: The Everyday World

The research presented here is part of a larger investigation of changes in the social institution of housing in the United States in the twentieth century. Thus, we began our research from the standpoint of older women located within the institution of housing. All the subjects were women living in the Phoenix metropolitan area at the time of the interviews. They were at least sixty years of age and had lived alone for at least six months. We excluded men from this study because women are rarely represented in housing studies (Luken & Vaughan 1991), and we chose older women living alone in order to capture their housing experiences over the life course (Luken & Vaughan 2001). After an initial contact we interviewed the women in their homes on at least four occasions for approximately two hours in 1992–3. Our interviews focused on their housing work throughout their lives and the conditions under which this work was done to unfold the institutional processes and connections fundamental to an IE analysis. We tape-recorded and transcribed approximately ten to twelve hours of conversation with each woman. In this article we use pseudonyms and change some of the information to ensure the anonymity of the women.

A word should also be said about sampling. Aside from the selection criteria mentioned above, we needed to capture a wide variety of housing experiences. As Smith notes, "Recognizing and incorporating into the project's ethnographic analysis the actual diversity of perspectives, biographies, positioning, and so on is integral to its ethnographic method" (2005: 125). In the course of conducting our interviews, it became apparent that our subjects had a diversity of housing experiences throughout their lives, including residing in company housing, living on ranches, rooming with others, squatting, renting apartments, receiving government subsidies, owning and renting houses, condos, or mobile homes, and so on. Thus, it was not necessary to make adjustments in our sampling. The reader should keep in mind, however, that the

practice of IE involves sampling an institutional process and social relations, not a population (Smith 2002: 26). Quoting Smith again:

> Institutional ethnographers are not using people's experiences as a basis
> for making statements about them, about the population of individuals,
> or about events or states of affairs described from the point of view of
> individuals. For IE, the speaking or writing of experience is essential to
> realizing the project of working from the actualities of people's lives as the
> people know them. (2005: 125)

As we examined the transcripts we noticed that the women spoke
at length of their girlhood and motherhood experiences. In addition to
telling us about the places where they lived as children and where they
raised their children, they made us aware of the things that they did,
the materials they used, the people with whom they interacted, and
their enjoyment or dislike of their activities and circumstances. Their
narratives opened up for us connections between housing and child-
rearing in the everyday world, and they provided an opportunity to
explore children's lives vis-à-vis housing and the social relations that
shaped these experiences.

Step 2: Textually-Mediated Social Relations

In her discussion of the child development discourse, Griffith writes:
"One discourse is often conceptually linked to others providing for coordination and articulation of institutional activities. Smith's unique
contribution to understanding everyday life has been to discover how
ideas, *legitimated through coordinated discourses*, organize knowledge and
action" (1995: 110, emphasis added). Thus, we began the "second stage"
of our research by exploring how each particular local setting is tied to
the larger general complex of social relations organizing the institution
of housing and child-rearing through textually-mediated discourses.
Keeping the institutional nexus of the state and housing in view, we
collected and read primary sources on child-rearing and housing between 1890 and 1930 from the US National Archives and Research Administration (NARA), the Library of Congress, historical societies and
museums in cities where each of the women lived as children and parents, and various library repositories across the United States. We put
primary emphasis on reviewing the archival data from the US Departments of Commerce and Labor, since during this period state concerns

about housing were located organizationally in these departments of the federal government. Following this path, our research extends the work done by Griffith (1995) and Hays (1996) on the historical linkages between the child development and mothering discourses to include the housing discourse.

We begin our exploration with brief housing biographies of the five women whose narratives form the experiential basis of this research. Next, we examine the ideological practices of three state-affiliated organizations and their organizational texts that embody the ideological code for rearing and housing children, which we call the "Standard American Home" (SAH). Finally, we present excerpts from the women's narratives and discuss the various ways SAH is evident in their talk and courses of action. At times SAH is obvious in the housing and child-rearing practices that the women produced, but it is also apparent in their commentary when they modify, reject, or are unable to attain the SAH.

Housing Biographies

Olive Jackson was born in 1905 and raised primarily on ranches owned by her father in western Wyoming. Much of her childhood was spent living with her family, consisting of six brothers and sisters, and doing chores. When she was old enough to attend high school, Olive lived with a family in a nearby town so that she could attend the school. After high school she briefly attended the state university, and then Olive moved to the plains of Wyoming, where she did home schooling and lived with several families. After two years as a teacher, she returned home and married a train checker. For the next two years, the Jacksons lived in company housing provided by the railroad. There Olive gave birth to a son, Ian, in 1928.

Within a year Olive moved with her son to Riverside, then a small town in the Southern California desert, for the child's health. She rented a small house for about a year, and then she returned to Wyoming with Ian and moved to her parents' house, since another woman had moved in with her husband in her absence. Recognizing that her marriage was probably over, Olive returned by herself to California to attend college and business school. There she sublet several small rooms.

Divorced from her husband in 1937 and needing to support herself, Olive began selling Fuller brushes. Through Fuller Brush she got another job opportunity in Idaho. She moved by herself, leaving Ian with her mother. In Idaho she roomed with two different families. After several months Olive left Idaho and moved to Long Beach, California, where she worked as a secretary. Again she lived with Ian for several years, and they moved a number of times to various rented apartments, small houses, and rooms in order to minimize living expenses and to reside closer to work. After her son left for military service, Olive continued to rent various apartments around the Los Angeles area. Eventually she moved to Arizona and continued to rent rooms or apartments or room and board with others.

Thelma Hay was born in Akron, Ohio, in 1911. Her mother was a housewife and her father a handyman and hardware store employee until the Great Depression. When Thelma was a child, her family moved frequently, renting various apartments and living with grandparents on their farm. Many of the moves were prompted by her father's lack of work or her grandparents' need for assistance in their house.

Thelma married an executive secretary for a large rubber company in 1938 and had two sons and two daughters. She and her husband rented an apartment at first and then a small house. When Thelma was pregnant for the first time, she and her husband moved in with her mother for about three months, and then they bought a house where they lived for twelve years.

In 1952 her husband's health forced them to relocate to a different climate, to a place they had never been before and where they had no prospects. They rented a home in Phoenix, Arizona, in the same subdivision as some friends whom they knew from Akron. Initially both Thelma and her husband found temporary jobs; and after her husband found a permanent personnel position with a large electronics firm, they began to look for new housing because they wanted more space for their children. In 1959 they bought their first house in Phoenix, a three-bedroom, and the following year they relocated to a four-bedroom home. When their children grew up and moved out, the Hays moved back to an apartment for a brief period and eventually bought a double-wide in a mobile home park.

Ursula Roberts was born in New Castle, Pennsylvania, in 1917. Her father worked as a sales manager for several car dealerships and her mother was a housewife, taking care of Ursula and her sister. Her parents lived in an apartment for a short time and then they purchased a home near her grandparents and other relatives. Ursula lived there throughout her childhood and continued to live there even after she was married in 1938. When the newlyweds saved enough money, they rented an apartment. Once her husband, Al, got a job with J.C. Penney they moved into a larger apartment; but during the Second World War, when Al was working in a defence industry, they decided to rent a house. After the war, the Roberts bought a house that they lived in for five years. At that time they had a son and a daughter.

Al began to work as an executive for a large life insurance company in 1952 and the family relocated often as he was transferred from one city to another. From that time on the Roberts always owned their own homes, which were single-family detached houses. Ursula stated that they "bettered" themselves with each move.

Nita Rodriguez was born in the state of Sonora, Mexico, in 1920. She had five half-brothers and half-sisters who were several years older than she was. Her widowed mother supported the family as a seamstress, and Nita did not know who her father was. Nita spent much of her childhood in mining towns in Mexico and in the United States. In an Arizona mining town Nita's family lived in an adobe house that they rented, but they had to move to another house when the landlord wanted the adobe for some of his relatives. In 1928 Nita's older sister received $1000 when her husband died in an auto accident, and her sister used the money to buy a house in the town. Nita and her mother also moved into this house, but soon afterward her mother died, leaving Nita in the care of her siblings.

During the Great Depression there was no longer work in the mines, and Nita travelled with family members for several years as they built a national highway in Mexico. They were moving constantly and often lived in shacks quickly constructed of mud and branches. They cooked out of doors and had very little furniture. Once they moved to a little town where the houses were made of adobe, and they lived there for a couple of months in an abandoned house. She also lived in mining towns in Mexico when her brothers or brothers-in-law could find temporary work.

Nita also lived on a farm for a while, land acquired by her brother through a land reform program after the Mexican Revolution. Soon after, she married Tony Rodriguez, a US citizen who had come to Mexico selling food and supplies to the miners. The couple moved to a house Tony built in the gold field near Santa Anna. Once Nita secured the documents that she would need to return to the United States, she and her husband moved to Phoenix, where he went back to his job as foreman in a brickyard. There they lived in an apartment near the plant. Later, as a bonus, the brick company gave Tony three acres of land, and in 1942 they moved into a large workshop/garage that they converted into a small house.

Tony took an opportunity to be a superintendent at a brick-making plant in Mexico. Nita and Tony remained in Mexico for two years, except when Nita returned to the United States in 1946 to give birth to her first child. After an unsuccessful venture, the Rodriguezes returned to the United States to the same warehouse they had converted to a small house. Upon returning Tony started his own brick-making company; however, in 1958, he was killed when a large office building under construction collapsed on him. Some time after her husband's death, Nita used money that she received in a settlement to buy another house for her four small children.

Edna Kepler was born in Akron, Ohio, in 1923. Her mother was a housewife and her father a circuit preacher, minister, and school custodian. Edna was the third of nine children in the family. Often the family did not have much money and they lived with Edna's grandparents on some occasions. Generally they rented apartments or houses near the places where her father worked. During the Second World War, when Edna's future husband went to England and her own parents moved to Mansfield, Ohio, she moved in with her fiancé's parents, where she paid room and board. In 1945 Edna married and the couple lived with her in-laws until her husband found a job driving a delivery truck for a major department store. With his first paycheque they rented an apartment by themselves. Soon they had two children.

In 1948 the Keplers purchased their first house, a bungalow that they lived in for five years. They moved from their first starter home because it was too small for the growing family of four children and because the neighbourhood was changing. In 1954 the family moved to a suburban neighbourhood. In 1962 they sold their suburban house to have money to send their children to college and to purchase a cheaper house in an old neighbourhood in the city. They lived there until 1980. When her husband died, Edna moved to Phoenix, Arizona, to be with her children, living with them until she found an apartment.

Ruling Relations and the Standard American Home

We propose that three state-affiliated organizations – the Children's Bureau, the Own Your Own Home movement, and the Better Homes in America campaign – through their ideological practices promoted the "Standard American Home" as the proper form of dwelling for infants and children. These organizations contributed to the textually-mediated discourse on housing and child-rearing and connected up with and regulated the housing activities of both businesses producing housing and parents. Although we do not claim that the child-rearing discourse originated with the agencies, the work of these organizations incorporated many pre-existing concerns about children with the discourse on home ownership as the proper way to raise children. In the text of these organizations, the SAH operates as an ideological code that reproduces normative organization and desire coordinated with the marketplace and the relations of ruling (Smith 1990c, 1999). Although SAH-ordered discourse ignores the material conditions of people's lives in the process, it ties people's child-rearing and housing work to a commercial market selling and leasing housing and offering household goods and services for young families and their children regardless of their material circumstances. The power of these three organizations is in their institutional practices, particularly their ability to reproduce SAH-ordered code at multiple sites and at different times regardless of context. Now let us look at some of the ideological practices of these organizations.

The Children's Bureau

The Children's Bureau was established by law on 9 April 1912 and was charged to "investigate and report ... upon all matters pertaining to the welfare of children and child life among all classes of people" (37 *Stat. L.* 79, quoted in Tobey 1925: 1). The original idea for the Children's Bureau is credited to Miss Lillian D. Wald, head of the House on Henry Street in New York City. She presented her idea to Mrs Florence Kelly of the National Consumers' League, who further developed the plan and obtained support from the National Child Labour Committee and prominent sociologists. The two women then presented the idea to President Roosevelt, who gave it his support. The Children's Bureau was originally created in the Department of Commerce and Labor, but in 1913 it moved to the newly established Department of Labor.

According to Tobey (1925), the bureau's early work included studying infant mortality; preparing pamphlets on prenatal care, infant care, and child care; reviewing child labour; initiating the national observance of Baby Week; shaping regulations to limit child labour; promoting birth registration; studying numerous problems of children residing in rural areas; and producing a number of popular pamphlets and research reports. Studies of infant mortality were undertaken initially because the topic was socially significant and of popular interest and because reports could be made public quickly as each study was completed. Ten studies were undertaken in industrialized cities and towns and twelve were done in rural communities (Children's Bureau 1977 [1914]). All these studies indicated that high infant mortality was associated with "low earnings, poor housing, the employment of the mother outside the home, and large families" (Abbott 1974 [1923]: 3).

The results of these studies led the Children's Bureau director Julia Lathrop to have Mrs Max West write several brochures, including *Infant Care* (1972 [1914]), which became the government's all-time bestseller. In the letter of transmittal to the secretary of labour, Lathrop notes that the booklet was compiled through an exhaustive study of the standard literature on child hygiene and in consultation with the best authorities in the medical and child development fields. In the 1914 monograph West describes in great detail the proper housing environment for growing children. She notes that separate houses, rather than apartments or tenement housing, are the places to raise children. These houses should be set in suburban locations where families can assure the proper growth and development of their children. Windows, sunshine, ventilation, play spaces indoors and out, and the locations of outhouses for proper drainage are essential for a child's well-being.

The 1929 Children's Bureau revised publication on infant care, written and compiled by the child hygiene director of the bureau and the advisory board of paediatricians from the American Child Health Association (ACHA) of the Child Division of the American Medical Association (AMA) and the American Pediatric Society (APS), describes the same information that was in West's 1914 monograph; however, the publication includes an expanded section on the home with more specificity about the necessary equipment and furniture needed for the nursery (see exhibit 10.1). In addition to providing a separate room with proper temperature and ventilation for their infant, parents are to acquire a long list of essential equipment specifically for the baby's room.

Exhibit 10.1 Instructions for care of infant in home from
***Infant Care*, 1929 (US Department of Labor, Children's Bureau)**

The Baby's Room

Whenever possible a room should be given up to the exclusive use of the baby, since it is hard to give him the quiet he should have in a room that must be used also by other members of the family. A bright sunny room should be chosen for the nursery.

Temperatures

In order that the baby may be dressed properly the temperature of his room should be known. This can be done by hanging a thermometer about 3 feet from the floor ...

For the first few weeks of the baby's life the daytime temperature of the room should be kept between 65° and 70° F. At night it may fall from 10° to 15° lower if the baby is properly dressed and protected. For older babies the day temperature may be 65° to 68° and the night from 15° to 30° lower. A healthy baby is much better off in a cool room. He should be protected by screens against drafts of cold air.

In winter the temperature of his room should be kept as even as possible. Oil or gas heaters may be used to give quick temporary heat, but gas heaters should not be used in a baby's room unless no other method of quick heating is available. They are likely to leak and give off poisonous fumes that are very dangerous; a slight leak day after day may make anyone exposed to it very ill ...

Ventilation

The best way to ventilate the baby's room is to keep the window open. Most of the time the window may be left open at the top, or at the bottom when a window board is used. It is possible to shield the crib in such a way that no direct draft falls on the baby.

For ventilating the nursery at night in cold and windy weather tack one or more thicknesses of cheesecloth on a wooden frame like that of an ordinary wire screen and insert in the open window. The cloth breaks up the air current and distributes it in various directions, thus preventing drafts. A narrow cloth screen a few inches wide may be inserted in an opening at the top of the window, thus making it possible to keep the window open most of the time even in very cold weather. (pp. 22–3)

Walls and Floors

The baby's room should be kept scrupulously clean. If the family moves into an old house, the nursery should be freshly papered and painted.

A bare floor is easily kept clean. Hardwood floors are better than soft for they do not splinter, but a softwood floor painted or varnished will do very well. If the floor is old, it may be covered with linoleum, which is easily cleaned. Heavy rugs and carpets are not suitable for a nursery, but washable rugs may be used. When the baby is old enough to sit on the floor to play, a heavy blanket folded or even a bed quilt may be used as a mat.

Furnishings

Everything not actually needed for the care of the baby should be kept out of the nursery. Furnishings must be washed often with soap and water and exposed to sunshine and open air. If old furniture is used, is should be painted with washable paint – white or light coloured. For cribs and play pens it is well to use paint containing no white lead, as a baby may bite the railing and swallow paint, and if it contains white lead he may be poisoned.

The following articles are essential:

Bed or crib.
Bedclothes.
Bureau or chest of drawers for clothing.
One or two low chairs.
Bed or couch for nurse or mother ...
Wall thermometer.
Low chair for the mother to use when nursing the baby.
Folding or stationary dressing table ...

Bathing equipment:
Tub – tin, enameled ware or rubber.
Washbasin.
Enamel-ware tray, or a box or drawer divided into compartments ...

Toilet equipment (kept in bathroom if possible).

Painted nursery toilet chair …, with a cushion.

Small toilet seat with back and sides, which can be fastened on the regular toilet.

Small enameled-ware chamber.

Covered enameled-ware slop pail or two for diapers.

Covered soiled-clothes hamper.

Other Useful articles are:

Clothes rack. Nursery ice box.

Balance scales. Bath thermometer.

Table to hold scales. Little chair and table.

Screen. Hinged gate at stairway. (pp. 21–4)

Source: Adapted from reprint *in Child Rearing Literature of Twentieth Century America*, Family in America Series (New York: Arno Press, 1972).

The orientation of this booklet is to no particular mother, but to typified mothers as producers of the skilled work of opening and closing windows, judging air temperatures and wind currents, controlling heating systems, cleaning and sanitizing, fastening screens, and furnishing a separate room for infants. The language of typification ("mother," "the baby") along with the use of the atemporal present provides a universalizing schema regardless of a mother's socio-economic conditions and housing arrangement. The discourse suggests that "the baby's room" must be a space separated from the parents' room, and furnished with a whole array of baby-specific belongings to which the tots are entitled. Not only must mothers be able to measure temperatures accurately, paint, paper, and clean, but implicitly inscribed in the text is the work they must do in planning, purchasing, and assembling baby-specific products.

In addition, in a 1922 report on a rural area in Kentucky, the bureau's recommendation for the spatial organization of children's sleeping is noted: "A separate bed in a separate room is usually considered the ideal sleeping arrangement for a child" (Roberts 1974 [1922]: 34). And while fresh air throughout the night is a requirement of the bureau, the manner in which the air enters the home is also important:

Fresh air in abundance day and night is requisite to the proper care of children. In the district studied it was the requirement most commonly fulfilled, but from compulsion and not from choice. It is probable that most of the children would not have any fresh air at night if it were not for poor housing, for 93 percent were sleeping in winter in rooms the windows of which were not opened. On account of the poor construction of homes, however, resulting in cracks in floors and walls and loose-fitting doors and windows, most of the children were receiving abundant fresh air. (35)

Finally, the Children's Bureau publications summarized the current child development expertise about children's play in the home. Although there was disagreement among Progressive Era experts about the proper activities for children, Zelizer (1985) and others have pointed out that activists, working to eliminate child labour by redefining children as sacred rather than as workers, focused on childhood as a time of growth and discovery best established through play activity. These experts tended to discourage children from doing chores in the home since they felt parents might exploit their labour. One publication, "Are You Training Your Child to be Happy?" written by a leading paediatric physician, discusses the importance of providing furniture that can be touched in the child's room, buying play things for children of different ages, and using the child's room for play and school work. It notes that *"Your child should have a corner of his own where he can work or play undisturbed when he wants to be alone. If there is only one child in your family, you should see that he also plays with other children"* (Thom 1972 [1930]: 52, emphasis in original).

The brochures and reports prepared by the Children's Bureau were widely distributed by the bureau itself through public health programs in cities, through agricultural extension services throughout rural areas, and as advertising supplements for infant formula (Macleod 1998; Richardson 1993). Mothers were encouraged to write to the bureau for more information and for additional free government publications on topics ranging from the use of milk in the home, the design of the home with children in mind, the duties of a good neighbour, and to how to get rid of bedbugs (Public Health Service 1976).

The Own Your Own Home Movement

A second government effort that helped to shape both housing and child-rearing practices was known as the Own Your Own Home (OYOH) campaign. It was a joint venture of the US Department of Labor, lumber companies, lending agencies, realtors, and municipalities to promote homeownership. Although largely directed to bankers, encouraging them to restructure mortgage-lending practices and to make more money available for home mortgages through builders and thrift institutions and directly to purchasers, the campaign developed and distributed extensive advertising materials to the public on the combined themes of good parenting and homeownership (National Archives and Research Association [NARA] N.d.a).

The Own Your Own Home campaign was initiated by the National Association of Real Estate Boards (NAREB) in 1917. The United States League of Building and Loan Associations, the National Federation of Construction Industries, and various lumber associations also joined the movement. The federal government became more involved when the Own Your Own Home section was established in the US Department of Labor's Division of Public Works and Construction Development and the Information and Education Division in February 1919 (NARA N.d.a). Franklin T. Miller, chairman of F.W. Dodge (which handled information services for the construction industry) and vice-president of the National Federation of Construction Industries, initially headed the section. Paul C. Murphy, a real estate broker and spokesperson for real estate boards from Portland, Oregon, and K.V. Haymaker, an executive for a savings and loan in Detroit who was connected to the United States League of Building and Loan Associations, assisted him.

The OYOH section acted as a clearinghouse for promotional materials to encourage growth of the movement, and they produced posters, newspaper copy, brochures, and advertisements and distributed these to over 137 local committees for their use. One poster, "Own a Home," presented here in figure 10.1, declares that parents should become homeowners "For your Children's Sake." Parents are instructed to write to Roger Babson, Chief, Information and Education Service, for copies of the brochure instructing parents on how to become homeowners.

The representation of SAH-ordered terms and phrases in the Department of Labor poster is compelling. The use of the abstract phrase, "For your children's sake," to refer to children's personal benefit and interests of no particular kind generates a common ordering in which parents' concerns for their children (the child's health, well-being, happiness, emotional development, educational progress, and so on) can be inserted. Not only are parents made responsible for their concerns, but also SAH-ordered terms – "yours," "own" – make the remedy theirs alone.

The OYOH campaign also published a solicited letter from the National Federation of Women's Clubs in newspapers throughout the

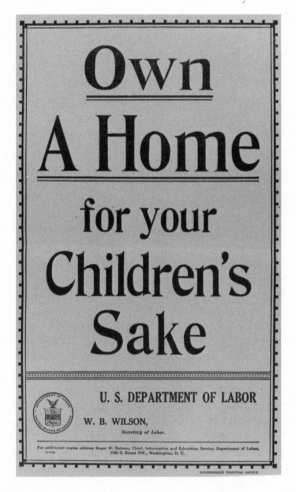

Figure 10.1 Own Your Own Home campaign advertising poster, 1919.
Source: National Archives and Research Administration (N.d.).

country suggesting that women's involvement in homeownership was important because it meant a "desirable neighborhood and proper environment in which to raise children." OYOH section often played on the fears of parents raising their children in certain neighbourhoods during this period. In remarkable newspaper copy, "A LETTER TO LITTLE GIRLS AND BOYS – AND BIG ONES," the Department of Labor not only portrays a proper home for a child, but also addresses the problems of overcrowding, malnutrition, abandonment, instability, family violence, child neglect, and the underachievement of children raised in rental apartments or flats. The suitable home for children includes a sunny room for each child, a big front and back porch on which to play, and suitable playmates in the neighbourhood (see exhibit 10.2).

Exhibit 10.2 Newspaper copy from the Own Your Own Home section, 1919.

A Letter to Little Girls and Boys – and Big Ones

Every baby bird and animal that is born comes into the world in its own little nest. Its father and mother choose a sheltered spot, and make the home comfortable with loving care. At night they gather there for protection against danger.

No bird or animal would even think of raising its little ones in a strange nest. Only the cuckoo, a very lazy bird, tries to save itself the trouble of building a nest, and lays its eggs in other birds [sic] nest. Birds hate the cuckoo, and will drive it away. But sometimes it lays its eggs unseen, and a bird mother hatches them as though they were her own, and feeds more little ones than she should have to. Or sometimes she finds that there are strange eggs in her nest and she builds over the top of it and lays more eggs, or chooses another nesting place altogether.

Of course we must shelter chickens and cows and horses. We have tamed them for our own use, and must keep them near by for our use. But if they were wild they would have the natural instinct that would tell them where and how they should find shelter – how to make *their own homes*.

Now what we are trying to make plain is this: If it is natural and right for little baby birds and animals to be born in their very own homes, it is the most natural thing in the world that you should have the right to be born in your own home.

When your father and mother pay rent they are paying someone else for the use of the place they live in. It is not a good thing to do that. It is like wearing someone else's clothes.

Besides, your father and mother want you to be healthy and strong. Now, in Oakland, California a doctor measured a lot of little boys and girls not long ago, and the children whose fathers and mothers lived in their own homes were bigger and stronger and smarter than others whose parents were not so well situated. It does not mean that some were rich and others poor, but that when your parents own your home they can keep it healthy and sanitary and comfortable.

When you live in a nice home you progress faster at school. If you change to a new school and new teachers every time your folks move you lose a lot of time, and must get used to a lot of new teachers and books and school-mates, and you don't get along as fast in your classes as you should.

Your home ought to have a nice big sunshiny room for you, and a sand pile under the back porch for little brother and sister, and a big front porch where you can watch for Daddy when he comes home in the evening. It will be where there are a lot of nice playmates, nice children, your own father and mother will be glad to have you play and go with, if they choose it rightly.

Read this letter all through, and ask your father and mother about anything in it you do not understand. And if they want more information themselves, have them ask us.

Source: National Archives and Records Administration, Own Your Own Home section, Real Estate Division, US Housing Corporation, Record Group 3, College Park, MD.

The welfare of children is further addressed in an OYOH press clipping from the *Washington Star* (17 May 1919). In the article "Mothers Grow Weary," the writer declares:

The children must start all over again making friends and forming those associations so dear to the heart of youth. It all seems so useless for already their short lives are overcrowded with a jungle of friends made one year and lost the next – are they to have no permanent memories of home to go with them through life? (NARA N.d.b)

"But what can I do?," you say. The answer is so easy if you just know how – "build your own home." Start building or buying today.

Are you fair to your family – are you doing for them all that is within your power?

The texts from the OYOH campaign use SAH-ordered discourse to universalize apprehension about overcrowding, malnourishment,

and so on, as the concerns of all parents raising children and to provide their solution. In very explicit ways, the selection and ordering
of words and sentences in these texts demonstrate how the universalizing features of ideological codes operate. Further, SAH-ordered discourse in the texts suppresses "alternative structuring devices" (Smith
1999: 166), which might treat those who rent, those who are poor, those
who do not own homes, those who are ethnically or racially different
in similar ways with regard to the provision of housing. Finally, SAH
code as written into these texts claims that raising one's children in a
stable and safe environment in an owner-occupied home with separate
rooms for children surrounded by porches, playmates, and play areas
in the yards is an innate parental behaviour. The normative organization in text portrays living in apartments or paying rent as defective
types of housing forms for child-rearing while simultaneously locating
and naming those children "at risk." These distinctions in the texts are
class and racially ordered, making poor, non-white renters the causes
of parents' concern.

   Although the Own Your Own Home campaign was short-lived, the
Department of Labor produced and distributed thousands of newspaper advertisements across the nation in multiple languages including
German, Polish, Yiddish, and Spanish. Much of their work that was
directed at working-class parents encouraged them to purchase homes
for their children's welfare despite current building costs and wages
(see Luken & Vaughan 2005). The texts direct concerned parents to the
market selling housing, a course of action to remedy their poor housing
situations.

Better Homes in America

The Better Homes in America movement also made significant contributions to the discourses on child-rearing and housing. It was a nation-
wide campaign begun in 1922 in the offices of the Butterick Publishing
Company and announced in their popular, mass-circulated, homemaking magazine for women, the *Delineator*. The campaign, which celebrated
and promoted homeownership, home maintenance, improvement, and
decoration in towns and cities across the country, not only served as a
means to educate consumers in responsible purchasing behaviour in an
ever-expanding market of housing goods, but also served powerful organizations and groups concerned with homebuilding, furnishing, and
maintenance (Library of Congress 1999).

The Better Homes in America movement received broad support from government and industry alike. President Coolidge served as honorary chairman of the advisory board and the then-secretary of commerce, Herbert Hoover, presided over the board of directors. Not only did Hoover play a major role in organizing local committees and coordinating homebuilding interests through the Department of Commerce by distributing Better Homes materials to industry specialists and groups, he also promoted what he said was the "spiritual" impact of homeownership on society, families, and children (Radford 1996: 51). In addition, volunteers drawn from local businesses (builders, lumber yards, real estate agents, suppliers, home decorating, and landscape businesses) formed hundreds of local committees that mounted widely advertised demonstration projects and yearly contests to develop enthusiasm for buying and maintaining houses appropriately for raising families.

One brochure, *School Cottages for Training in Home-Making*, distributed by the Better Homes in America committee to schools throughout the United States, outlines the importance of skills for girls and boys in house-making for the "development of our civilization" and "character of our people":

In this generation, due partly to the increasing urbanization of American life and the increasing demands made upon the time and energy of both parents and children outside the home, the training of children by their parents in the art of home-making has become more meager and inadequate. Meanwhile, the standards of home-making, as outlined by specialists, have become better defined and have developed with the changing needs of our civilization. Home economics is becoming an applied science; child training is a developing art borrowing increasingly from psychology; and with the new recognition of the ethics of personality, the household itself has changed from a limited monarchy to a democracy with rights and duties for all members.

The development of our civilization demands that we give the younger generation training for home-making – the most universal of occupations. And it should be a training which will make up for the lack of apprenticeship in the home, which will cull the best from our developing household sciences and impart it in a usable form to all future housekeepers. Above all, the program of instruction should conserve and develop the finer values of family life including the spirit of cooperation and service. (Library of Congress 1999)

Each year the movement sponsored a Better Homes Week that highlighted a demonstration house built, remodelled, and decorated by local architects, builders, and home economists with donated materials from sponsoring community businesses (see figures 10.2 and 10.3).

The images and their accompanying text posit visually an SAH-ordered discourse about houses as sanitary, painted, papered, landscaped, and single-family detached, surrounded by large, open yards for children. Again, the representation of SAH-ordered terms and phrases, "old shacks" and "poorest paid farm laborer," generates a common ordering in which any shack or worker can be inserted by making the poor parent the doer of skilled work in painting, trellising, and landscaping. On the other hand, the implicit contrast of the image of the two-storey house is also the project of poor parents' work. Here desire is constructed in relation between the middle-class image of the home in the text and the forever-imperfect actuality of the shack or their own homes. Thus, the images themselves and their ordering in the texts generate implicit class differences and provide women with an explicit yardstick to compare their own housing circumstance against the discourse.

In one plan book, *Better Homes in America Plan Book for Demonstration Week, October 9 to 14, 1922*, the bedrooms for boys and girls that are to be replicated in model homes are described. The booklet was developed in consultation with the combined expertise of home economists, child development specialists, home decorators, architects, and doctors, and was based on the current scientific understanding of the way children developed and learned (Leavitt 2002). It was distributed to local committees and duplicated for parents attending the demonstration project, and on its cover instructed parents to write for additional information.

The text in exhibit 10.3 describes in detailed and near endless lists the appropriately gendered furniture, textures, colours, and equipment for sleeping, playing, and studying for boys and girls. While boys' rooms should be made interesting, girls' rooms should reflect their personalities and disclose their potential as housekeepers. Although the nursery should have a wide array of washable furnishings appropriate in size for an infant, decoration with designs and bright colours should be kept to a minimum to ensure happiness and meaningful impressions that will have a "lasting influence on the adult life."

BETTER HOMES IN AMERICA

Old shack in Pulaski County, Arkansas, which for years had been used as a storage barn. Re-conditioned by the Better Homes Committee of Mabelvale. See opposite page.

The Better Homes Committee of Mabelvale, Arkansas, took the shack shown on the opposite page, painted and papered it, built trellises, planted vines and garden, and successfully demonstrated the possibility of providing a comfortable, sanitary and attractive home within the reach of the poorest paid farm laborer.

Figure 10.2 Before and after demonstration home from Better Homes in America, publication no. 11, *Guide Book for Better Homes Campaigns in Rural Communities and Small Towns*, 1927.
Source: Library of Congress (1999).

Figure 10.3 Demonstration house built in suburbs. Exterior of house in Better Homes in America exhibit. *Source*: Library of Congress, Prints and Photographs Division, Theodor Horydczak Collection.

Exhibit 10.3 Pages from *Better Homes in America Plan Book for Demonstration Week*, October 9 to 14, 1922.

Bedroom for Either Boys or Girls

It has been proven that furnishings and colour produce either desirable or disastrous effects upon the sensitive minds of children. As all children's rooms are usually a combination of bedroom, play room, and study, it is well to keep in mind colours, design, arrangement, and practicality for all purposes.

To most children, a spotty or too often repeated design is distracting. Blues and violets soothe, while reds, yellows, and sometimes greens are exciting and stimulating colours.

We so often send our children to study and amuse themselves in their room, but have we done our share in providing them with the comforts and necessities that will assist them to produce better school work?

Boys – With no frills, light fabrics, or woodwork for them to soil and mar, their rooms may be made interesting – even beautiful – but convenience and masculinity should be kept foremost in mind.

Girls – A girl's room, on the other hand, should be dainty, bright, and frivolous. Her personality, even at a very tender age, will clearly be disclosed by the way she cares for her room. There is no need of a great expenditure of money in buying furniture or hangings for a girl's room. Some of the cheaper fabrics and simplest furniture will make the most charming room.

Boys' Rooms

A Suggested Colour Scheme
  Walls – Buff-coloured paint, or tinted walls.
  Woodwork – Stained mission oak or walnut.
  Floors – Hardwood floor, strips of coco matting, or wool-braided
  rugs. Softwood – a large square of linoleum.
Suggested List of Furnishings
  Bed – Something of the day bed type.
  Bedspread of blue denim, with stitched bands of yellow sateen at
  edge.
  Chest of Drawers – Painted buff or brown, or walnut or mission oak.
  A Mirror – Antique gilt, or of wood to match chest of drawers, hung
  low.
  A Desk – Of the craftsman type, with stool or bench to match.
  Two Wooden Chairs – Either painted or of mission oak.
  A Table – Low, plain wooden table, of walnut, or stained to match the
  woodwork.
  One Comfortable Chair – Brown wicker or the Windsor type.
  A Lamp – Of the student type, or on a bracket, securely fastened to the
  wall.
  A Tie Rack – Hung near chest of drawers.
  One or two shelves – For books, trophies, etc. Made of plain wood,
  stained to match the woodwork of a plain bookcase or mission oak.

Curtains – Of blue denim, with stitched bands of sateen at edge – hung straight.

Girls' Rooms

A Suggested Colour Scheme
Walls – Papered in a soft grey-rose, allover design paper.
Woodwork – Cream paint.
Floors – Hardwood – Rag rugs, with rose stripes or a grey chenille carpet. Softwood – Battleship grey paint, with rag rugs or rose chenille carpet.
Suggested List of Furnishings
Bed – *Single* – Painted ivory or cream – four posts, or with some low, simple headboard.
Bedspread of rose dotted swiss, with wide ruffle.
A Dressing Table – To match bed, with rose coloured sateen mats – bound in pale-grey with drawers.
A Large Box – For waists, etc. Covered in rose and grey cretonne.
A Desk – To correspond with painted furniture; a grey blotter and rose coloured pen.
Two Chairs – One of natural wicker with cushions of rose sateen, and one of wood to correspond with painted furniture, caned seat.
A Sewing Table – Of mahogany or cherry.
A Lamp – China base with a shade of silk, dotted swiss, or rose-coloured paper.

The Nursery

The ideal nursery is also a play room. It should, as nearly as possible, meet the ideals of the child's own world. In that room are received early impressions which are never forgotten, and which have a lasting influence on the adult life.

Don't bedeck the cribs, beds, or curtains with ribbons and laces and expect your child to be happy. The "don'ts" and "be carefuls" make children irritable and unhappy. Choose the room with a thought to sunlight, and be sure it has outside blinds which will darken the room without keeping out the air.

The walls and woodwork should be painted, if possible, a cream or light grey. Some fairy tale friezes are attractive, and afford opportunities of introducing colour, but if used, should not be placed too high on the wall – about three-quarters of the way up from the floor is a reasonable height. Child-study has taught that many and oft-repeated designs and subjects become meaningless, especially to older children.

The furniture in the nursery should be practical. Painted furniture and wicker chairs are attractive. A comfortable winged or overstuffed chair for the grown-ups is essential. Low shelves and cupboards built for toys and books are necessary if the room is to be kept neat and tidy. A stationary blackboard, and a large box for books and cherished belongings, are very welcome additions.

A Suggested Colour Scheme for the Nursery
   Walls – A soft, misty, grey paint, tint, or plain paper.
   Woodwork – A dull white.
   Floors – Plain hardwood, with a rag or braided rug in sapphire blue – or softwood, entirely in taupe Jaspe linoleum.
Below Is a Suggested List of Furnishings Which
The Nursery Might Contain
   A Crib – White iron or wood, on ball bearing casters.
   Bedspread of yellow and white seersucker, or a silky yellow sunfast.
   A Tall Chest of Drawers – Painted cream or white, with plenty of drawers.
   Table – Low nursery table or tall one which has had its legs cut.
   Two Chairs – Low, with wooden seats, and painted to match the furniture.
   A Desk – Flat top with plenty of paper and pencils.
   Waste Paper Basket – White or natural wicker.
   One Large Fireside Chair – With slip cover of blue and yellow striped linen.
   Glass Curtains – Of best quality of cream coloured cheesecloth, bound in yellow tape.
   Overdraperies (If desired) – Of primrose yellow silk or sunfast, or striped yellow and blue linen to match slip cover.
   Clothes Rack – Low wooden rack, painted white, with at least four hooks.
   Closet – Should have a low pole on which could be hung plenty of hangers. Also a shelf about 6 inches from the floor for shoes, etc.
   Large Cushions for the floor – One each of blue, yellow, nile green and orange.

Colour Scheme – If you desire another colour scheme, such as blue-and-white, or pink-and-white, write for information.

Pages from *Better Homes in America Plan Book for Demonstration Week, October 9 to 14, 1922.*

Source: Adapted from *Better Homes in America Plan Book for Demonstration Week, October 9 to 14, 1922.* "Prosperity and Thrift: The Coolidge Era Collection," Library of Congress (1999).

Here SAH code generated in-text universalizes colours, furniture, textures, and arrangements in children's rooms across gender and age through the language of typification: boys mar, and therefore the furniture in boys' rooms must be strong and masculine; girls are tender, and therefore their rooms must be dainty, frivolous, and low cost to produce as compared to boys'; infants are sensitive and impressionable, and thus, their rooms must be soft, misty, and white. The ideological code of SAH ties child-rearing to housing practices specifically through a gender and age discourse about the "don'ts" and "be carefuls," warning parents about the negative consequences of poor decorating practices. In this way, the code organizes parents responsible for decorating, furnishing, and purchasing for their children's rooms not only in relation to the work of experts in child development and home economics, but also to a newly emerging market selling gender- and age-specific products to anxious parents desiring to assure their children's emotional and physical well-being (Stearns 2003).

By 1930 there were 7279 Better Homes local committees established in numerous cities and rural areas including Ohio, Pennsylvania, Wyoming, and Arizona. Not only did hundreds of community business people contribute to these expositions, but thousands of people attended and participated in them over the year both in ongoing home economics classes for girls and in infant care classes taught by agricultural extension workers. Often demonstration homes were reassembled at state fairs and used to distribute pamphlets and brochures and to provide a venue for speaking about how good homes build character in children. The Better Homes in America movement, in stressing cooperative efforts between government and private enterprise and demonstrating what housing purchases parents might make, helped to guarantee the appropriately raised child of the early twentieth century (Wright 1983).

SAH Discourse and Women's Narratives

The ideological code of the "Standard American Home" provided a point of reference for the organization of housing and child-rearing for the women in this study. It informed their assessments of their living arrangements and the activities of their own children. It is important to note that SAH did not cause or influence the women (and their parents) to act in the manners in which they did. Rather, SAH provided a framework for how their children should be housed and how they should act in the home and for how the women should remedy or change their housing situations. The actual conditions of their lives are not a feature of this universalized discourse. At times the women were unable to produce "proper" housing and at times they modified or rejected this form of housing. Nonetheless, SAH formed part of a discursive terrain that was often referenced in the narratives of the women who participated in this research.

Although we have no direct evidence that the women in this study or their parents actually read the pamphlets, brochures, or advertising materials produced by these three state-affiliated organizations, literacy rates markedly increased between 1890 and 1930 (US Bureau of the Census 1975) and the discourse and the ideological code were pervasive in other organizational sites. Olive Jackson's mother probably was well aware of the discourse through academic texts she read in the process of receiving her degree in home economics at a land-grant institution that distributed expertise about housing, homemaking, cooking, and child care (Rutherford 2003). Nita Rodriguez lived in an ethnically diverse company town owned by a major US mining company that was headquartered in Philadelphia. Shareholder reports (University of Pennsylvania 1930) show expenditures for building single-family detached housing, for providing community wells and electricity, and for conducting "Americanization" classes for employees. These classes were probably much like those taught by the Ford Motor Company in the early part of the twentieth century, which included classes on proper housing and child-rearing (see Meyer 1980). In addition, the notion of privacy in homes, so pervasive in North American discourse at the time, did not characterize the living arrangements of families in Mexico (Pader 1993, 1994). Ursula, Thelma, and Edna grew up in cities where both the Better Homes in America and the Own Your Own Home campaigns were organized locally and extensively advertised (Luken & Vaughan 2005). In addition, all three women purchased homes from developers and builders locally engaged in those campaigns (NARA N.d.b). More importantly, however, as children the women connected with the discourse through schooling and textbooks picturing the proper housing for raising children. By 1935, the ubiquity of the discourse was evident even in popular culture. For example, Charlie Chaplin's film *Modern Times* portrays the ideal home for raising children in candid contrast to the defective home in which the movie couple lived.

Despite the lack of direct evidence, the ubiquitous standards of SAH discourse to which women felt accountable, but not necessarily compelled to enact, are evident in their narratives with respect to housing type, privacy and household accoutrements, decorating and remodelling, stability, and work and play.

Housing Type: The Single Family Home

The single-family, detached, suburban house was strongly promoted as the ideal form of accommodation for children. This home was to be constructed, equipped, and furnished in such a manner that it would provide for adequate ventilation, a comfortable temperature, privacy for the occupants, sleeping quarters for children that were separate from the adults, gender-appropriate decoration, and space for play. This standard was at times characteristic of the housing actually obtained by the women's parents when the women were still girls and by the women when they were parents. Yet, knowledge of SAH came to bear on their lives even when the ideal was not attained.

Ursula Roberts lived in accordance with SAH through most of her childhood and during the child-rearing period of her life. She told us that after living in apartments with grandparents, "then I moved on the north side, which is the best side of New Castle, Pennsylvania. They bought their house on Maryland Avenue when I was five years of age, and, let's see, I lived there until after I was married. And that's a standard home with a reception hall, living room, dining room, kitchen, and three bedrooms and a bath upstairs." As a married woman and the mother of two children, Ursula and family stopped living in apartments and moved into "a home in a new section that was built of small little brick homes." The Roberts continued to purchase single-family detached houses as long as their children lived with them.

Thelma Hay told us about fond memories of one house where she resided with her parents and little brother: "Yeah, we rented in our first two places. Then we had our own home after that. A three-storey. It had an attic and basement, and that was fully equipped, you know what I mean. It had electric and everything. I mean it was a real home. It was a brand new house, uh-huh. I was only eleven, I guess, when we moved in there." Regarding her housing as a mother, she spoke mostly of a house that the Hays purchased and lived in with their four children for twelve years in Akron: "Three-bedroom, bath, living room, dining room, kitchen, and garage, of course. Nice front porch. Little back porch. I liked it. And it was great for our kids too."

Edna Kepler was born into a large family that often moved from apartment to apartment because her family did not have much money. As she recalled:

We moved a lot because as our family was increasing and we needed a bigger place. We moved to something larger by the time the sister next to me was born. And there was a couple of times we lived with my grandparents. [Once] we rented a suburban house. We loved that place "cause us kids had lots of room. It was actually a double house. It was the old stone house, 100 years old. And it was on this farm, so us kids had access to this barn."

When Edna had children of her own, she said that her first two children were born in a large duplex, but

when Sheila was a baby we moved to the first home we bought. Late '48. It was a two-storey bungalow. Two large bedrooms. We moved out of there when [my daughter] Joanie was a year old, in November of '54. The neighbourhood was changing and it wasn't good for raising children safely. We bought a new home, which was suburban to Akron. This house was ranch type, three bedrooms, living room, dining room, kitchen, and frame with brick trim ... with a big yard. It was perfect for raising children.

Of course, not all the women we interviewed actually lived in dwellings that conformed to SAH. The single-family, detached, suburban home rarely entered Olive Jackson's experience as a child or as a mother. For a number of years she lived in a two-room cabin with her parents and six siblings. She did live in a detached house in a small town, however, where she was boarded with a family while attending high school. When she was first married and had a child, Olive lived in a company house. She told us: "You know how companies house families ... filthy, like sheep; it was no good." When Olive moved to Riverside with her son, she resided in several apartments. A few years later, when Olive was divorced with a young son she described her first home in Long Beach as "a little shanty."

Similarly, Nita Rodriguez spent much of her childhood in mining towns where she and her large family rented houses in the towns near the mines.

[One] was a big house. It was made of adobe, but then it wasn't stuccoed, not painted, but whitewashed. We did have wood floors, however. It had a big porch and I think it had four rooms. In Superior [Arizona] I don't remember ever being without electricity. We had to walk down stairs in the back [to] an outhouse. It was far from the house. We didn't have no well. It was a like a community pipe and that's where you would go and get your buckets full of water, and that would supply quite a few homes, but you wouldn't have one inside. We had wood stoves. I don't think we did have an icebox.

After her half-brothers lost their jobs in the United States because of the Depression, the family moved to Mexico to find work. There, Nita lived in a variety of dwellings.

In Magdalena they were all adobe homes, and we rented an adobe home. That's the first real home we lived in, and from there we went to a huge house that used to be a warehouse where they had hay because my sister started working there. Then we were moving from Magdalena to Hermosillo building the [Pan American] highway, and we lived in shacks. You'd have to build your own shack because it was just temporary. They would build them out of ocotillo, out of the trees. The houses were pretty small. Because you didn't know if tomorrow you'd be leaving. They were made of mud and they'd stand up and were very sturdy and they had dirt floors. When we had to cook, we cooked outside. Management would supply the water in barrels. We had these cots. My family had cots. It was like camping. Everyday was camping. I was 13 at the time.

After Nita married, the Rodriquezes moved to Phoenix and lived in a converted warehouse on the property of a brick-making business for which her husband worked. Although Tony intended to build a house on the property, Nita recalled, "We didn't get to build the other house that he intended. He had everything to build the home and never did."

After Tony was killed and with four young children, Nita told us: "I was in shock. It was three or four years that I was ill. After I received the money from the state I bought a three-bedroom house for my little ones and me. It was really home."

Clearly the women's accounts point to a wide diversity of experiences with housing and the conditions under which housing work was carried out, and just as clearly the form of housing promoted by SAH was not always attained by the women or their parents. When they were babies none of the women lived in single-family, detached, suburban, owner-occupied homes, although the parents of Ursula Roberts, Edna Kepler, and Thelma Hay eventually rented or owned these types of homes. Olive Jackson and Nita Rodriguez's families struggled with what they had – a cabin, an adobe, a warehouse, or a shelter made with mud. As adults, the women, except for Olive Jackson, eventually purchased dwellings similar to the ideal described by the discourse.

More importantly, however, we note that in their narratives all the women make explicit or implicit reference to a "standard" home, by using terms such as standard, ideal, real, normal, and shanty; the homes that they describe and contrast to the standard capture the notion of the SAH-ordered discourse of a single-family, detached dwelling surrounded by a yard. Their use of the terms "standard," "real," and so on communicates what they understand as common knowledge about the proper home for growing children, one that was exalted in SAH code. As these narratives make clear, SAH discourse does not determine what the women do; rather it provides a rhetorical terrain and framework on which to pursue their own child-rearing and housing activities.

Privacy and Household Accoutrements

Notions of privacy (separate beds and rooms), proper ventilation, and equipping children's rooms with proper furniture – vital to raising children correctly according to SAH discourse – were of concern in the women's accounts, although the women and children often had to make do by attempting to organize their own housing situation to conform to the discourse. Olive Jackson recalled her mother's work in trying to provide bedrooms that separated the children from the parents.

For a while we were all in that two-room house. I think there were three beds in the bedroom. Momma had it partitioned with sheets so each had a room of their own. We were three in a bed. I slept three in a bed with those girls. I slept three in a bed until we had two little brothers because they had a baby bed that was big enough for two babies. So the oldest boy was in the bed first, then the second boy was in the bed. I always had to sleep with somebody. When there's six kids in a small house, it isn't really too easy. So they put me in the kitchen. It was a nice big room. It was a dining room, living room, and kitchen. And I had a little cot in the corner and I had it all by myself, and I didn't bother anybody. I was never warm. I was always cold … because I had a little thin mattress, about three inches.

Years later, when Olive Jackson moved with her own son to Riverside, they had very little space of their own. There, her first home was "a place where I could move in and have a room and a kitchen privilege. So Ian and I … slept in the same bed. And we ate in this little kitchen. They had a table about this big for two people. You cooked your meal, and used their dishes, and ate in the dining room, and went back in your bedroom. She noted to us that she could not afford "much else" because she was living on the meagre cheque her husband sent her.

Later, describing another place she rented with her son in southern California, Olive alludes to the discourse on poor housing and ventilation presented by the Children's Bureau. Her description of her own dwelling highlights its deficiencies in SAH terms, revealing the importance of SAH in her own evaluation.

I got it for $15 a month! A house! The house didn't have a window in the bedroom. It had a flap that came down. It had a screen on it. In the summer time you lifted the screen and stuck a pole under it. And there was a place not much bigger than that hallway for our kitchen. And there was a bathroom. There was grass that grew up and came up between the floor and the wall. There wasn't much of anything there.

Nita Rodriguez also described concerns about privacy. She noted that there were separate rooms in which her brothers and sisters slept in the three-room house her brother eventually purchased from the mining company, and added: "I always slept with my mother, and my sister would try and [move me], saying it wasn't proper to sleep that way and she would say, 'Oh just leave her.' And I would sleep." She also commented that while living in a warehouse where the family did not have to pay rent in Sonora, Mexico, "we had to put in dividers out of sheets to make rooms," and her husband also put up "boards in a warehouse to make room dividers" in their home in Phoenix. Nita repeatedly picks up SAH discourse about privacy in her assessment of her varied living arrangements. Her family attempts to enact the ideological code of American family privacy by disapproving of her sleeping arrangement, hanging sheets, and erecting board dividers.

The taken-for-granted notion that proper mothers will remedy their children's concerns about space and privacy discursively transcribed in SAH is linguistically structured in Thelma Hay and Edna Kepler's narratives about purchasing new homes and goods and services for home improvements for their children's sake. Thelma Hay stated that her daughters virtually demanded more room for themselves: "The girls said, 'We don't have enough room!' So we ... bought a bigger one with four bedrooms so each kid could have a room of their own. Sara was nineteen, and Bill was sixteen, and Ann would be fifteen. They got big enough that we needed a bigger house. And by that time we could see our way clear." Thelma noted to us that soon after her children complained about the space, she and her husband began searching for a larger home, reading the newspaper, driving around looking for FOR SALE signs, contacting realtors, banks, and purchasing a new, larger house in a good, suburban neighbourhood.

Similarly, the Keplers did not have separate rooms for their children, but the importance of having extra space for a growing family is evident is Edna's description of one of their homes, where they hired a contractor to finish off the basement and purchased furniture for a recreation room for their children: "This house was ranch type, three bedrooms, living room, dining room, kitchen, and frame with brick trim. A beautiful basement. As our kids got bigger, we finished off the basement and had a kitchen and everything down there too. It was nice. We had a freezer down there, but you needed all that stuff when you had growing kids."

In contrast, the Hays and the Roberts were able to provide their children rooms of their own. Ursula was quick to tell us that when her first child was born, she created a baby's room that was sparsely furnished, but had a window for air circulation and sunshine. Echoing SAH discourse, she describes her family dwelling: "The apartment was a living room, dining room, and kitchen, bedroom. And then off of the living room was another small room, which I used as a nursery. When Annie was born we fixed that up as a nursery. It had a rocking chair in it and a baby's bed we purchased. It had a window ... I could open to let fresh air and sunshine in." She also told us that they painted and purchased new curtains for the room. Not only does Ursula's narrative replicate the prescriptions about creating a special room for her baby, but also it shows how her work connects up with department stores and businesses selling baby furniture and goods for the home. The SAH discourse she uses in her talk provides both the prescriptive framework and appropriate courses of action that connect her to the market of the home furnishing industry.

Decorating and Remodelling

The mothers we interviewed often took up home decorating and remodelling projects for the benefit of their children, thus conforming to the gendered ideological forms presented by SAH discourse. In each instance, underlying their description of their activities is the taken-for-granted assumption implicated in SAH code that a good mother would attend to or remedy her family's home for the sake of her children. For example, Ursula Roberts spoke about wallpapering her daughter's bedroom: "The paper had pink feathers in it and I papered the room. I bought curtains and sheets to match." In addition, the Keplers had their first home remodelled and redecorated by a professional company. Edna said: "The kids were real excited about their rooms afterwards. They had done them up with new furnishings, curtains and things ... Fit better for our boys and girls."

Olive Jackson described the decorating work that she did after talking with her son about their "shanty" in Long Beach:

And I said to Ian, "What's the matter, honey? I'll fix things here so you can invite your friends in and offer them an apple or something." And he said, "I wouldn't want any of my friends to know that I live in this hovel." And I didn't know he was upset about it.

I had read a thing: anything that's on the child's mind should not be on its body. And I figured that house was on his body, so I got rid of it. So I called my boss's wife and I said, "I just looked at an apartment. I think I want it if you'll help me furnish it." She's an interior decorator. I had to buy the furniture and she gave me the curtains, drapes, and so forth. It was absolutely beautiful. It was the nicest place I've ever had. Ian's in school. He had about five little girls chasing him. They always were running with him when he came home from school after that.

In a very explicit way, Olive describes to us not only the evaluation process she uses when her son judges their housing as substandard, but how that assessment in relation to the discourse leads to courses of action to remedy the circumstances: locating a new apartment, moving from her home, consulting another mother, hiring a decorator, buying new furniture, and so on. Olive's SAH-imbued narrative describes the sequences of action she takes to remedy her son's distress. She connects to the market of owners leasing apartments, home decorators selling their services, and department stores offering housewares.

Home Ownership and Stability

SAH discourse promotes home ownership as a strategy for ensuring stability, which, among other things, is beneficial to children's emotional and physical well-being. Some of the women we interviewed and their families experienced this stability from home ownership; others did not. However, for those women and their families that relocated frequently, their reasons for moving were always cast in the context of the SAH discourse and children's welfare. In their narratives they acknowledged that while uprooting might have harmed their children, some were quick to say that the moves were always to benefit their children. Others noted that the lack of stability in their or their children's lives might have been a problem.

While Ursula Roberts, Edna Kepler, and Thelma Hay moved frequently as infants, all three proudly told us that after they moved to their new suburban homes as young children, they lived in the same house for many years. Ursula's parents bought their first house when she was five. "I lived in that same house until I was married," she recalled. "Wonderful neighbourhood, wonderful friends ... I remember Daddy was concerned because we were the only house on the street when we moved in and I did not have any friends to play with. Families moved in on both sides, and I'm still friends with one of the girls next door." Edna moved a lot early in her childhood, but when her parents moved to a large, suburban, 100-year old house, she recalled: "We lived there until I got engaged and moved with my in-laws ... We kids always thought that was the best place after moving so much." Thelma's parents bought a three-storey home when she was eleven. She told us: "I lived there until 1938, [the] year I got married. That was about sixteen years. We had real nice neighbours and kids all around and we always had a lot of fun. We knew all our neighbours and played."

Even when the contingencies of the lives of the women did not permit them to own homes or live in homes for long periods of times, the notion that moving might harm children's emotional and physical well-being structured by the SAH discourse is contained in their narratives of relocating. They acknowledged it, sometimes accepting it and sometimes rejecting it. The Rodriguezes were living in Mexico and moved back and forth across the US-Mexico border when Nita became pregnant with her children, even though they owned a nicely furnished, large, single-family dwelling that Tony built. She told us that "we left the house [because] I came back and had [my son] John and I was pregnant with [my daughter] Eileen when I came back. I came back for all my little ones. You know, it wasn't bad for them; they were so small."

Olive Jackson told us that because the ranch that she lived on was far from a high school, "Dad bought a house in town. We lived there for the first year, but it was hard on Mom being away. So Dad found another couple and he boarded my sister and me in town. It was a bad situation." Later, when a doctor advised her that her ailing son needed a drier climate than Wyoming, Olive asked her husband to "order a pass on the train to Riverside." Relying on a small cheque from her husband, she rented a two-room house. Her assessment: "It wasn't good to raise a son in a place like that." Similarly, the Keplers sold their owner-occupied home in which they had lived for seventeen years and moved into a cheaper house so they could afford to send their children to college. Edna explained: "So we decide to get rid of the house and move to another place, so we could help the kids with school when the time came. We worried that it might be a problem since the kids just loved this house, but they became okay with it." She also noted that her parents did move a lot, but Edna asserted: "With each child you needed more space, you know, even if it's hard to adjust."

Work and Play in the Home

The SAH discourse advocated that child labour should be replaced by play in the home and the process of learning "the art of homemaking" should become more formalized since parents no longer had the inclination or time to instruct children properly. Further, child development advocates recommended providing children with age- and gender-appropriate toys to spark individual imagination and growth. In this way the discourse on child's play directly connects to the newly emerging US industry of mass-produced dolls, bicycles, children's books, and board games for families with children (Formanek-Brunell 1998; Whittaker 2002).

The women we interviewed did not take up the discourse of child development through play promoted by SAH discourse in a straightforward manner. As we noted above, textually-mediated discourse ignores the particular, historical, local circumstances of women's lives. In so doing, SAH discourse disregards knowledge mothers have in raising their children and contingencies in their lives. Thus, four of the women we interviewed told us that they were encouraged to make friends and play with their friends in their house, but they still had tasks to perform as children and their parents often delegated household labour to them. In some respects, then, our analysis suggests a disjunction between the standards elaborated in the SAH code and what the women did in their lives. On the other hand, they did acknowledge that play was or should have been an important part of growing up, although sometimes their narratives involved rejecting what SAH discourse noted as culturally appropriate and improvising in the face of their families' material conditions.

Ursula Roberts told us that her parents did provide her and her sister with toys and a room of her own in which to play. She said:

On my twelfth birthday my father and mother gave me a birthday party. And my father gave me three things for my birthday. He gave me a set of golf clubs, a tennis racket, and a bicycle. They gave me lessons at the country club too. When I was younger he gave me roller skates and a tricycle. We lived on a slight hill, we got sidewalks and I thoroughly enjoyed doing that. I was pretty athletic for a girl.

In addition, her parents encouraged her to play with her younger sister, but after other families moved in next door much of the play she described involved a great deal of improvising with toys:

I played a little bit with my sister, but see, she was five years younger; so I played a lot with my sister when she got a little older. We used to play jacks a lot. Now when I became around eleven or twelve, people moved in next door on both sides, and they both had girls my age. Then I played with the girl next door. I wasn't much for baby dolls even though I had lots of them. But we had little celluloid dolls, and we used to make clothing for them, then we pretend we were smoking and we'd put talcum powder in paper. And she'd be in her house in her bedroom and I'd be in my house in the bedroom and we'd be talking to each other. We did the thing with the cans, you know, put it up to your ears.

Ursula Roberts's narrative invokes many of the culturally prescribed standards elaborated in SAH discourse on play, albeit sometimes in a contrary manner. She did use her own room for girl-appropriate activities as the discourse prescribes, but she also liked sports and she played outdoors a lot – bicycling, roller skating, and taking tennis and golf lessons. By prominently noting to us that she "wasn't much for dolls" and "athletic compared to most girls," her narrative includes the concepts and notions inscribed by the gender-ordered SAH discourse, although her actual play was not like that envisioned by child development specialists.

Unlike Ursula Roberts, Thelma Hay, Edna Roberts, and Nita Rodriquez helped with housework as they were growing up and improvised much of their play with the few toys their families could afford. The women often continued these practices as mothers, particularly when they themselves had to work. In spite of this, their narratives allude to SAH discourse in various ways. For example, Thelma Hay told us that she worked around the house:

> Like keeping your own room straight. Things like that. Yes, and dusting and doing dishes, and you know, we had to do those things. We helped do those things, but we always had time to play.
>
> Unlike kids who had all sorts things … We had real nice neighbours and kids all around and we always had a lot of fun. We knew all our neighbours and played. We just kinda made up our own entertainment along the way. And my Dad [would] get out and play with us. We played duck on the rock. We played board games. In high school there was a whole big bunch of us that were together (in the neighbourhood) that would have a party at least once a month. We had bunko parties then and we played partners, you know. And it'd be at least sixteen to twenty of us there at one time.

Later, her children worked around the house when she went to work at a bank to help support her family after moving to Phoenix:

> When we came out here and my kids were just little ones. My oldest daughter was only twelve, but when I went to work in the bank they had to do things too. I had to rely on them. We worked on Saturdays so I didn't

even have Saturday home to do things. So I had to teach them how to wash clothes and hang them up and things like that, you know. My girls learned to cook in school. [My son] Bill was young; he was a good cook too ... I never let it interfere with school or their activities.

Thelma Hays's narrative of housework and play points repeatedly to the notion that the housework that she did as a child was "help" rather than work. In addition, although her children took over many of the household tasks when she went to work, as a proper mother who is concerned with making sure that her children develop properly, she reminds us that these tasks did not interfere with their doing appropriate children's activities.

Thelma's description of play in her family, although not in accordance with the type of play advocated in the SAH discourse for children, is structured around the discourse with the beginning phrase "kids who had a lot of things." While her parents purchased cards and board games for the whole family's entertainment, they seldom could afford separate toys for their children. Edna Kepler invokes a similar notion when she tells us that imagination and creativity in children cannot be purchased, but "you make do with what you have." She fondly recalled playing with her siblings as a child, but the play did not require special toys or specifically designed play areas. Earlier she told us:

Parents think they have to buy everything for their children, [but] we entertained ourselves. There was enough of us as we were growing – up to ten years old, we would play grocery store. My mother would give us cans and kids were creative and you entertained yourselves. But we learned to be creative. We would take orange crates and they were cupboards for girls' play dishes and all kinds of things.

In this way, both women reference the discourse in their speech by conceding what other kids have or what other parents think they must do; however, in describing their own experience as a contrast, they reject the tenets prescribed by SAH discourse.

Nita Rodriguez had playmates in the mining camps; yet, she worked intermittently to help her family on farms and with housework. In the mining town Nita told us that that she played a lot in the neighbourhood with other children when she was little, but that her mother made sure that she played only girls' activities and not with boys. At the time, Nita's family rented a two-room house where other Mexican families lived in town. She said: "There were quite a few playmates, more girls around. We played ring-around-rosy and things like that, that girls play. My mother would never allow me playing with boys. That's for sure." Nita also told us that her sisters encouraged her to read and do well in school: "I used to like to read a lot since I was little. My sisters would get me books. And the school books, oh I loved to read the stories. I remember reading readers from school. Oh, I had a place for my books. My sisters wanted me to go to school, not just work like they did." She had chores to do once she moved to Mexico and the family was struggling to find work: "I wasn't very good working on the farm. They didn't really want me to do hard work either. I was still little and a girl. They preferred for me to do the cooking and the cleaning and everything around the house." Later, she added that as she got older, "I did work for the superintendent of the mine. I learned how in school. I worked at their home, cooking and washing and cleaning."

Similarly, Nita Rodriquez's narrative of her actual play and housework as a child does not correspond to the prescriptions of SAH discourse; however, the discourse is inscribed in her narrative as she discusses what is appropriate play activity for girls and children her age. She also told us that her sisters wanted her to be in school, to "be a child," in other words, in contrast to working like her other siblings. Unlike the other women we interviewed, as a teenager Nita worked to help support the family. When the family returned to Mexico because her brothers were laid off from the mines during the Great Depression, she worked in the fields and did much of the housework for the family, clearly activities for children discouraged in the discourse. She noted that some of her housekeeping skills were learned in school, as prescribed by SAH discourse, and she used what she learned to help support her family. Although Nita Rodriquez's narrative of work is inscribed with the idea that her family did not want her to work because she was a girl or still small, her work as a child brings to our attention the disjunction between the discourse on children's work and play dominating American life and the conditions of her family's life, particularly during the Great Depression. In this respect, the discourse ignores the contingencies and material conditions of women's lives, particularly the historical, local contingencies in which parents raised children during this period. Olive Jackson's narrative of work and play is similar.

Olive Jackson spent much of her childhood performing many of the productive tasks for sustaining the ranch and house. Olive rode around the ranch on horseback to check the fences, and she took care of her youngest brother, bathing and dressing him, when her mother did not have the time. Before telling us about these activities, she said: "Play? I didn't play. It wasn't a good situation. I worked all the time. When [my son] Ian was small, he played with friends and I even got him a kitten for $15." Olive recalled that most of her childhood involved work on the ranch:

> Mom and Dad made sure we went to school ... [but] I used to go out and help Dad with the chores. Dad had a blacksmith shop and when he worked in the blacksmith shop it was necessary for me to go out and help because I would have to hold things on the anvil while he pounded it into shape. He used to get mad at me because I wasn't very strong and couldn't hold things in place for him or climb fences.
>
> I helped my mother in the kitchen. I stood on a chair and washed or wiped dishes. And if she was making bread, she would measure out the flour and the yeast and the stock and put it in on the chair, and I stood and got my little paddies in it and got it all kneaded up nicely and got it in good shape. When I got older I did that myself. Pretty well took over many of my mother's duties.

Olive remembered one summer when she was ten or twelve and did all the cooking for the men who were taking in hay: "I baked ten, twelve loaves of bread every morning, and cooked beef roasts and other kinds of roasts that I could barely lift and put ... into the oven."

Much like Nita Rodriquez, Olive Jackson's narrative about actual play and work does not follow SAH discourse standards for proper child development; however, she references this discourse in the beginning of her narrative by contrasting her experience as a child with what she did as a mother. Although her parents did not enact SAH discourse surrounding play, Olive structures her story in such a way to tell us that she knows that a child should play and have things to play with and that as a mother she did her mothering properly. On the other hand, the disjunction between Olive Jackson's play and work experience as a child and the SAH discourse is not surprising since some who debated the issue of child labour during the period noted that the recommendations about play and work were only applicable to non-farm families, since farm households continued to rely on household labour (Trattner 1970).

Discussion

Beginning with the experiences of five ordinary women whose lives span the twentieth century, we have examined ruling relations as they operated through a textually-mediated Standard American Home discourse organizing parents' experience of child-rearing in the home. Our findings show that the work of the Children's Bureau, the Own Your Own Home campaign, and the Better Homes in America movement – their advertising campaigns, brochures, studies, manuals, and demonstration projects – established connections between proper child-rearing practices and appropriate housing for children and codified a form of housing that held parents responsible for their children's well-being. These agencies coordinated the work of lumber companies, savings and loans, real estate associations, builders, contractors, child development specialists, doctors, home decorators, academics, and newspaper and magazine publishers. Further, through the ideological code of SAH, parents were connected to the newly professionalized child welfare experts, to an emerging market of consumer goods and services for the home, and to the depressed consumer market for housing between 1900 and 1930.

Our findings indicate that SAH is a specific gendered, class- and race-based discourse about appropriate housing arrangements for child-rearing. From the texts we conclude that the Standard American Home is a conceptualization of the home with a wide array of features: owned and not rented; a house and not a flat or an apartment; suburban or, if it must be in a city, near a park so that there is an outdoor play area; clean, well-ventilated, dry, sunny, with temperature control and screens on the windows; away from sewage; and easily cleaned. It has separate bedrooms for each child – or at least separates the boys from the girls and the children from the parents. The bedrooms have appropriate colour schemes, furnishings, and toys for the children's ages and genders. And the family should reside in the same home for many years. This type of housing is not presented as an ideal, but as a standard home that should be available to all children regardless of class or ethnicity. Not only does the SAH code discursively construct the home and household as the site of proper child-rearing and family life, as Gubrium and Holstein (1990) have shown, but, much like Schlossman's (1977) Progressive Era analysis of the juvenile courts' sponsors, our analysis demonstrates how SAH discourse holds parents, rather than other institutional authorities, responsible for their children's welfare.

By establishing the ideological code of the Standard American Home, this Progressive Era discourse was transformed from one of concern for children who were housed in poor, inadequate shelters to a capitalist concern for home ownership and for stimulating consumer demand for manufactured housewares, children's toys, and home services.

The extension of the ruling relations into the everyday world of working-class parents and the coordination of these relations with a consumer market selling both houses and child-care products for the home transformed the institution of housing. Working-class parents were informed that they could have the prescribed "family environment" and hence the "normal child" by buying a home where activities, ages, and genders were separated appropriately. To assure proper development of their children, they could purchase, through growing catalogue and department store housewares and home-service businesses, the medically and academically recommended furniture and equipment for their infants and gendered "identity kits" (Bauman 1990) for aptly decorating their daughters and sons' bedrooms. In spite of their material conditions, working-class parents could redeem their children and give them a stake in America.

Although SAH discourse generalizes and is generalized, the parents of women we interviewed and the women themselves did not appropriate this discourse into their housing work in a straightforward manner. Their narratives show a diversity of housing experience that the discourse disregards, but it is precisely at these disjunctions, where SAH and women's experience – particularly of home ownership or children's work and play activity – contradict each other that we see how the ideality of SAH code operates to disregard the contingencies and demands of women's everyday lives. At the same time, SAH provides a discursive framework for the women when carrying out their own housing work. Indeed, the women's narratives show there is a constant tension between the local experiences and extra-local ruling relations.

On the other hand, mothers often took up SAH discourse to organize their children's housing either to conform to the ideological forms, to make do, to reject or seek alternatives in relation to the discourse given the material conditions of their lives, or to evaluate their own housing circumstances against the standard proposed by the discourse. While the women and their mothers did not always act in accordance with SAH discourse, this is not to say that the code was not operating in their narratives. Rather, while sometimes rejecting SAH or choosing other alternatives, they organized and framed their talk in relation to the code. In fact, their narratives are SAH-ordered through and through.

Many scholars note the irony of the child welfare rhetoric of Progressive Era activists exalting the family home as the proper venue for raising children while at the same time proposing that control over child-rearing be given to those professionals outside it. By investigating SAH discourse as a complex of actual relations vested in texts and as constituent of social relations it organizes, we uncovered in this research the "symbolic terrain" and material practices by which the state and other agents within the institution of housing, including parents themselves, brought into being the Standard American Home. Thus, our analysis extends the historical understanding of what Holstein and Gubrium (1999) call "deprivatization of the family home" by showing how women's child-rearing and housing work was directly and indirectly organized and standardized, and how women participated in these processes as active subjects.

Finally, as we have noted above, in some instances the mothers of the women we interviewed attempted to order their households around the Standard American Home, but not always successfully. Often they had to make do with their material circumstances. They hung sheets to separate family members, they boarded their children with other families, they shared houses with extended family members, they created makeshift play areas and toys, they relocated to have more space for their growing families, they moved a child to a cot in the kitchen to sleep, they slept under the trees, they had outhouses and community pipes, and they sometimes let their kids sleep with them. While some of the women's parents were able to eventually replicate the practices of SAH, others were not. The Progressive Era reformers realized that it was unlikely the parents of recent immigrants and the working class could be saved, but their children surely could be (Cohen 1985). On becoming mothers themselves, the women in our study returned to the housing market again and again, each time attempting to remedy "the textually reflected imperfections" (Smith 1990b: 206) of their own childhoods and adult lives. As Ursula Roberts said poignantly, "Each time we bought up, something bigger, always trying to better ourselves."

Further Implications

Institutional ethnography investigations are never complete. The strategy of beginning in everyday experience is one that encourages others to recall their own experiences, to compare their experiences to the participants in the study, and to consider the researchers' explications by searching for the social determinants of their own experiences. Institutional ethnography invites others to add their stories to the narratives in the research and to extend the investigation in ways that reveal other threads of the configuration of social relations. While conducting this investigation we found that often we were comparing and contrasting aspects of our own experiences with that of the women even though we are of different generations, and we wondered how children's housing is organized today and what the child-rearing and housing connection is like.

Unlike the women in the study, we are baby boomers and we were brought up and housed in a manner more akin to the participants' children. We can recall the emphasis on cleanliness in our homes. We had our own beds and even our own bedrooms in single-family, detached houses. We can remember the games we played, the toys we had, household tasks that we performed, and the television programs that we watched. Both of us grew up in the same houses for our entire childhoods or, at least, the vast majority of it. And these houses were important to us.

The question of whether the housing experiences of children differ today is, of course, empirical, and as institutional ethnographers we can begin in our own experience. Neither of us have children of our own, but the ones that we know and have done activities with spend much less time at home. We help out our friends and family members by picking their children up at school and attending their children's concerts, sports events, or award activities with their parents or in place of them. The children often refer to us as their "other" mother or father. Their parents are not at home much either, largely because their mothers work outside the home and their fathers frequently live elsewhere. We babysit and often provide a house to come to after school or during summer breaks. We sometimes prepare meals for them or stop along the way to pick up food to eat in the car as we take them to soccer practice, circus school, and numerous other after-school activities. In some instances we even ferry these kids to their own jobs – babysitting, working in restaurants, or department stores – which they tell us they do because "I can buy all sorts of things now." We ask them to come over to our houses to teach us how to use and program a wireless phone and video players we just purchased. We read the *New York Times*, telling us of a government report advising that co-sleeping is dangerous to children; we see digital signs on the roadway and hear radio reports that a child has been abducted or that a sexual predator is assaulting children; we watch television advertisements telling us what every child needs and adores; and we scan newspaper supplements and stores to find the "perfect gift" for these children. We talk and argue with our friends and family members who have children about child-rearing and the advice they read in parenting manuals. And we complain among ourselves and with others without children about the annoying instances when friends or family members tell us we "just don't understand; you're not a mother or father."

As the beginning place to unfold that complex of institutional relations governing and organizing child-rearing and housing in the beginning of the twenty-first century, our narrative of our everyday experience points us to an exploration of the actual practices of the school, food industry, state, marketplace, and media, among other institutional agents in the housing enterprise. It directs us to an investigation of how discourse that privileges parents as the experts about child-rearing or that identifies "other" parents is textually-mediated and replicated across multiple sites. Nonetheless, further research begins in experience.

NOTE

1 This research was partially supported by grants from the Scholarly Research and Creative Activities Program, Arizona State University West. The authors would like to thank the women who graciously participated in this study. They also thank James Holstein and the many anonymous reviewers for their comments on prior versions of this paper. Authors' names are listed in alphabetical order. The contents of this article represent a cooperative effort. This paper was originally published in 2006 as "Standardizing Child Rearing through Housing," *Social Problems* 53 (3): 299–331.

Afterword

DOROTHY E. SMITH
AND SUSAN MARIE TURNER

Our purpose in this book has been to gather together and make available some of the finest institutional ethnographies in which texts appear "in action." To write of texts as "in action" doesn't mean that texts somehow operate on their own. In institutional ethnography, texts are always seen and explored as they enter and are brought into people's actual courses of action; texts are not taken up in or for themselves. For institutional ethnographers, people are always there as texts come into play in coordinating our doings – whether the text is being produced or being taken up and activated by an individual or individuals. In each case, people are active and what they are doing is an actual occurrence in an actual place and taking whatever time it takes. The chapters in this collection do not focus on texts *as such*, nor do they begin and end in a theoretical concept.

Each chapter explicitly makes visible how texts coordinate individuals' doings. All chapters follow institutional ethnography's method of inquiry beginning in people's actualities and experience with issues or problems or questions arising for them that are also the concern of the researcher. The traditional sociological dominance of theory and theoretical categories is displaced. Recognizing texts as in action makes it possible for institutional ethnographies to return to people and their doings as sociology's ethnographic ground and yet to reach beyond into regions ordinarily the province of theory. Thus, in the studies collected here, texts are consistently seen as people take them up. There are accounts of text–reader conversations (Eastwood, Warren, Turner, D.E. Smith), of how governing text categories are deployed in producing textual representations (G.W. Smith, de Montigny), of the implementing of governing or boss texts (G.W. Smith, Wagner, McCoy, Warren, Rankin and Campbell), and of how governing texts organize people's work and daily lives (Wagner, Rankin and Campbell, Luken and Vaughan) and so on.

Though each study is coherent and complete in itself, it is important to recognize that what we've called the "ruling relations" are a vast transnational complex into which each researcher has chosen to delve. What we call corporations or large-scale organizations, government, institutions in general, and so on exist only as distinctive modes of textually coordinated work done by actual people at particular times and places (Smith 2001). Carving out the *textual modes of coordination visible as a distinctive sequence* is a discursive move. What every instance of ethnography collected here has carved out for description is fully articulated to, indeed is only a brief moment in, that vast complex of relations. Nonetheless we can see that together they have much to tell us about how that complex is organized as it is mediated textually. We can see, for example, how the actualities of people's lives are produced as textual representations or realities. It is the latter that become what institutional or organizational procedures (as prescribed in, or at least authorized by, governing or "boss" texts) can recognize *for action*. It is only when the detectives have written and submitted a description of gays enjoying themselves in the steam bath that action can be taken against them within the law (see G.W. Smith's chapter). De Montigny's experiential ethnography describes what G.W. Smith explicates as *the work of translating actuality into categories that fit the governing texts*. Organic farmers in British Columbia have to be certified as such before they can sell their produce as organic; its textual representation is integral to the organization of the market for organic food. The work of instructors in colleges in Ontario comes to be calculated using an imaginary but standardized count of hours which can then be incorporated into measurements of the relative costs of different programs or courses used as a basis for making decisions about which will be run. Each chapter brings into view the work that produces a textual reality.

That the specific focus of every institutional ethnography is tied in to an undefined complex of relations becomes an ordinary problem for the ethnographer. Choices have to be made about the direction of interest in order to be able to keep the ethnographic project under control. Any institutional ethnography opens up possible lines of exploration which would take the research beyond what the ordinary economies of research make practicable. Each of these studies discovers not just how texts of different kinds are implicated in coordinating what people are doing. It is also discovering some distinctive aspect or function of how that concerting works or is getting done: while gay men in the steam bath are represented textually in the police account in ways they surely did not intend, organic farmers work intently to perform to the book, writing up their own activities and responding to the inspector in a way that fits certification requirements. Warren describes the shift from governing technologies built into musical scores that left performance open to interpretation and contemporary score construction that has radically tightened the composer's control. Rankin and Campbell show us something of the work that is governed by, but never becomes visible within, the textual representations. We also have some prescient explorations of governing texts: Eastwood shows us something of the work of building policy texts; Luken and Vaughan investigate and bring to light the development of a standardized moral representation identified with images of the American suburban home that has tied home purchases to parental virtue.

Each chapter *discovers* texts of different kinds in people's actions in distinctive ways and settings, and tells us how to recognize people's reading and interpretation as actual embodied and situated actions. Some ethnographers have drawn on their own experience of reading, responding to, or producing texts. For example, de Montigny describes how the categories of the discourse he deploys in preparing to write a report organize what he sees, senses, and makes note of on his visit to an apartment suspected of a child abuse problem and D.E. Smith opens up discourse as an active practice engaging intertextually. Other ethnographers, for example, G.W. Smith and Luken and Vaughan, rely on standpoints in the experience of people actually involved, whether it is implicit, as in G.W. Smith's study, or explicit as it is in Luken and Vaughan's interviews with older women living in Phoenix. There are examples where ethnographers such as McCoy and Warren draw on specialized skills in the readings of the texts on which they focus; Turner also shows the specialized skills of reading a text in practices coordinating a course of action producing "political decision making." In most studies (though not all) there have been interviews and here we can see the characteristic stance of the institutional ethnographer who is learning from the informant's own expert knowledge of just how she or he is taking up, working towards, or being governed by a text.

All these studies open doors to further exploration; each contributes to our knowledge of how to take exploration further. Through such discoveries we learn also how to find out what is going on in our own lives and work. It is this particular conception of the significance and role of "texts in action" in the organization of contemporary society, *but never without* institutional ethnography's stipulation of "preserving the presence of subjects" and subjects' "work knowledges" in the organization of the everyday activities, that hooks them in ordinary ways into institutional work and shapes their consciousnesses and doings. The original (Smith 1987) goal of an alternative discourse that is a collaborative conversation among people whose work investigates different terrains and shares that new knowledge is being put into practice and developed at meetings and workshops and via the Internet. The editors' (necessarily limited) knowledge informs us of workshops and conferences across the world (including Australia, Canada, the United States, Denmark, Norway, Greece, Iceland, Japan, Taiwan, and Brazil and no doubt other places we haven't yet connected with). Institutional ethnographers are always learners. Questions and discussions of how to do the inquiry, the particular explorations on the particular institutional terrains ethnographers are exploring, take place among groups and networks of learners. The development of institutional ethnographic concepts comes out of the practice, like a science, aiming to understand the world as it is sensuously experienced and lived, and to improve its tools for looking and learning.

Overall, our book aims at enabling further research that discovers particular terrains of governing and relations that go beyond notions of state or corporation, beyond concepts of civil society, however expanded or revised. It is the significant use of Smith's concept of *text-mediated social relations and their observable practices* that allows the move of ethnography into the complex of ruling or governing relations and forms of organization, that in our daily lives we are active in and yet over which we have no control. Bringing texts into ethnography in this way – and using the kinds of strategies presented in the preceding chapters – makes it possible to expose and lay out as a "map" the material concrete operations of these forms of organization. Incorporating "texts in action," ethnography can begin in and explore "front line work" so that people can see how to enter and act in these text-mediated social relations and contemporary forms of organization. They can learn about and assemble a working knowledge of this realm of coordinated work and organization and so learn how it might be possible to work with others to change them.

References

Abbott, Grace. 1974 [1923]. *Ten Years' Work for Children*. Children's Bureau, US Department of Labor. Reprinted in *The United States Children's Bureau, 1912–1972*. Youth and Society: Social Problems and Social Policy Series. New York: Arno.

Alexander, Jeffery C. 1995. *"Fin de Siècle" Social Theory: Relativism, Reductionism, and the Problems of Reason*. London: Verso.

Arnett, Gordon, and David C. Hadorn, and the Steering Committee of the Western Canada Waiting List Project. 2003. "Developing Priority Criteria for Hip and Knee Replacements: Results from the Western Canada Waiting List Project." *Canadian Journal of Surgery* 46 (4): 290–4.

Bakhtin, M.M. 1981. *The Dialogic Imagination: Four Essays*. Ed. Michael Holquist. Trans. Caryl Emerson and Michael Holquist. Austin: University of Texas Press.

Bakhtin, Mikhail M. 1986a. "The Problem of Speech Genres." In M.M. Bakhtin, *Speech Genres and Other Late Essays*, 60–102. Trans. Vern W. McGee. Austin: University of Texas Press.

Bakhtin, Mikhail M. 1986b. *Speech Genres and Other Late Essays*. Trans. Vern W. McGee. Austin: University of Texas Press.

Bauman, Zygmunt. 1990. *Thinking Sociologically*. Cambridge, MA: Basil Blackwell.

Bernard, Jessie. 1973. My Four Revolutions: An Autobiographical History of the ASA. In Joan Huber, ed.,*Changing Women in Changing Society*. Chicago: University of Chicago Press.

Bologh, Roslyn Wallach. 1979. *Dialectical Phenomenology: Marx's Method*. London: Routledge and Kegan Paul.

Bronner, Simon J. 1989. *Consuming Visions: Accumulation and Display of Goods in America, 1880–1929*. New York: W.W. Norton.

Bruner, Arnold. 1981. "Out of the Closet: A Study of Relations between the Homosexual Community and the Police." In *Report to Mayor Arthur Eggleton and the Council of the City of Toronto*. Toronto: City Clerk's Office.

CAN (Canadian Nurses Association). 2002. Code of Ethics for Registered Nurses. Ottawa: Author.

Campbell, Marie, and Ann Manicom, eds. 1995. *Knowledge, Experience and Ruling Relations: Studies in the Social Organization of Knowledge*. Toronto: University of Toronto Press.

Campbell, Marie, and Frances Gregor. 2002. *Mapping Social Relations*. Aurora, ON: Garamond Press.

Canadian Association of Emergency Physicians (CAEP). 2001. "Submission of the Commission on Health Care in Canada. Emergency Medicine: Change and Challenge. Section C – The Case of National Standards for Hospital Emergency Services." www.caep.ca/advocacy/romanow-commission/case-national-standards.

Certified Organic Association of British Columbia (COABC). 2007. http://www.certifiedorganic.bc.ca/standards/docs/Book_2_V9.pdf.

Chapman, Paul D. 1988. *Schools as Sorters: Lewis Terman, Applied Psychology, and the Intelligence Testing Movement, 1890–1930*. New York: New York University Press.

Children's Bureau. 1972 [1929]. *Infant Care*. US Department of Labor. Children's Bureau. Bureau Publication, 8. Reprinted in *Child Rearing Literature of Twentieth Century America*. Family in America Series. New York: Arno.

Children's Bureau. 1977 [1914]. *Baby-Saving Campaigns: A Preliminary Report on What American Cities Are Doing to Prevent Infant Mortality*. Children's Bureau, US Department of Labor. Infant Mortality Series, 1. Bureau Publication, 3. Reprinted in *The Health of Women and Children*. Public Health in America Series. New York: Arno.

Cohen, Ronald D. 1985. "Child-Saving and Progressivism, 1885–1915." In J.M. Hawes & N.R. Hiner, eds, *American Childhood: A Research Guide and Historical Handbook*, 273–309. Westport, CT: Greenwood.

Couch, David, and Joan Sutherland. 2004. OCCI Current and Future. Ontario Ministry of Health. http://www.healthinformation.on.ca/symp2004/presentations/Ontario%2Case%20Cost%20Database_Couch_Sutherland.ppt.

Cremin, Lawrence A. 1961. *The Transformation of the School: Progressivism in American Education*. New York: Vintage.

Cyr, Mary. 1992. *Performing Baroque Music*. Portland: Amadeus.

De Montigny, Gerald A.J. 1995. *Social Working: An Ethnography of Front-Line Practice*. Toronto: University of Toronto Press.

Dennison, John D., and Paul Gallagher. 1986. *Canada's Community Colleges: A Critical Analysis*. Vancouver: UBC Press.

DeVault, Marjorie L., ed. 2008. *Power at Work: Life, Power, and Social Inclusion in the New Economy*. New York: New York University Press.

DeVault, Marjorie L., and Liza McCoy. 2001. "Institutional Ethnography: Using Interviews to Investigate Ruling Relations." In J.F. Gubrium & J.A. Holstein, eds, *Handbook of Interviewing*, 751–76. Thousand Oaks, CA: Sage. http://dx.doi.org/10.4135/9781412973588.d43.

Diamond, Timothy. 1992. *Making Gray Gold: Narratives of Nursing Home Care*. Chicago: University of Chicago Press. http://dx.doi.org/10.7208/chicago/9780226144795.001.0001.

Dimen, Marcia. 1989. "Power, Sexuality, and Intimacy." In Alison M. Jaggar & Susan R. Bordo, eds, *Gender/Body/Knowledge: Feminist Reconstructions of Being and Knowing*, 34–51. New Brunswick: Rutgers University Press.

Durkheim, Emile. 1964. *The Rules of Sociological Method*. New York: Free Press.

Eastwood, Lauren. 2005. *The Social Organization of Policy: An Institutional Ethnography of UN Forest Deliberations*. New York: Routledge.

Fairclough, Norman. 1995. *Critical Discourse Analysis*. Boston: Addison Wesley.

Fairclough, Norman. 2003. *Analysing Discourse: Textual Analysis for Social Research*. London: Routledge.

Finkelstein, Lawrence S. 1988. *Politics in the United Nations System*. Durham: Duke University Press.

Formanek-Brunell, Miriam. 1998. *Made to Play House: Dolls and the Commercialization of American Girlhood, 1830–1930*. Baltimore: Johns Hopkins University Press.

Foucault, Michel. 1970. *The Order of Things: An Archaeology of the Human Sciences*. London: Tavistock.

Foucault, Michel. 1972. *The Archaeology of Knowledge and the Discourse on Language*. New York: Pantheon.

Foucault, Michel. 1981. "The Order of Discourse." In Robert Young, ed., *Untying the Text: A Post-structuralist Reader*, 51–78. London: Routledge.

Frankel, Noralee, and Nancy S. Dye, eds. 1991. *Gender, Class, Race, and Reform in the Progressive Era*. Lexington: University Press of Kentucky.

Gardiner, Michael. 1992. *The Dialogics of Critique: M.M. Bakhtin and the Theory of Ideology*. New York: Routledge. http://dx.doi.org/10.4324/9780203203828.

Garfinkel, Harold. 1967. "Good Organizational Reasons for 'Bad' Clinical Records." In *Studies in Ethnomethodology*, 186–207. Englewood Cliff, NJ: Prentice-Hall.

Giddens, Anthony. 1987. *Social Theory and Modern Sociology*. Stanford. Stanford University Press.

Giltrow, Janet. 1995. *Academic Writing*. Toronto: Broadview.

Gordon, Linda, ed. 1990. *Women, the State, and Welfare*. Madison: University of Wisconsin Press.

Graham, Hilary, and Ann Oakley. 1981. "Competing Ideologies of Reproduction: Medical and Maternal Perspectives on Pregnancy." In Helen Roberts, ed., *Women. Health and Reproduction*, 50–74. London: Routledge & Kegan Paul.

Greenspan, Edward L., ed. 1984. *Martin's Annual Criminal Code 1984*. Aurora, ON: Canada Law Book.

Griffith, Alison I. 1995. "Mothering, Schooling, and Children's Development." In M. Campbell & A. Manicom, eds, *Knowledge, Experience, and Ruling Relations: Studies in the Social Organization of Knowledge*, 108–21. Toronto: University of Toronto Press.

Grout, Donald J. 1980. *A History of Western Music*. 3rd ed. Toronto: McLeod.

Gubrium, Jaber F., and James A. Holstein. 1990. *What Is Family?* Mountain View, CA: Mayfield.

Hacker, Sally L. 1988. *"Doing It the Hard Way:" Investigations of Gender and Technology*. Ed. D.E. Smith and S.M. Turner. Boston: Unwin Hyman.

Harries, Meirion, and Susie Harries. 1981. *The Academy of St. Martin in the Fields*. London: Michael Joseph.

Haydn, Franz Joseph. 1962. *Concerto in C Major for Violoncello and Orchestra, Hob. VIIb: 1*. Prague: Statni Hudebni Vydavatelstvi.

Haydn, Franz Joseph. 1989. *Concerto in C Major for Violoncello and Orchestra, Hob. VIIb: 1. Urtext from Joseph Haydn Werke*. Basel: Barenreiter Kassel.

Hays, Sharon. 1996. *The Cultural Contradictions of Motherhood*. New Haven, CT: Yale University Press.

Hodges, Andrew. 1983. *Alan Turing: The Enigma*. New York: Simon and Schuster.

Holstein, James A., and Jaber F. Gubrium. 1999. "What Is Family? Further Thoughts on a Constructionist Approach." *Marriage & Family Review* 28 (3–4): 3–20. http://dx.doi.org/10.1300/J002v28n03_02.

Hopper, Trevor, and Peter Armstrong. 1991. "Cost Accounting, Controlling Labour and the Rise of Conglomerates." *Accounting, Organizations and Society* 16 (5–6): 405–38. http://dx.doi.org/10.1016/0361-3682(91)90037-F.

Hopwood, Anthony. 1989. "Accounting and the Pursuit of Social Interests." In Wai Fong Chua, Tony Lowe, & Tony Puxty, eds, *Critical Perspectives in Management Control*, 141–57. London: Macmillan.

Hopwood, Anthony. 1990. "Accounting and Organization Change." *Accounting, Auditing & Accountability Journal* 3 (1): 7–17. http://dx.doi.org/10.1108/09513579010145073.

Hoskin, Keith, and Richard Macve. 1994. "Writing, Examining, Disciplining: The Genesis of Accounting's Modern Power." In Anthony G. Hopwood & Peter Miller, eds, *Accounting as Social and Institutional Practice*, 67–97. Cambridge: Cambridge University Press.

Hurston, Zora Neale. 1937. *Their Eyes Were Watching God*. Philadelphia: J.B. Lippincott.

Jack, Dana Crowley. 1991. *Silencing the Self: Women and Depression*. Cambridge, MA: Harvard University Press.

Jackson, Nancy. 1995. "'These Things Just Happen:' Talk, Text and Curriculum Reform." In Marie Campbell & Ann Manicom, eds, *Knowledge, Experience, and Ruling Relations: Studies in the Social Organization of Knowledge*, 164–80. Toronto: University of Toronto Press.

Kerr, Christine A., J. Colin Glass, Gillian M. McCallion, and Donal G. McKillop. 1999. "Best Practice Measures of Resources Utilization for Hospitals: A Useful Complement in Performance Assessment." *Public Administration* 77 (3): 639–50. http://dx.doi.org/10.1111/1467-9299.00172.

Kress, Gunther, and Robert Hodge. 1979. *Language as Ideology*. London: Routledge & Kegan Paul.

Landon, H.C. Robbins. 1983. Joseph Haydn Cello Concertos, notes to recording by the Academy of Ancient Music (Christophe Coin, cello; Christopher Hogwood conducting, #414 615-2). Florelegium, Éditions de l'Oiseau-Lyre. London: Decca Records.

Latour, Bruno, and Steve Woolgar. 1979. *Laboratory Life: The Social Construction of Scientific Facts*. London: Sage.

Leavitt, Sarah A. 2002. *From Katharine Beecher to Martha Stewart: A Cultural History of Domestic Advice*. Chapel Hill: University of North Carolina Press.

Levine, Murray, and Adeline Levine. 1970. *A Social History of Helping Services: Clinic, Court, School, and Community*. New York: Appleton-Century-Crofts.

Library of Congress. 1999. *Prosperity and Thrift: The Coolidge Era and the Consumer Economy, 1921–1929*. http://memory.loc.gov/ammem/coolhtml/coolhome.html.

Luken, Paul C., and Suzanne Vaughan. 1991. "Elderly Women Living Alone: Theoretical and Methodological Considerations from a Feminist Perspective." *Housing and Society* 18: 37–49.

Luken, Paul C., and Suzanne Vaughan. 2001. "Life History and the Critique of American Sociological Practice." In N.K. Denzin & Y.S. Lincoln, eds, *The American Tradition in Qualitative Research: Benchmarks in Research Methodology*, 151–72. Los Angeles: Sage.

Luken, Paul C., and Suzanne Vaughan. 2005. "'… be a genuine homemaker *in your own home*': Gender and Familial Relations in State Housing Practices,

1917–1922." *Social Forces* 83 (4): 1603–25. http://dx.doi.org/10.1353/sof.2005.0073.

Lynch, Michael. 1983. "Discipline and the Material Form of Images: An Analysis of Scientific Visibility." Paper presented at the Annual Meeting of the Canadian Sociology and Anthropology Association, Vancouver.

Macleod, Davis I. 1998. *The Age of the Child: Children in America 1890–1920*. New York: Twayne.

Malhotra, Valerie Ann. 1981. "The Social Accomplishment of Music in a Symphony Orchestra: A Phenomenological Analysis." *Qualitative Sociology* 4 (2): 102–25. http://dx.doi.org/10.1007/BF00987214.

Mannheim, Karl. 1936. *Ideology and Utopia*. New York: Harcourt Brace.

Marx, Karl. 1973. *Grundrisse: Introduction to the Critique of Political Economy*. Trans. Martin Niklaus. New York: Random House.

Marx, Karl, and Friedrich Engels. 1976. *The German Ideology*. Moscow: Progress.

Marx, Karl, and Friedrich Engels. 1998. *The German Ideology*. New York: Prometheus.

Maurer, David W. 1964. *Whiz Mob: A Correlation of the Technical Argot of Pickpockets with Their Behavior Pattern*. New Haven: College and University Press.

Maurer, David W. 1981. *Language of the Underworld*. Lexington: University Press of Kentucky.

McCoy, Liza. 1995. "Activating the Photographic Text." In Ann Manicom and Marie L. Campbell, eds, *Experience, Knowledge and Ruling Relations: Explorations in the Social Organization of Knowledge*, 181–92. Toronto: University of Toronto Press.

McCoy, Liza. 1999. "Accounting Discourse and Textual Practices of Ruling: A Study of Institutional Transformation and Restructuring in Higher Education." PhD dissertation. Department of Sociology and Equity Studies in Education, University of Toronto.

McDonagh, Eileen L. 1999. "Race, Class, and Gender in the Progressive Era: Restructuring State and Society." In S.M. Milkis & J.M. Mileur, eds, *Progressivism and the New Democracy*, 145–91. Amherst: University of Massachusetts Press.

Mead, George Herbert. 1934. *Mind, Self and Society: From the Perspective of a Social Behaviorist*. Ed. Charles W. Morris. Chicago: University of Chicago Press.

Meyer, Stephen. 1980. "Adapting the Immigrant to the Line: Americanization in the Ford Factory, 1914–1921." *Journal of Social History* 14 (1): 67–81. http://dx.doi.org/10.1353/jsh/14.1.67.

Miller, Peter. 1994. "Accounting as Social and Institutional Practice: An Introduction." In Anthony G. Hopwood & Peter Miller , eds, *Accounting* as *Social and Institutional Practice*, 1–39. Cambridge: Cambridge University Press.

Miller, Peter, and Ted O'Leary. 1987. "Accounting and the Construction of the Governable Person." *Accounting, Organizations and Society* 12 (3): 235–65. http://dx.doi.org/10.1016/0361-3682(87)90039-0.

Mykhalovskiy, Eric. 2001. "Troubled Hearts, Care Pathways and Hospital Restructuring: Exploring Health Services Research as Active Knowledge." *Studies in Cultures, Organizations and Societies* 7 (2): 269–96. http://dx.doi.org/10.1080/10245280108523561.

Mykhalovskiy, Eric, and George Smith. 1994. *Getting Hooked Up: A Report on the Barriers People Living with HIV/AIDS Face Accessing Social Services*. Toronto: Ontario Institute for Studies in Education.

National Archives and Research Administration (NARA). N.d.a *Records of the "Own Your Own Home" Section*. Real Estate Division. US Housing Corporation. Record Group 3, box 450. College Park, MD.

National Archives and Research Administration (NARA). N.d.b *Records of the "Own Your Own Home" Section*. Real Estate Division. US Housing Corporation. Record Group 3, box 460. College Park, MD.

National Archives and Research Administration (NARA). N.d.c *Records of the "Own Your Own Home" Section*. Real Estate Division. US Housing Corporation. Record Group 3, box 464. College Park, MD.

Nelson, Barbara J. 1984. *Making an Issue of Child Abuse: Political Agenda Setting for Social Problems*. Chicago: University of Chicago Press.

Ng, Roxana. 1996. *The Politics of Community Services: Immigrant Women, Class and State*. 2nd ed. Halifax: Fernwood.

Pader, Ellen. 1993. "Spatiality and Social Change: Domestic Space Use in Mexico and the United States." *American Ethnologist* 20 (1): 114–37. http://dx.doi.org/10.1525/ae.1993.20.1.02a00060.

Pader, Ellen. 1994. "Sociospatial Relations of Change: Rural Mexican Women in Urban California." In I. Altman and A. Churchman, eds, *Women and the Environment*, 73–103. New York: Plenum. http://dx.doi.org/10.1007/978-1-4899-1504-7_4.

Pence, Ellen. 1996. *"Safety for Battered Women in a Textually-Mediated Legal System."* PhD dissertation. University of Toronto.

Petrie, P. 2003. "Maintaining Quality Care at West Coast General Hospital." Consultants' report presented to Port Alberni mayor & VIHA CEO.

Pfohl, Stephen J. 1977. "The 'Discovery' of Child Abuse." *Social Problems* 24 (3): 310–23. http://dx.doi.org/10.2307/800083.

Platt, Anthony M. 1969. *The Child Savers: The Invention of Delinquency*. Chicago: University of Chicago Press.

Porter, Theodore. 1992. "Quantification and the Accounting Ideal in Science." *Social Studies of Science* 22 (4): 633–51. http://dx.doi.org/10.1177/030631292022004004.

Preston, John. 1983. *Franny, the Queen of Provincetown*. Boston: Alyson.

Prior, Lindsay. 2011. *Using Documents and Records in Social Research*. New York: Sage.

Public Health Service. 1976. "200 Years of Child Health in America." In Edith H. Grotberg, ed., *200 Years of Children*, 61–122. Washington, DC: US Department of Health, Education, and Welfare, Office of Human Development and Office of Child Development.

Radford, Gail. 1996. *Modern Housing for America: Policy Struggles in the New Deal Era*. Chicago: University of Chicago Press. http://dx.doi.org/10.7208/chicago/9780226702216.001.0001.

Registered Nurses Association of British Columbia (RNABC). 2003. *Standards for Nursing Practice in British Columbia*. Vancouver: RNABC.

Reimer, Marilee. 1995. "Downgrading Clerical Work in a Textually-Mediated Labour Process." In Marie Campbell & Ann Manicom, eds, *Knowledge, Experience, and Ruling Relations: Studies in the Social Organization of Knowledge*, 193–208. Toronto: University of Toronto Press.

Richardson, Diane. 1993. *Women, Motherhood, and Childrearing*. London: MacMillian.

Robson, Keith. 1992. "Accounting Numbers as "Inscription": Action at a Distance and the Development of Accounting." *Accounting, Organizations and Society* 17 (7): 685–708. http://dx.doi.org/10.1016/0361-3682(92)90019-O.

Rothenbuhler, Eric W. 1990. "The Liminal Fight: Mass Strikes as Ritual and Interpretation." In Jeffery C. Alexander, ed., *Durkheimian Sociology: Cultural Studies*, 67–87. Cambridge: Cambridge University Press.

Rothman, David J. 2002. *Conscience and Convenience: The Asylum and Its Alternatives in Progressive America*. New York: Aldine de Gruyter.

Roweis, Shoukrey T. 1988. "Knowledge-Power and Professional Practice." In P. Knox, ed., *The Design Professions and the Built Environment*. London: Croom Helm.

Rubin, I.I. 1973. *Essays on Marx's Theory of Value*. Montreal: Black Rose.

Rutherford, Janice Williams. 2003. *Selling Mrs. Consumer: Christine Frederick and the Rise of Household Efficiency*. Athens: University of Georgia Press.

Saber, Mostafa, & Mansour Hekmat. 1992. "Labour Law against Workers' Rights: A Critique of Labour Law." *Labour Solidarity* (January–February): 4.

Salmins, Sandra. 1999. The Rigors of Organic Inspector Training. Online: http://eap.mcgill.ca/MagRack/COG/cog_foot.htm.

Schafer, R. Murray. 1980. *Adieu, Robert Schumann*. London: Universal Editions. http://www.universaledition.com/Raymond-Murray-Schafer/composers-and-works/composer/634/work/1051.

Schlossman, Steven L. 1977. *Love and the American Delinquent: Theory and Practice of "Progressive" Juvenile Justice, 1825–1920*. Chicago: University of Chicago Press.

Schutz, Alfred. 1964. "Making Music Together: A Study in Social Relationship." In Arvid Broderson, ed., *Collected Papers, Volume II: Studies in Social Theory*. The Hague: Martinus Nijhoff.

Schutz, Alfred. 1973. "On Multiple Realities." In M. Natanson, ed., *Alfred Schutz Collected Papers: The Problem of Social Reality*, vol. 1. The Hague: Martinus Nijhoff.

Sears, Alan. 2011. "30 Years On: The Toronto Bathhouse Raids and Sexual and Gender Liberation." *The Bullet (Socialist Project E-bulletin)*, 471 (26 February). www.socialistproject.ca/bullet/471.php.

Shanahan, Marian, Marni D. Brownell, M. Lloyd, and Noralou P. Roos. 1993. "A Comparative Study of the Costliness of Manitoba Hospitals." *Medical Care* 37 (Supplement): JS101.

Shanahan, Marian, Marni D. Brownell, & Noralou P. Roos. 1999. "The Unintended and Unexpected Impact of Downsizing: Costly Hospitals Become More Costly." *Medical Care* 37(6) (Supplement): JS123–34.

Skocpol, Theda. 1992. *Protecting Soldiers and Mothers: The Political Origins of Social Policy in the United States*. Cambridge, MA: Harvard University Press.

Smith, Dorothy E. 1974a. "The Ideological Practice of Sociology." *Catalyst* 8 (Winter): 39–54.

Smith, Dorothy E. 1974b. "The Social Construction of Documentary Reality." *Sociological Inquiry* 44 (4): 257–68. http://dx.doi.org/10.1111/j.1475-682X.1974.tb01159.x.

Smith, Dorothy E. 1981. "The Experienced World as Problematic: A Feminist Method." The Sorokin Lectures no. 12. Regina: University of Saskatchewan.

Smith, Dorothy E. 1982. "The Active Text: A Textual Analysis of the Social Relations of Public Textual Discourse." Paper presented at the World Congress of Sociology, Mexico City.

Smith, Dorothy E. 1983. "No One Commits Suicide: Textual Analysis of Ideological Practices." *Human Studies* 6: 309–59.

Smith, Dorothy E. 1984. "Textually-Mediated Social Organization." *International Social Science Journal* 36 (1): 59–74.

Smith, Dorothy E. 1987. *The Everyday World as Problematic: A Feminist Sociology*. Toronto: University of Toronto Press.

Smith, Dorothy E. 1990a. "The Active Text." In D.E. Smith, ed., *Texts, Facts and Femininity*, 120–58. London: Routledge.

Smith, Dorothy E. 1990b. *The Conceptual Practices of Power: A Feminist Sociology of Knowledge*. Boston: Northeastern University Press.

Smith, Dorothy E. 1990c. *Texts, Facts and Femininity: Exploring the Relations of Ruling*. London: Routledge. http://dx.doi.org/10.4324/9780203425022.

Smith, Dorothy E. 1999. *Writing the Social: Critique, Theory, and Investigations*. Toronto: University of Toronto Press.

Smith, Dorothy E. 2001. "Texts and the Ontology of Organizations and Institutions." *Studies in Cultures, Organizations and Societies* 7 (2): 159–98. http://dx.doi.org/10.1080/10245280108523557.

Smith, Dorothy E. 2002. "Institutional Ethnography." In T. May, ed., *Qualitative Research in Action*, 17–52. Thousand Oaks, CA: Sage.

Smith, Dorothy E. 2005. *Institutional Ethnography: A Sociology for People*. Lanham, MD: Rowman & Littlefield.

Smith, Dorothy E. 2006. "Incorporating Texts into Ethnographic Practice." In D.E. Smith, ed., *Institutional Ethnography as Practice*, 65–88. Lanham, MD: Rowman & Littlefield.

Smith, George W. 1988. "Policing the Gay Community: An Inquiry into Textually-Mediated Social Relations." *International Journal of the Sociology of Law* 16: 163–83.

Smith, George W. 1990. "Political Activist as Ethnographer." *Social Problems* 37 (4): 629–48. http://dx.doi.org/10.2307/800586.

Smith, George W., and Liza McCoy. 1991. *Meeting the Training Demands of Labour Market Adjustment and Industrial Restructuring: The Case of the Steel Industry and Ontario Colleges of Applied Arts and Technology*. Report produced for the Canadian Steel Trade and Employment Congress. CSTEC.

Smith, George W., and Dorothy E. Smith. 1998. "The Ideology of 'Fag': The School Experience of Gay Students." *Sociological Quarterly* 39 (2): 309–35. http://dx.doi.org/10.1111/j.1533-8525.1998.tb00506.x.

Stearns, P.N. 2003. *Anxious Parents: A History of Modern Childrearing in America*. New York: New York University Press.

Takemitsu, Toru. 1989. *I Hear the Water Dreaming*. Tokyo: Schott Japan.

Tobey, James A. 1925. *The Children's Bureau: Its History, Activities, and Organization*. Baltimore: Johns Hopkins Univeersity Press.

Trattner, Walter I. 1970. *Crusade for Children: A History of the National Child Labor Committee and Child Labor Reform in America*. Chicago: Quadrangle.

Trattner, Walter I. 1984. *From Poor Law to Welfare State: A History of Social Welfare in America*. New York: Free Press.

Turner, Susan Marie. 1995. "Rendering the Site Developable: Texts and Local Government Decision Making in Land Use Planning." In Marie Campbell & Ann Manicom, eds, *Knowledge, Experience, and Ruling Relations: Studies in the Social Organization of Knowledge*, 234–48. Toronto: University of Toronto Press.

Turner, Susan Marie. 2003. "Municipal Planning, Land Development and Environmental Intervention: An Institutional Ethnography." Unpublished PhD dissertation, Department of Sociology and Equity Studies in Education, University of Toronto.

Turner, Susan Marie. 2006. "Mapping Institutions as Work and Texts." In D.E. Smith, ed., *Institutional Ethnography as Practice*, 139–61. Lanham, MD: Rowman & Littlefield.

Turner, Victor. 1969. *The Ritual Process: Structure and Anti-structure*. Chicago: Aldine.

University of Pennsylvania. 1930. *Magma Copper Company Annual Report*. Lippincott Library of the Wharton School Corporate Annual Reports Collection.

US Bureau of the Census. 1975. *Historical Census of the United States, Colonial Times to 1970*. Washington, DC: Government Printing Office.

Vološinov, V.N. 1973. *Marxism and the Philosophy of Language*. Trans. I.R. Titunik. New York: Academic.

Walsh, Kieron. 1995. "Quality through Markets: The New Public Service Management." In Adrian Wilkinson & Hugh Willmott, eds, *Making Quality Critical: New Perspectives on Organizational Change*, 82–104. London: Routledge.

Warren, Leanne. 2001. "Organizing Creation: The Work of the Musical Text in Concert Performance." *Studies in Cultures, Organizations and Societies* 7 (2): 327–53.

Weeks, Peter A.D. 1990. "Musical Time as a Practical Accomplishment: A Change in Tempo." *Human Studies* 13 (4): 323–59. http://dx.doi.org/10.1007/BF00193569.

Weeks, Peter A.D. 1996. "A Rehearsal of a Beethoven Passage: An Analysis of Correction Talk." *Research on Language and Social Interaction* 29 (3): 247–90. http://dx.doi.org/10.1207/s15327973rlsi2903_3.

White, D., and P. Sheppard. 1981. "Report on Police Raids on Gay Steambaths." Submitted to Toronto City Council, 26 February.

Whittaker, Nicholas. 2002. *Toys Were Us: A History of Twentieth Century Toys and Toy-Making*. London: Orion.

Willis, Eileen. 2004. "Accelerating Control: An Ethnographic Account of the Impact of Micro-economic Reform on the Work of Health Professionals."

Unpublished PhD dissertation. Department of Social Inquiry, University of Adelaide.

Wright, Gwendolyn. 1983. *Building the American Dream: A Social History of Housing in America*. Cambridge, MA: MIT Press.

Zelizer, Viviana. 1985. *Pricing the Priceless Child: The Changing Social Value of Children*. New York: Basic Books.

Zimmerman, D.H. 1969. "Record-keeping and the Intake Process in a Public Welfare Agency." In S. Wheeler, ed., *On Record: Files and Dossiers in American Life*. New York: Russell Sage.

Contributors

Marie L. Campbell is professor emerita at the University of Victoria, British Columbia, Canada. Until retirement she taught in the Faculty of Human and Social Development's Interdisciplinary Graduate Program, Studies in Policy and Practice. Her research and publications focus primarily on the social organization of front-line, professional, human service work. Her books include, with Janet Rankin, *Managing to Nurse: Inside Canada's Health Care Reform* (University of Toronto Press, 2006); and, with Fran Gregor, *Mapping Social Relations: A Primer in Doing Institutional Ethnography* (Garamond Press, 2002; AltaMira Press, 2004). Appointed in 2005–6 by the Open Society Institute as an international scholar in American University of Central Asia, Bishkek, she and Elena Kim, a professor at AUCA, undertook some studies of international development funded by the Social Sciences and Humanities Research Council of Canada, that resulted in several publications, including, in 2010, M. Campbell and K. Teghtsoonian, "Aid Effectiveness and Women's Empowerment: Practices of Governance in the Funding of International Development," *Signs: Journal of Women in Culture and Society* 36 (1): 177–202; and, in 2013, Campbell and Kim, "Violence against Women and Peace Building: Tracking Ruling Relations in a Women's Development NGO in Kyrgyzstan," in A. Choudry and D. Kapoor, eds, *NGOization: Complicity, Contradictions and Prospects* (Zed Books).

Gerald A.J. de Montigny is an associate professor in the School of Social Work, Carlton University, in Ottawa, Ontario, Canada. His publications include his book *Social Working: An Ethnography of Front-Line Practice* and his chapter "The Power of Being Professional," in Marie Campbell and Ann Manicom, eds, *Knowledge, Experience, and Ruling*

Relations: Studies in the Social Organization of Knowledge (University of Toronto Press, 1995).

Lauren Eastwood is an assistant professor in the Department of Sociology and Criminal Justice at the State University of New York at Plattsburgh, New York, US. Her book *The Social Organization of Policy: An Institutional Ethnography of UN Forest Deliberations* (Routledge, 2005) maps the work of non-governmental organizations in UN processes, focusing on civil society participation and indigenous peoples' issues within the UN negotiating forums. She has recently expanded her work to incorporate an analysis of civil society participation in the United Nations Convention on Biological Diversity as well as the United Nations Framework Convention on Climate Change. She is also pursuing research that explores community responses to resource extraction in the western United States. Her focus is how community members engage in concerted action to attempt to influence both policy and practice associated with resource extraction for energy purposes. She teaches environmental sociology, sociological theory, and the sociology of gender.

Paul Luken is an associate professor of sociology at the University of West Georgia, Georgia, US. Along with Suzanne Vaughan he has been studying the social relations that have organized and reorganized the social institution of housing in the United States in the twentieth century and is beginning an investigation of the work of home buying. He is very active in the Institutional Ethnography Division of the Society for the Study of Social Problems and in the International Sociological Association Thematic Group on Institutional Ethnography.

Liza McCoy is an associate professor of sociology at the University of Calgary, Alberta, Canada. Her research focuses on the social organization of knowledge and everyday practice in the areas of health, immigration, employment, education, and visual representation. She is the author, among other works, of "Activating the Photographic Text," in Marie Campbell and Ann Manicom, eds, *Knowledge, Experience, and Ruling Relations: Studies in the Social Organization of Knowledge* (University of Toronto Press, 1995); "Institutional Ethnography and Constructionism," in J.A. Holstein and J.F. Gubrium, eds, *Handbook of Constructionist Research* (Guilford, 2008) and "Producing 'What the Deans Know': Cost Accounting and the Restructuring of Post-Secondary Education," *Human Studies* 21 (1998).

Janet M. Rankin, PhD, RN, is member of the Faculty of Nursing at the University of Calgary, Alberta, Canada. She has been involved in nursing work since 1975. Her practical background was in hospitals. She has worked as a nurse educator since 1990 and has been doing research in nursing since 1995. Her research focuses on the impacts of hospital restructuring and health care reforms on nurses and patients. Most recently Rankin has been exploring the social organization of nursing education at the intersection of nursing practice. She co-authored with Marie L. Campbell, *Managing to Nurse: Inside Canada's Health Care Reform* (University of Toronto Press, 2006).

Dorothy E. Smith is professor emerita of the Ontario Institute for Studies in Education / University of Toronto and an adjunct professor in the Sociology Department of the University of Victoria, British Columbia, Canada. She is the founder of the approach now known as institutional ethnography. She has published widely both articles and books. Her published books are, edited with Sarah David, *Women Look at Psychiatry: I'm not mad, I'm angry* (Press Gang, 1975); *The Everyday World as Problematic: A Sociology for Women* (University of Toronto Press, 1987); *The Conceptual Practices of Power: A Feminist Sociology of Knowledge* (Northeastern University Press, 1990); *Texts, Facts and Femininity: Exploring the Relations of Ruling* (Routledge, 1990); *Writing the Social: Critique, Theory, and Investigations* (University of Toronto Press, 1999); *Institutional Ethnography: A Sociology for People* (Rowman & Littlefield, 2005); with Alison Griffith, *Mothering for Schooling* (Routledge, 2005); an edited collection *Institutional Ethnography as Practice* (Rowman & Littlefield, 2006); and, with David Livingstone and Warren Smith, *Manufacturing Meltdown: Reshaping Steelwork* (Fernwood, 2011). She has at least two books in the works. She lives back and forth in Toronto, Ontario, and Vancouver, British Columbia.

George W. Smith was a scholar activist and research associate at the Ontario Institute for Studies in Education and worked with Dorothy E. Smith for many years. His publications include "Political Activist as Ethnographer," *Social Problems* 37 (4) (1990) and "Accessing Treatments: Managing the AIDS Epidemic in Toronto" in Marie Campbell and Ann Manicom, eds, *Knowledge, Experience, and Ruling Relations: Studies in the Social Organization of Knowledge* (University of Toronto Press, 1995). They are key early works of institutional ethnography.

Susan Marie Turner is an independent educator and researcher. She is currently a research consultant with the Aboriginal Sexual Violence Community Response Initiative, based at the Federation of Ontario Indigenous Friendship Centres and funded by the Ontario Women's Directorate. She is associate scholar at the Centre for Women's Studies in Education, Ontario Institute for Studies in Education, University of Toronto, Canada. Her publications include "Rendering the Site Developable: Texts and Local Government Decision Making in Land Use Planning," in Marie Campbell and Ann Manicom, eds, *Knowledge, Experience, and Ruling Relations: Studies in the Social Organization of Knowledge* (University of Toronto Press, 1995); "Texts and the Institutions of Municipal Government: The Power of Texts in the Public Process of Land Development," *Studies in Cultures, Organizations and Societies* 7 (2) (2001), reprinted in Lindsay Prior, ed., *Using Documents and Records in Social Research* (Sage Publications, 2011) and "Mapping Institutions as Work and Texts," in Dorothy E. Smith, ed., *Institutional Ethnography as Practice* (Routledge, 2006). She has a book in preparation on institutional ethnography.

Suzanne Vaughan is an associate professor of sociology in the Division of Social and Behavioral Sciences at Arizona State University, US. She and her colleague Paul Luken have published several articles on homeownership, child-rearing, retirement housing, and independence in old age using institutional ethnography and historical texts to explicate the ways in which the ordinary work of agents of the housing enterprise have transformed the organization of housing in the United States over the twentieth century. Professor Vaughan teaches graduate classes in institutional ethnography in the Social Justice and Human Rights program.

Katherine Wagner has studied sociology, literature, and creative writing, and has her Masters of Arts from the University of Victoria, British Columbia. She lives on Vancouver Island with her partner and their two children.

Leanne Warren is currently a PhD candidate at the University of Victoria, British Columbia. Her research focuses on the intersection between public prescription-drug funding policies and the work of caring for patients with diabetes. She works for the BC Ministry of Health and has also been a research coordinator and analyst in health services research. She and her husband own a shop in Victoria specializing in fine stringed instruments.